23482

9-4   17-31
  9-23   200-210
✕9-25   47-58
 10-21   234-82
  10-30   188-96   293-302
 11-6   17-31
 11-13   211-33
 11-18   110-63
 11-20   164-86   302-312

BOOKS BY HENRY KISSINGER

Does America Need a Foreign Policy?:
Toward a Diplomacy for the 21st Century

Years of Renewal

Diplomacy

Observations: Selected Speeches and Essays, 1982–1984

Years of Upheaval

For the Record: Selected Statements, 1977–1980

White House Years

American Foreign Policy: Three Essays

Problems of National Strategy: A Book of Readings (editor)

The Troubled Partnership: A Reappraisal of the Atlantic Alliance

The Necessity for Choice: Prospects of American Foreign Policy

Nuclear Weapons and Foreign Policy

A World Restored: Metternich, Castlereagh
and the Problems of Peace: 1812–22

HENRY KISSINGER

Does America Need a Foreign Policy?

◇ ◇ ◇ ◇ ◇ ◇ ◇ ◇ ◇ ◇   *Toward a Diplomacy for the 21st Century*

A Touchstone Book
Published by Simon & Schuster
New York London Toronto Sydney Singapore

TOUCHSTONE
Rockefeller Center
1230 Avenue of the Americas
New York, NY 10020

First Touchstone Edition 2002

TOUCHSTONE and colophon are registered trademarks
of Simon & Schuster, Inc.

For information regarding special discounts for bulk purchases,
please contact Simon & Schuster Special Sales at
1-800-456-6798 or business@simonandschuster.com

Designed by Karolina Harris

Manufactured in the United States of America

10 9 8 7 6 5 4 3 2 1

Library of Congress Cataloging-in-Publication Data
Kissinger, Henry, date.
   Does America need a foreign policy? : toward a diplomacy
for the 21st century / Henry Kissinger.
       p.   cm.
   Includes bibliographical references and index.
   1. United States—Foreign relations.   I. Title.
JZ1480 .K57   2001
327.73—dc21   2001020564
ISBN 0-684-85567-4
ISBN 0-684-85568-2 (Pbk)

ACKNOWLEDGMENTS

No one has done more to make this book possible than my wife, Nancy. She has been my emotional and intellectual support for decades, and her incisive editorial comments were only a small part of her contribution.

I have been fortunate in my friends and associates, some going back to years together in government service, who permitted me to impose on them for advice, editing, research, and general comments. I will never be able to thank them enough for what they have meant to me over the years and in preparing this volume.

Peter Rodman, my tutee at Harvard, friend, and counselor of a lifetime, read, reviewed, and helped edit the entire manuscript, and I am grateful for his perceptions and critique.

The same is true of Jerry Bremer, another long-time associate, whose pithy advice and editorial comments sharpened my thinking.

William Rogers continued educating me on the chapter dealing with Latin America and regarding the legal aspects of the concept of universal jurisdiction.

Steve Graubard, professor at Brown University and former editor of *Daedalus*, and I were graduate students together and have been friends ever since. He read and commented on the manuscript, greatly improving it by suggesting new avenues for exploration.

The following prepared helpful and indispensable research: Alan Stoga, on Latin America and globalization; Jon Vanden Heuvel, on Europe and the American philosophical debate on foreign policy; John Bolton, on the International Criminal Court; Chris Lennon, on human rights issues; Peter Mandaville, as a fact-checker, researcher, and editorial advisor on portions of several chapters; and Rosemary Niehuss, who was invaluable in collecting and annotating background materials.

John Lipsky and Felix Rohatyn commented with characteristic perspicacity on the chapter on globalization.

Gina Goldhammer went over the entire manuscript several times with a fine editorial eye and unfailing good humor.

No one has ever had a more dedicated staff than the group I have been fortunate enough to assemble. Faced with tight deadlines made even tighter when my writing was interrupted by illness, they worked indefatigably, often late into the night.

Jody Iobst Williams expertly deciphered my handwriting, typing the manuscript through several drafts, and in the process made innumerable extremely valuable editorial suggestions.

Theresa Cimino Amantea supervised the entire process, from ensuring that research and comments arrived on time and collating them to seeing to it that every target date of the publisher's was met and the manuscript properly prepared. She did all of this with great efficiency matched by extraordinary good cheer.

Jessica Incao and her associates, on whom fell the burden of having to see to the smooth operation of my office while their colleagues were working on the book, performed admirably and with great dedication.

This is the third book I have published with Simon & Schuster, and my gratitude for their support and affection for their staff continues to grow. Michael Korda is both a friend and advisor in addition to being a subtle editor and psychologist practicing without a license. Rebecca Head and Carol Bowie in his office were invariably cheerful and helpful. John Cox assisted subtly and ably with the editing. Fred Chase did his customary careful and thoughtful job of copyediting. Sydney Wolfe Cohen wrote the index with perspicacity and patience.

The irrepressible Gypsy da Silva, assisted by Isolde Sauer, coordinated all the various copyediting aspects of the book at Simon & Schuster with unflagging enthusiasm and endless patience matched by great efficiency.

Karolina Harris, in charge of the interior design, and George Turianski, the production manager, both have my deep gratitude.

I alone am responsible for the shortcomings of this volume.

I have dedicated this book to my children, Elizabeth and David, and to my daughter-in-law, Alexandra Rockwell, who have made me very proud of them and of the close friendship that exists between us.

To my children, Elizabeth and David,
and to my daughter-in-law, Alexandra Rockwell

❖ ❖ ❖ ❖ ❖ ❖ CONTENTS

Does America Need a Foreign Policy?

ONE

America at the Apex: Empire or Leader?

A T the dawn of the new millennium, the United States is enjoying a preeminence unrivaled by even the greatest empires of the past. From weaponry to entrepreneurship, from science to technology, from higher education to popular culture, America exercises an unparalleled ascendancy around the globe. During the last decade of the twentieth century, America's preponderant position rendered it the indispensable component of international stability. It mediated disputes in key trouble spots to the point that, in the Middle East, it had become an integral part of the peace process. So committed was the United States to this role that it almost ritually put itself forward as mediator, occasionally even when it was not invited by all the parties involved—as in the Kashmir dispute between India and Pakistan in July 1999. The United States considered itself both the source and the guarantor of democratic institutions around the globe, increasingly setting itself up as the judge of the fairness of foreign elections and applying economic sanctions or other pressures if its criteria were not met.

As a result, American troops are scattered around the world, from the plains of Northern Europe to the lines of confrontation in East Asia. These way stations of America's involvement verge, in the name of peacekeeping, on turning into permanent military commitments. In the Balkans, the United States is performing essentially the same functions as did the Austrian and Ottoman empires at the turn of the last century, of keeping the peace by establishing protectorates interposed between warring ethnic groups. It dominates the international financial system by providing the single largest pool of investment capital, the most attractive haven for investors, and the largest market for foreign exports. American popular culture sets standards of taste around the world even as it provides the occasional flash point for national resentments.

The legacy of the 1990s has produced a paradox. On the one hand, the United States is sufficiently powerful to be able to insist on its view and to carry the day often enough to evoke charges of American hegemony. At the same time, American prescriptions for the rest of the world often reflect either domestic pressures or a reiteration of maxims drawn from the experience of the Cold War. The result is that the country's preeminence is coupled with the serious potential of becoming irrelevant to many of the currents affecting and ultimately transforming the global order. The international scene exhibits a strange mixture of respect for—and submission to—America's power, accompanied by occasional exasperation with its prescriptions and confusion as to its long-term purposes.

Ironically, America's preeminence is often treated with indifference by its own people. Judging from media coverage and congressional sentiments—two important barometers—Americans' interest in foreign policy is at an all-time low.[1] Hence prudence impels aspiring politicians to avoid discussions of foreign policy and to define leadership as a reflection of current popular sentiments rather than as a challenge to raise America's sights. The last presidential election was the third in a row in which foreign policy was not seriously discussed by the candidates. Especially in the 1990s, American preeminence evolved less from a strategic design than a series of ad hoc decisions designed to satisfy domestic constituencies while, in the economic field, it was driven by technology and the resulting unprecedented gains in American productivity. All this has given rise to the temptation of acting as if the United States needed no long-range foreign policy at all and could confine itself to a case-by-case response to challenges as they arise.

At the apogee of its power, the United States finds itself in an ironic position. In the face of perhaps the most profound and widespread upheavals the world has ever seen, it has failed to develop concepts relevant to the emerging realities. Victory in the Cold War tempts smugness; satisfaction with the status quo causes policy to be viewed as a projection of the familiar into the future; astonishing economic performance lures policymakers to confuse strategy with economics and makes them less sensitive to the political, cultural, and spiritual impact of the vast transformations brought about by American technology.

Coinciding with the end of the Cold War, the combination of self-satisfaction and prosperity has engendered a sense of American destiny that expresses itself in a dual myth: On the left, many see the United States as the ultimate arbitrator of domestic evolutions all over the world. They act as if America has the appropriate democratic solution for every other society regardless of cultural and historical differences. For this school of thought, foreign policy equates with social policy. It deprecates the significance of victory in the Cold War because, in its view, history and the inevitable trend toward democracy would have by themselves brought about the disintegration of the Communist system. On the right, some imagine that the Soviet Union's collapse came about more or less automatically as the result of a new American assertiveness expressed in the change in rhetoric ("the Evil Empire") rather than from bipartisan exertions spanning nine administrations over almost half a century. And they believe, based on this interpretation of history, that the solution to the world's ills is American hegemony—the imposition of American solutions on the world's trouble spots by the unabashed affirmation of its preeminence. Either interpretation makes it difficult to elaborate a long-range approach to a world in transition. Such controversy on foreign policy as takes place is divided between an attitude of missionary rectitude on one side and a sense that the accumulation of power is self-implementing on the other. The debate focuses on an abstract issue: whether values or interest, idealism or realism, should guide American foreign policy. The real challenge is to merge the two; no serious American maker of foreign policy can be oblivious to the traditions of exceptionalism by which American democracy has defined itself. But neither can the policymaker ignore the circumstances in which they have to be implemented.

THE CHANGING NATURE OF THE INTERNATIONAL ENVIRONMENT

For Americans, understanding the contemporary situation must begin with the recognition that its disturbances are not temporary interruptions of a beneficent status quo. They signal instead an inevitable transformation of the international order resulting from changes in the internal structure of many of its key participants, and from the democratization of politics, the globalization of economies, and the instantaneousness of communications. A state is by definition the expression of some concept of justice that legitimizes its internal arrangements and of a projection of power that determines its ability to fulfill its minimum functions—that is, to protect its population from foreign dangers and domestic upheaval. When all these elements are in flux simultaneously—including the concept of what is foreign—a period of turbulence is inevitable.

The very term "international relations" is, in fact, of relatively recent vintage, since it implies that the nation-state must inevitably be the basis of its organization. However, this is a concept that originated in Europe only in the late eighteenth century and was spread around the world largely by European colonialism. In medieval Europe, obligations were personal and traditional, based neither on common language nor on a single culture; they did not interpose the bureaucratic machinery of a state between the subject and the ruler. Restraints on government derived from custom, not constitutions, and from the universal Catholic Church, which preserved its own autonomy, thereby laying the basis—quite unintentionally—for the pluralism and the democratic restraints on state power that evolved centuries later.

In the sixteenth and seventeenth centuries, this structure collapsed under the dual impact of the Reformation, which destroyed religious unity, and of printing, which made the growing religious diversity widely accessible. The resulting upheaval culminated in the Thirty Years' War, which, in the name of ideological—at that time, religious—orthodoxy, killed 30 percent of the population of Central Europe.

Out of this carnage emerged the modern state system as defined by the Treaty of Westphalia of 1648, the basic principles of which have shaped international relations to this day. The treaty's foundation was the doctrine of sovereignty, which declared a state's domestic conduct and institutions to be beyond the reach of other states.

These principles were an expression of the conviction that domestic rulers were less likely to be arbitrary than crusading foreign armies bent on conversion. At the same time, the balance of power concept sought to establish restraints by an equilibrium that prevented any one nation from being dominant and confined wars to relatively limited areas. For over two hundred years—until the outbreak of World War I—the state system emerging from the Thirty Years' War achieved its objectives (with the exception of the ideological conflict of the Napoleonic period, when the principle of nonintervention was, in effect, abandoned for two decades). Each of these concepts is under attack today, to a point where it is forgotten that their purpose was to limit, not expand, the arbitrary use of power.

Today the Westphalian order is in systemic crisis. Its principles are being challenged, though an agreed alternative has yet to emerge. Noninterference in the domestic affairs of other states has been abandoned in favor of a concept of universal humanitarian intervention or universal jurisdiction, not only by the United States but by many West European countries. At the United Nations Millennium Summit in New York in September 2000, it was endorsed as well by a large number of other states. In the 1990s, the United

States undertook four humanitarian military operations—in Somalia, Haiti, Bosnia, and Kosovo; other countries took the lead in two, in East Timor (led by Australia) and Sierra Leone (led by the United Kingdom). All of these interventions except Kosovo had United Nations sanction.

Simultaneously, the heretofore dominant concept of the nation-state is itself undergoing metamorphosis. True to the dominant philosophy, every state calls itself a nation but not all are such in terms of the nineteenth-century concept of a nation as a linguistic and cultural unit. Of the "great powers" at the turn of the new millennium, only the democracies of Europe and Japan fulfill that definition. China and Russia combine a national and cultural core with multiethnic attributes. The United States has increasingly equated its national identity with multiethnicity. In the rest of the world, states with mixed ethnic composition are the rule, and the cohesion of many of them is threatened by subject ethnic groups seeking autonomy or independence on the basis of nineteenth- and early-twentieth-century doctrines of nationalism and self-determination. Even in Europe, falling birthrates and growing immigration are introducing the challenge of multiethnicity.

Historic nation-states, aware that their size is insufficient to play a major global role, are seeking to group themselves into larger units. The European Union represents the most sweeping expression of this policy thus far. But similar transnational groupings are emerging in the Western Hemisphere in such institutions as the North American Free Trade Agreement (NAFTA) and Mercosur in South America, and in Asia in the Association of Southeast Asian Nations (ASEAN). The idea of a rudimentary free trade area has made its appearance in Asia under joint Chinese and Japanese sponsorship.

Each of these new units, in defining its identity, is driven, sometimes subconsciously, often deliberately, to do so in distinction to the dominant powers in its region. For ASEAN, the foils are China and Japan (and, in time, probably India); for the European Union and Mercosur, the foil is the United States, creating new rivalries even as they overcome traditional ones.

In the past, transformations of far lesser magnitude have led to major wars; indeed, wars have occurred with considerable frequency in the present international system as well. But they have never involved the current great powers in military conflict with each other. For the nuclear age has changed both the significance and the role of power, at least as far as the relationship of the major countries to one another is concerned. Until the beginning of the nuclear age, wars were most often sparked by disputes over territory or access to resources; conquest was undertaken to augment a state's power and influence. In the modern age, territory has lost much of its significance as an element of national strength; technological progress can enhance a country's power far more than any conceivable territorial expansion. Singapore, with literally no resources other than the intelligence of its people and leaders, has a much higher per capita income than much larger and more favorably endowed countries. And it uses this wealth in part to build up—at least locally—impressive military forces to discourage the designs of covetous neighbors. Israel is in a similar position.

Nuclear weapons have rendered war between countries possessing them less likely—though this statement is unlikely to remain valid if nuclear weapons continue to proliferate into countries with a different attitude toward human life or unfamiliar with their catastrophic impact. Until the advent of the nuclear age, countries went to war because the consequences of defeat and even of compromise were deemed worse than those of war; this kind of reasoning led Europe to consume its substance in the First World War. But, among nuclear powers, this equation holds true in only the most desperate circumstances. In the minds of most leaders of major nuclear powers, the devastation of nuclear war is likely to appear more calamitous than the consequences of compromise, and perhaps even of defeat. The paradox of the nuclear age is that the growth in nuclear capability—and hence the acquisition of vast total power— is inevitably matched by a corresponding decline in the willingness to use it.

All other forms of power have been revolutionized as well. Until the end of the Second World War, power was relatively homogeneous; its various elements—economic, military, or political—complemented one another. A society could not be militarily strong without commanding a similar position in other fields. In the second half of the twentieth century, however, the various strands seemingly began to diverge. Suddenly a country could become an economic power without possessing a significant military capacity (Saudi Arabia, for example) or develop vast military power despite an obviously stagnant economy (witness the late Soviet Union).

In the twenty-first century, these strands are likely to merge again. The fate of the Soviet Union demonstrated that one-sided emphasis on military power is impossible to sustain—especially in an age of economic and technological revolution linked by instant communications that bring the vast gaps in the standards of living into living rooms worldwide. In addition, in a single generation, science has made leaps that exceed the accumulated knowledge of all previous human history. The computer, the Internet, and the growing field of biotechnology have invested technology with a scope unimaginable by any past generation. An advanced system of technological education has become a prerequisite for a country's long-term power. It supplies the sinews of a society's strength and vitality; without it, all other types of power will wither.

Globalization has diffused economic and technological power around the world. Instantaneous communications make the decisions in one region hostage to those in other parts of the globe. Globalization has produced unprecedented prosperity, albeit not evenly. It remains to be seen whether it accelerates downturns as efficiently as it did global prosperity, creating the possibility for a global disaster. And globalization—inevitable as it is—also has the potential of giving rise to a gnawing sense of impotence as decisions affecting the lives of millions slip out of local political control. The sophistication of economics and technology is in danger of outrunning the capacities of contemporary politics.

AMERICA'S CHALLENGE

The United States finds itself in a world for which little in its historical experience has prepared it. Secure between two great oceans, it rejected the concept of the balance of power, convinced that it was either able to stand apart from the quarrels of other nations or that it could bring about universal peace by insisting on the implementation of its own values of democracy and self-determination.

I shall discuss these concepts in greater detail in a later chapter; for present purposes, it is sufficient to point to the impossibility of applying a single formula to the analysis and interpretation of the contemporary international order. For in today's world, at least four international systems are existing side by side:

• In relations between the United States and Western Europe and within the Western Hemisphere, America's historic ideals have considerable applicability. Here the idealist version of peace based on democracy and economic progress demonstrates its relevance. States are democratic; economies are market-oriented; wars are inconceivable except at the periphery, where they may be triggered by ethnic conflicts. Disputes are not settled by war or the threat of war. Military preparations are a response to threats from outside the area; they are not aimed by the nations of the Atlantic region or the Western Hemisphere at one another.

• The great powers of Asia—larger in size and far more populous than the nations of nineteenth-century Europe—treat one another as strategic rivals. India, China, Japan, Russia—with Korea and the states of Southeast Asia not lagging far behind—consider that some of the others, and certainly a combination of them, are indeed capable of threatening their national security. Wars among these powers are not imminent, but they are not inconceivable either. Asian military expenditures are rising, and they are designed principally as protection against other Asian nations (though some of China's military effort includes as well the contingency of a war with the United States over Taiwan). As in nineteenth-century Europe, a long period of peace is possible—even likely—but a balance of power will necessarily play a key role in preserving it.

• The Middle East conflicts are most analogous to those of seventeenth-century Europe. Their roots are not economic, as in the Atlantic region and the Western Hemisphere, or strategic, as in Asia, but ideological and religious. The maxims of the Westphalian peace diplomacy do not apply. Compromise is elusive when the issue is not a specific grievance but the legitimacy—indeed, the existence—of the other side. Therefore, paradoxically, attempts to bring about a definitive resolution of such conflicts have a high potential for backfiring, as President Clinton and Prime Minister Ehud Barak discovered in the aftermath of the Camp David summit in the summer of 2000. For an attempt to "compromise" on the question of what each party considers to be its holy place was bound to bring home to them the irreconcilable aspect of their positions.

• The continent for which there is no precedent in European history is Africa. Though its forty-six nations call themselves democracies, they do not conduct their policies on the basis of a unifying ideological principle. Nor are African politics dominated by an embracing concept of balance of power. The continent is too vast, the reach of most of its countries too short, to be able to speak of an African balance of power. And, with the end of the Cold War, the great power rivalry over Africa has largely disappeared as well. Moreover, Africa's legacy of colonial rule endows it with explosive potential, ethnic conflict, serious underdevelopment, and dehumanizing health problems. Borders drawn to facilitate colonial rule divided tribes and ethnic groups and assembled different religions and tribes in administrative subdivisions that later emerged as independent states. Hence Africa has produced savage civil wars that spread into international conflicts, as well as epidemics that rend the human conscience. In this continent, there is a challenge to the democracies to compensate for their histories in finding a way to help Africa to participate in global growth. And the world community has an obligation to end, or at least to mitigate, the political and ethnic conflicts.

The very range and variety of international systems renders much of the traditional American debate about the nature of international politics somewhat irrelevant. Whether it is values or power, ideology or raison d'état that are the key determinants of foreign policy, in fact depends on the historical stage in which an international system finds itself. For American foreign policy, ever in quest of the magic, all-purpose formula, the resulting need for ideological subtlety and long-range strategy presents a special and as yet unsolved challenge.

Unfortunately, domestic politics is driving American foreign policy in the opposite direction. Congress not only legislates the tactics of foreign policy but also seeks to impose a code of conduct on other nations by a plethora of sanctions. Scores of nations now find themselves under such sanctions. Successive administrations have acquiesced, in part as a compromise to gain approval for other programs, in part because, absent an immediate outside danger, domestic politics has become more important to political survival than the handling of foreign policy. What is presented by foreign critics as America's overweening quest for domination is very frequently a response to domestic pressure groups, which are in a position to put the spotlight on key issues by promising support or threatening retribution at election time and which support each other's causes to establish their own claims for the future.

Whatever the merit of the individual legislative actions, their cumulative effect drives American foreign policy toward unilateral and occasionally bullying conduct. For unlike diplomatic communications, which are generally an invitation to dialogue, legislation translates into a take-it-or-leave-it prescription, the operational equivalent of an ultimatum.

Simultaneously, ubiquitous and clamorous media are transforming foreign policy into a subdivision of public entertainment. The intense competition for ratings produces an obsession with the crisis of the moment, generally presented as a morality play between good and evil having a specific outcome and rarely in terms of the long-range challenges of history. As soon as the flurry of excitement has subsided, the media move on to new sensations. At their peak, the Gulf and Kosovo crises or the Camp David summit were covered twenty-four hours a day by print and television media.

Since then, except during occasional flare-ups, they have received very little day-to-day attention, even though the underlying trends continue, some of them becoming more unmanageable the longer they remain unresolved.

But the deepest reason for America's difficulty in the 1990s with developing a coherent strategy for a world in which its role is so central was that three different generations with very different approaches to foreign policy were disputing America's role. The contending forces were: veterans of the Cold War strategy of the 1950s and 1960s seeking to adapt their experience to the circumstances of the new millennium; stalwarts of the Vietnam protest movement seeking to apply its lessons to the emerging world order; and a new generation shaped by experiences which make it hard for them to grasp the perceptions of either the Cold War generation or those of the Vietnam protesters.

The Cold War strategists sought to manage the conflict of the nuclear superpowers by the policy of containment of the Soviet Union. Though far from oblivious to the nonmilitary issues (after all, the Marshall Plan was as important as NATO to the overall design), the Cold War generation insisted that there was an irreducible element of power involved in international politics and that it was measured by the ability to prevent Soviet military and political expansion.

The generation of Cold War strategists reduced and, for a while, nearly eliminated the historic tension in American thinking between idealism and power. In the world dominated by the two superpowers, requirements of ideology and equilibrium tended to merge. Foreign policy became a zero sum game in which the gains of one side translated into losses for the other.

Beyond containment, the major thrust of American Cold War diplomatic foreign policy was to return the defeated enemies, Germany and Japan, to the emerging international system as full-fledged members. This task, unprecedented in respect to nations on which unconditional surrender had been imposed less than five years earlier, made sense to a generation of American leaders whose formative experience had been overcoming the Great Depression of the 1930s. The generation that organized resistance to the Soviet Union had experienced Franklin D. Roosevelt's New Deal, which had restored political stability by closing the gap between American expectations and economic reality. The same generation had prevailed in World War II, fought in the name of democracy.

It was Vietnam that broke the fusion of ideology and strategy that characterized the thinking of what is now termed "the greatest generation."[2] Though the principles of American exceptionalism continue to be affirmed by all participants in the domestic discussions of foreign policy, their application to concrete cases became subject to a profound and continuing dispute.

Shaken by disillusionment with the Vietnam experience, many erstwhile intellectual supporters of Cold War policies either retreated from the field of strategy or, in effect, rejected the essence of postwar American foreign policy. The administration of President Bill Clinton—the first staffed by many individuals who came out of the Vietnam protest—treated the Cold War as a misunderstanding made intractable by American intransigence. They recoiled from the concept of national interest and distrusted the use of power unless it could be presented as being in the service of some "unselfish" cause—that is, reflecting no specific American national interest. On numerous occasions and on several continents, President Clinton fell to apologizing for actions of his predecessors that, in his view, stemmed from what he derogatorily described as their Cold War attitudes. But the Cold War was not a policy mistake—though some mistakes were, of course, made in the pursuit of it; profound issues of survival and national purpose were involved. Ironically, that claim to unselfishness was interpreted as a special kind of unpredictability, even unreliability, by nations that have historically treated diplomacy as a reconciliation of interests.

Obviously the United States cannot—and should not— return to the policies of the Cold War or of eighteenth-century diplomacy. The contemporary world is far more complex and in need of a much more differentiated approach. But neither can it afford the self-indulgence or self-righteousness of the protest period. These schools of thought, in any event, mark the end of an era whose disputes seem to the generation born after 1960 as abstruse and academic.

That generation has not yet raised leaders capable of evoking a commitment to a consistent and long-range foreign policy. Indeed, some of them question whether we need any foreign policy at all. In the globalized economic world, the post–Cold War generation looks to Wall Street or Silicon Valley in the same way their parents did to public service in Washington. This reflects the priority being attached to economic over political activity, partly caused by a growing reluctance to enter a calling blighted by relentless publicity that all too often ends in destroying careers and reputations.

The post–Cold War generation is concerned very little with the debates over the war in Indochina, being largely unfamiliar with its details and finding its liturgy nearly incomprehensible. Nor does it feel guilty about professing a doctrine of self-interest which it pursues strenuously in its own economic activities (though it sometimes enlists appeals to national unselfishness as a sop to the conscience). As the product of an educational system that puts little emphasis on history, it often lacks perspective about foreign affairs. This generation is subject to being seduced by the idea of riskless global relations as compensation for the intense competitiveness of its private lives. In this environment, the belief comes very naturally that the pursuit of economic self-interest will ultimately and almost automatically produce global political reconciliation and democracy.

Such attitudes are possible only because the danger of general war has largely disappeared. In such a world, the post–Cold War generation of American leaders (whether graduated from the protest movements or the business schools) finds it possible to imagine that foreign policy is either economic policy or consists of instructing the rest of the world in American virtues. Not surprisingly, American diplomacy since the end of the Cold War has turned more and more into a series of proposals for adherence to an American agenda.

But economic globalism is not a substitute for world order, though it can be an important component of it. The very success of the globalized economy will generate dislocations and tensions, both within and between societies, which will exert pressures on the world's political leaderships. Meanwhile, the nation-state, which remains the unit of political accountability, is being reconstituted in many regions of the world on the basis of two seemingly contradictory trends: either by breaking down into ethnic components or by dissolving itself into larger regional groupings.

So long as the post–Cold War generation of national leaders is embarrassed to elaborate an unapologetic concept of enlightened national interest, it will achieve progressive paralysis, not moral elevation. Certainly, to be truly American, any concept of national interest must flow from the country's democratic tradition and concern with the vitality of democracy around the world. But the United States must also translate its values into answers to some hard questions: What, for our survival, must we seek to prevent no matter how painful the means? What, to be true to ourselves, must we try to accomplish no matter how small the attainable international consensus, and, if necessary, entirely on our own? What wrongs is it essential that we right? What goals are simply beyond our capacity?

Stop
Here

TWO ◆ ◆ ◆ ◆ ◆ ◆ ◆ ◆ ◆ ◆ ◆ ◆

America and Europe: The World of Democracies I

THE Wilsonian ideal of an international order based on a common devotion to democratic institutions and settling its disputes by negotiations rather than war has triumphed among the nations bordering the North Atlantic. The governments are democratic, and the label "democracy" denotes genuinely pluralistic states with regular and peaceful alternation of parties in office. This is in contrast to much of the rest of the world where the word is often invoked to legitimize whoever is in power and where changes in government occur, if at all, by coups or couplike procedures. In the Atlantic area, war is no longer accepted as an instrument of policy; in the past half-century, force has been used only at the fringes of Europe and between ethnic groups, not between traditional nation-states.

This is why, for half a century, the partnership of nations bordering the North Atlantic has served as the keystone of American foreign policy. Even after the disappearance of the Soviet threat, the Atlantic partnership has remained for the United States the crucial buttress of international order. Beyond the definition of mutual defense of a traditional alliance, the nations of the North Atlantic have evolved a web of consultations and relationships to affirm and achieve a common political destiny. In the immediate aftermath of the Second World War, American assistance staved off Europe's economic collapse. And when the Soviet Union became threatening, the North Atlantic Treaty Organization was called into being. Its military arm has been an integrated military command; its permanent Council of ambassadors has coordinated allied diplomacy. More recently, globalization has deepened economic ties to a point where investments by the two sides in each other have linked the well-being of North America and Europe in a nearly inextricable manner.

And yet—paradoxically—relations between North America and Europe are beset by controversy. It is not that allied relations have been traditionally idyllic or even smooth. Controversy marked the Alliance's growing pains—as was to be expected when nations which had dominated global affairs for three centuries found themselves suddenly largely dependent on decisions being made three thousand miles away in Washington. During the Suez crisis in 1956, the Eisenhower administration dissociated from its British and French allies and actively worked to defeat them; the Kennedy administration's handling of the Berlin Crisis in the 1960s was greeted with misgivings in both Germany and France; the Nixon administration's attempt to define a new transatlantic relationship in the 1970s was widely resisted, especially by France; and the placement of American nuclear missiles in Europe in the 1980s was opposed by demonstrations all over the continent.

There is now, however, an important qualitative difference. The early crises within the Alliance were generally in the nature of family disputes, having to do with differing interpretations of the requirements of an agreed common security. Today the very definition of common security and, indeed, of common purpose is being questioned. The issue of American dissociation from European colonial interests now seems almost historically quaint. At this writing, it is our European allies who dissociate from American policies outside the NATO area, often demonstratively—from sanctions against Cuba, Iraq, or Iran to America's policy in the Taiwan Strait and the plan to build a national missile defense. While, in the past, opposition parties in European countries often denounced American deployment decisions, it is unprecedented for heads of NATO governments to attack publicly, or side by side with a Russian leader, the strategic judgments of an ally on whom their security depends. Yet that is what happened when Russian President Vladimir Putin visited Paris in October 2000. At a joint press conference with his guest, President Jacques Chirac, speaking on behalf of the European Union—of which France held the presidency for six months—attacked the Clinton administration's plan to explore revision of the ABM Treaty:

> The European Union and Russia have an identical view. We have condemned any potential revision of the ABM Treaty, believing that such a revision will involve a risk of proliferation that will be very dangerous for the future.[1]

More challenging was the dispatch of a conciliation team from the European Union to explore possibilities of easing tensions on the Korean peninsula, with a mission the declared opposite of the American policy proclaimed by President Bush barely two weeks earlier. The merits of the two views are not at issue. But, at a minimum, greater patience and restraint in an explosive region where the United States is taking all the military risks would have been in order.

During the Cold War, European integration was urged as a method of strengthening the Atlantic partnership; today many of its advocates view it as a means of creating a counterweight to the United States. The distinctive feature of the European Union military force, which will come into being by 2003, is to create a capacity to act outside the NATO framework. In the same spirit, German Foreign Minister Joschka Fischer has stated that, henceforth, the United Nations would play a larger role in German foreign policy and, in some cases, a larger role than NATO.[2]

When the Alliance was formed, its unifying element was a common policy toward the Soviet Union. Today the principal allies on both sides of the Atlantic are seeking to define their own "special relationships" with Moscow. While their efforts are not necessarily directed against each other, neither are they especially solicitous of the views of their allies. What they seek is to magnify their own options—to some extent as an insurance policy against each other—by gaining Moscow's goodwill.

What passes for a common Alliance policy toward Russia is often a sentimental interpretation of the personality of the current Russian leader—at one time Boris Yeltsin, now (at least initially) Vladimir Putin—leaving each ally free to gear national policy to the psychological criteria it chooses to elaborate for itself.

The disagreements in the economic field are, if anything, even sharper. Major trade frictions have erupted in a variety of threats of United States retaliation against Europe over bananas and beef, and by the European Union against the United States over American taxation of exports. The two sides of the Atlantic are at this writing deadlocked on how, or even whether, to launch a new multilateral trade negotiation in the World Trade Organization. They disagree over both the substance and the process. On the horizon looms another confrontation over energy policy, especially if oil prices continue to remain high.

Even more worrisome is the loss of human contact between the two sides of the Atlantic, which is occurring despite unprecedented travel. More Americans and Europeans are visiting the other continent than ever before. But they move about in the cocoon of their preconceptions or professional relationships, without acquiring a knowledge of the history and intangible values of the other side of the Atlantic. What the current generation of Americans knows about Europe grows far more out of business deals than political or cultural ties. On the other hand, the United States, about which most Europeans learn through their mass media, is defined by the death penalty, the allegedly inadequate system of medical insurance, the vast American prison population, and other comparable stereotypes.

To be sure, the principal leaders of Europe have used George W. Bush's accession to the presidency to reaffirm their commitment to Atlantic ties. The question remains, however, whether the Alliance is still considered the expression of a common destiny or whether it is turning into a safety net for essentially national or regional policies. The leaders of both sides of the Atlantic face no more important challenge than to answer this question.

THE TRANSFORMATION OF
THE ATLANTIC RELATIONSHIP

The drift in Atlantic relations is not caused by specific policies of individual leaders; rather, these policies reflect reactions to four fundamental changes in the traditional relationship:

- the disintegration of the Soviet Union;
- the unification of Germany;
- the increasing tendency to treat foreign policy as a tool of domestic policy;
- the burgeoning of a European identity.

Ever since America's entry into the First World War in 1917, its policy has been based on the recognition that it is in its geopolitical interest to prevent a potentially hostile power from dominating Europe. To defend that interest, the United States abandoned its tradition of isolation after the Second World War and confronted the Soviet Union in a protracted struggle. Europe hailed America's role in both instances even when its missionary zeal and tendency to equate foreign policy with moral improvement grated on leaders whose national history had taught them the virtue of more limited ambitions. The consciousness that the Soviet threat could only be met by a joint effort of the nations bordering the Atlantic and by subordinating largely national interests to the common good spawned the existing Alliance structure—perhaps the most effective in history.

In the process, there developed an attitude on both sides of the Atlantic that went beyond the traditional framework of common defense: the members of the Atlantic Alliance thought of themselves as belonging to a unique and special community of values and not simply as an aggregation of national interests. But the end of the Soviet threat has revived the temptations of both more traditional patterns of national diplomacy and of domestic politics, as will be discussed later in the chapter.

The unification of Germany accelerated these tendencies. It is one of the ironies of history that Germany should have emerged stronger in relation to its neighbors after each of the world wars it lost than it had been before they began. Nothing proves more clearly the limitations of human foresight than the outcome of these wars. Germany was instrumental in starting the first—though the other European states eagerly seized the opportunity—and it single-handedly provoked the second to achieve European, and possibly world, domination. Had it never fought these wars, Germany would have reached almost automatically the preeminent position, at least within Europe, which it is now approaching on the basis of the strength of its economy and the vitality of its people—this in spite of two defeats, the occupation of its territory by foreign troops, and its partition into two competing states for more than four decades. The debacle of the Nazi period, the country's division, and the fact that the Cold War demarcation line ran through its center convinced the founders of the new German democracy that they must avoid above all any repetition of a solitary national course.

Germany, the last major European state to be unified, became a nation not as the result of a popular movement, but because the princes of the various German principalities proclaimed the state in 1871, following the lead of a Prussia which had defeated them militarily five years earlier. In Germany, unlike in the other major European states, nationalism and democracy evolved on separate—often conflicting—tracks for the better part of a century. As a result, German nationalism frequently had about it an abstract, emotional, and romantic quality.

Above all, it lacked a sense of proportion. This turned the strategic problems produced by Germany's central geographic location into a permanent source of instability for Europe. Before unification in 1871, Germany's division into dozens of small states had, for two centuries, enabled its neighbors to contest the European balance of power on German soil. After unification, Germany moved to the other extreme, seeking to ensure security against all its neighbors simultaneously. But if Germany was strong enough to defeat all its neighbors if they were allied, it was clearly strong enough to overwhelm them individually. Thus Germany's effort to escape its strategic predicament produced its worst nightmare: a coalition of all the neighboring states against it. Germany has been for centuries either too weak or too strong for the peace of Europe.

In the end, this problem has been solved only twice in German history: by Otto von Bismarck in the first decades of a unified Germany in the nineteenth century, and after World War II by Konrad Adenauer and his successor chancellors of the Federal Republic. Bismarck opted for security via diplomatic dexterity. He sought to arrange the relations of European states toward each other in such a manner that Germany would always have more options than any possible rival, thereby preventing the formation of hostile coalitions. This tour de force proved too subtle and complex for his successors who substituted an arms race for diplomatic skill and slid into the First World War by the excessive flexing of muscles.

Adenauer and his successors inherited a defeated, partitioned, and devastated Germany, whose taste for solitary adventures had been exhausted by two wars. They had learned that Germany's past conduct had generated too much distrust to allow for the Bismarck style of subtle combinations, and that the German romantic tendency would overwhelm the sense of proportion on which the Bismarckian diplomacy was based. In any event, a national diplomacy was precluded by the realities of allied occupation.

As the Cold War division of Germany stretched into decades, the Federal Republic emphasized both its Atlantic and European vocations. It sought security from Soviet military pressures by supporting American leadership in the Atlantic Alliance, and it strove for legitimacy vis-à-vis the East German Soviet satellite by accepting French political leadership on European integration. Playing second fiddle to the United States within NATO and to France within Europe, the Federal Republic emerged a few decades after its unconditional surrender as the strongest military and economic power in Europe and as a key building block of Atlantic solidarity.

In the early stages of the Cold War, there was considerable opposition to the Adenauer course. It was expressed mostly in the Social Democratic Party, which had heroically resisted the Nazis and included among its members some of the most admirable figures in German politics. In the early days of the Federal Republic, its leaders advocated what amounted to a national policy in neutralist garb—in concrete terms, what they proposed was to give up Western military ties in return for unification.

By the 1970s, the SPD (in its German acronym) had come to terms with Germany's integration into the West. Two distinguished Social Democratic chancellors, Willy Brandt and Helmut Schmidt, reinforced Germany's Atlantic and European ties, albeit with a greater willingness to explore diplomatic options with the Communist East, and supported by the United States, at first hesitantly, later with conviction. Brandt's "opening to the East" in negotiations with Moscow led to the formal acceptance of Germany's division and laid the basis for a four-power agreement on Berlin which, in 1971, ended the threat to that city. The lingering interest in Germany's eastern option as a road to unification and a different approach to military strategy on the part of the SPD's rank and file brought down Chancellor Schmidt when, in 1982, he was preparing to implement the NATO decision to deploy American intermediate-range missiles on German soil.

In 1998—after being out of office for sixteen years—the SPD took over the direction of Germany in coalition with the so-called Green (Environmental) Party, whose platform had been historically hostile to the Atlantic Alliance. In office, neither of these parties has stressed the issues that characterized them in opposition—due in part to the fact that the post–Cold War world has overtaken many of the debates of the 1980s.

Inevitably, and independent of the party in office, the new international alignment has brought about greater emphasis on the German national interest. When the collapse of the Soviet Union reduced (and, for a time, eliminated) the fear of military attack from the East and when, in 1990, unification destroyed the East German Soviet satellite, the political balance within Europe and NATO basically changed. Germany's willingness to accept a subordinate status in NATO as well as in Europe has diminished. As Russian recovery gains momentum, the traditional temptation of special German relations with Russia has reappeared.

Three basic trends are likely to emerge as Germany becomes less dependent on the United States for security and on France for legitimacy:

• A greater assertiveness will become evident within both the Atlantic Alliance and European institutions. Gradually Germany may well seek for itself the role within Europe that France insists Europe should play within the Atlantic Alliance.

• Germany will always be far less prepared to put at risk its links to the United States than is provided for by French prescriptions for Atlantic relations. In that sense, it provides a limit to the implementation of French rhetoric.

• As Germany's relative role and power grow, and as Russia recovers, there will emerge temptations for a special Russo-German rapprochement based on the Bismarckian tradition that the two countries prospered when they were close and suffered when they were in conflict.

These tendencies will not be confined to the governing parties. Not only did the younger generation of Germans not experience the postwar trauma—not to speak of the Nazi one—but the former Communist third of Germany did not participate in the democratic experience until the last decade of the twentieth century. Thus a new kind of nationalism is likely to develop, not militarily aggressive but resistant to discrimination based on a past which the vast majority of Germans never knew and insistent on political influence for Germany commensurate with its economic and military potential.

These trends will tempt other European nations to court Russia, in part as a reaction to American dominance, in part as a counterweight to Germany—though, in such a contest, Germany's bargaining position vis-à-vis Russia would appear to be much stronger. Were the United States eventually to enter the same game, the Atlantic relationship would change its character and become more like the traditional European diplomacy of balancing rewards and penalties.

THE CHANGE IN ATLANTIC AND EUROPEAN LEADERSHIP

The leaders who created the Atlantic relationship had learned in the crucible of the Second World War that divisions among the democracies in the period of appeasement of the 1930s and during the long road to victory had nearly caused a worldwide catastrophe. They launched the Marshall Plan and NATO, overcame a series of direct and indirect Soviet challenges, and laid the basis for the eventual defeat of Communism.

The generation in office or dominating elections in the 1990s in the countries bordering the Atlantic emerged from quite a different set of experiences. Their fathers were reared on confidence in American power and the importance of allied unity. The sons and daughters grew up during the protest movements of the 1960s and 1970s that had at their cores a profound distrust of American power and, indeed, of the role of power in international affairs in general. They identified foreign policy with nonstrategic causes and were uncomfortable with the notion of national interest. The question their attitude raised was not whether such issues are important but whether they can be sustained if the traditional framework of security is neglected.

The generation in office at the turn of the millennium in almost all the countries of Western Europe represented center-left parties that had had their formative experiences in some type of anti-American protest. Even in the United States, many in the foreign policy establishment of the Clinton administration had grown up with the conviction that America had no right to project its power abroad until it faced up to and overcame its own domestic short-comings or, if it did, that it should do so only on behalf of causes other than its own interests. Some of them held the view that it was the United States that bore a heavy responsibility for the origins of the Cold War, by awakening Soviet fears through an excessive concern with military power.[3]

While the founding generation treated the Atlantic Alliance as the point of departure for a union of democracies, the protest generation views the Atlantic Alliance as a relic of the Cold War, if not an obstacle to overcoming it. Thus President Clinton, in a joint press conference with Russian President Boris Yeltsin in March 1997, stated that the "old NATO" was "basically a mirror image of the Warsaw Pact," in effect equating a voluntary association of democratic nations with a structure the Soviet Union had imposed on the subjugated countries of Eastern Europe.[4] The protest generation's goal was less to strengthen an Atlantic community than to "erase dividing lines." A good example is a speech by Clinton at West Point in May 1997, during which he gave four reasons for NATO enlargement:

- to strengthen the Alliance for "addressing conflicts that threaten the common peace of all" in the new century (presumably ethnic and out-of-area conflicts);
- to "help to secure the historic gains of democracy in Europe;"
- to "encourage prospective members to resolve their differences peacefully;" and
- along with the Partnership for Peace and the special arrangements with Russia and Ukraine, to "erase the artificial line in Europe that Stalin drew, and bring Europe together in security, not keep it apart in instability."[5]

While each of these arguments had merit, they omitted the most important reason for admitting Poland, Hungary, and the Czech Republic into NATO: to eliminate once and for all the strategic vacuum in Central Europe that in the twentieth century had tempted both German and Russian expansionism. It was left to the United States Senate, in its resolution of advice and consent to NATO enlargement a year later, to affirm that geopolitical truth.

The senators declared firmly that NATO was "first and foremost a military alliance," and that it existed for the purpose of preventing "the reemergence of a hegemonic power confronting Europe."[6]

In the Clinton era, affirmations of the Alliance had a liturgical quality which, step by step, edged the original concept of the Alliance ever closer toward the doctrine of collective security.

The distinction between the two concepts is not a legal quibble; it marks an important philosophical difference. An alliance comes into being when a group of nations decides to defend a specified territory or a particular cause; it in effect draws a line, the violation of which constitutes a *casus belli*. By contrast, a system of collective security defines neither the territory to be defended nor the means or machinery for doing so; it is essentially a judicial concept. NATO is an alliance; the United Nations is a collective security system. An alliance deals with a definite and defined threat and often designates the forces to meet it. A system of collective security is juridically neutral; far from defining the threat, it is obliged to wait for it to emerge before action can be considered.

In a system such as the United Nations, the aggressor cannot be named in advance and has a right to participate in the deliberations regarding its actions; to do otherwise would be to abandon the impartial and quasi-judicial character of the organization. When a threat arises, the participants in the collective security system are supposed to agree on its nature, and only then are they free to assemble collective forces to meet it. In the United Nations, if the aggressor happens to be one of the permanent members of the Security Council, it has the right to veto the determination of who is the guilty party or the collective actions to be undertaken.

This is why both the League of Nations and the Pact of Locarno failed in the 1930s, as has the contemporary United Nations, against the principal threats. The United Nations has occasionally been helpful in peacekeeping, especially when all the parties agree and when the issue is the technical implementation of an agreement. But the United Nations has never succeeded in imposing peace on reluctant parties or on a party backed by a permanent member of the Security Council. When all the participants agree, the need for collective security is minimal; when they split, it is impossible to apply. When every member of an international system has the same obligations, no country or group of countries has the special obligation which is the essence of an alliance. Though the terms "alliance" and "collective security" are often used interchangeably, the two concepts are, in fact, incompatible with one another.

As a result of this confusion, NATO has in the 1990s been diluted in both concept and execution. A host of institutions has been created, which bid fair to turn NATO into a mini–United Nations. There is the North Atlantic Council, composed of the ambassadors of the nineteen countries belonging to NATO; the Permanent Joint Council, which includes the North Atlantic Council plus Russia; the Euro-Atlantic Partnership Council, grouping NATO and twenty-eight former East bloc countries; and the Partnership for Peace, in which countries of Eastern Europe—including Russia—are invited to engage in joint training for unspecified multilateral missions. All these countries, which extend as far east as Kazakhstan, Azerbaijan, and Uzbekistan, are represented at NATO summits; all are serviced out of NATO headquarters, diverting the historic Alliance missions into a plethora of multilateral collective security enterprises of vague purpose.

Where is the limit of NATO? And how do these new structures differ conceptually from U.N.-type organizations? To extend the reach of American or Atlantic influence into other regions of the world may be desirable. But is NATO the right instrument for that mission? Seeking to direct this plethora of institutions from the headquarters of a military alliance diffuses NATO's focus and confuses its priorities. The annual summits of NATO chiefs of state are now attended by nearly fifty leaders of the various groupings, including the nineteen formal allies. All this threatens to dissolve NATO into a multilateral mishmash.

This is evident in the way NATO has formalized its relations with Russia. In the so-called Founding Act on Mutual Relations, Cooperation, and Security signed on May 27, 1997 in Paris, partly to pacify Russian concerns over NATO enlargement, a NATO-

Russia Permanent Joint Council was created, composed of the original North Atlantic Council plus a Russian ambassador. The jurisdiction of the Permanent Joint Council, required to meet at least once a month, was explained at great length, and its structure guarantees that Russia, if it wants, can have the major voice in setting the agenda. This is because the Russian representative, the Secretary General of NATO, and one rotating ambassador from the North Atlantic Council will chair the permanent council. (Russia is to be permanently in the chair, while the United States presides only one nineteenth of the time.) If Russia fully exploited the opportunities open to it (it has not done so at this writing), North Atlantic Council sessions and Permanent Joint Council sessions could end up merging.

The ambiguous priorities of NATO reflect the disappearance of the immediate threat. As a result, it has become increasingly safe in all NATO countries to give priority to domestic politics over foreign and security policy. Since almost all European center-left governments have disappointed their core followers by carrying out market economic reforms, they are reluctant to inflame the radical wings even further by implementing national security policies identified with the United States. Much of the European resistance to a U.S. national missile defense program replays the 1980 arguments against the deployment of offensive missiles—in some instances, by the same leaders.

The Clinton administration fell in with distinguishing its priorities from those of its predecessors in much the same way as the European left. Though it affirmed the importance of NATO, it did so in the context of values that scarcely related it to NATO's traditional strategic objectives. Nevertheless, in the face of the weakening of historic ties, personal relations between the leaders of the Atlantic nations remained remarkably close during the Clinton administration. Because of the congruence of domestic politics, European leaders saw no contradiction between their personal admiration for Clinton and vocal opposition to many of his policies, which they considered as having been partly imposed on him by a fractious right.

As a result, the most freewheeling and satisfying encounters of Atlantic leaders occurred not at formal summit meetings but at "Third Way" get-togethers of world—mostly European—Social Democratic Party heads of government. The ostensible aim of these meetings has been to seek a middle way between traditional capitalism and socialism. This is why the Socialist Prime Minister of Portugal was invited, and the conservative Prime Minister of Spain was not; why the Socialist Prime Minister of France attended, but the conservative President of France was excluded. President Clinton, in attending these meetings as a regular participant, threw the prestige of his office behind one side in the domestic politics of the countries represented.

Before the collapse of the Soviet Union, there existed a fixed set of foreign policy criteria to which all allies might appeal. It was then generally true that the American approach to foreign policy was somewhat more ideological and missionary, the European approach more traditional and realistic. America thought of itself as lifting Europe's sights while European leaders prided themselves on helping the United States discover the limits of the possible. The relationship did not depend on which party was in office on either side of the Atlantic. A return to such an attitude is necessary if Atlantic policy is to develop a coherent sense of direction.

The advent of a Republican administration will inevitably change the forum for consultation with Europe's leaders. President George W. Bush will not be eligible for Third Way meetings or, if he is, the European leaders heretofore excluded will have to be admitted as well, turning the conference into a heads-of-government meeting. And the leaders of Europe will find, once they get used to a relationship based on congruent national interests, that Atlantic relations will have a more permanent character.

Nostalgia for Cold War certitudes is no guide to a wise policy, but neither is the rote repetition of slogans of Atlantic solidarity in the face of a crumbling underlying reality. A new approach is needed to deal with a set of unanswered questions which are the legacy of the 1990s. Is the Atlantic Alliance still at the heart of transatlantic relations? If so, how does it define its purposes in the post-Cold War world? How will a unified Europe affect the concept of an Atlantic partnership? Is the Alliance a set of common purposes or a safety net?

THE FUTURE OF EUROPEAN INTEGRATION

The emergence of a unified Europe is one of the most revolutionary events of our time. The impetus for it has sprung from a variety of motives, not all of them compatible. Initially, Europe saw integration as a way to overcome the suicidal rivalry that had led it into two catastrophic world wars, and to overcome the economic ravages of those wars by cooperative action. France supported European integration so that Germany would not again emerge as a national threat. The Federal Republic committed itself to the ideal of an integrated Europe as a way of differentiating itself from the East German Soviet satellite and as an emotional substitute for national unity. Britain, heir to a tradition that has historically considered a unified Europe a threat to British independence, went along grudgingly, supporting pragmatic technical and economic arrangements but always wary of any undertaking that might turn the United Kingdom into a province of Europe and jeopardize its special relationship with the United States.

A new impetus for European integration developed when Germany was unified in 1990. To assuage European fears of dominance by a united Germany, Chancellor Helmut Kohl made himself the principal advocate of the 1992 Maastricht Treaty, which called forth a European currency—the Euro—and initiated significant steps toward a common European foreign and security policy. France supported this process, partly to contain German strength, partly to enlist it in a policy of gaining greater freedom of action vis-à-vis the United States.[7]

Throughout this process of unifying Europe, the United States has played a major supporting role—at first as passionate advocate, more recently as foil. Since the first stirrings of European integration in the aftermath of the Second World War, the United States has strongly endorsed the project and sometimes even urged it on initially reluctant allies. As early as 1963, President Kennedy advocated the unification of Europe in order to bring about a more equal relationship with Europe:

> It is only a fully cohesive Europe that can protect us all against fragmentation of the alliance. Only such a Europe will permit full reciprocity of treatment across the ocean, in facing the Atlantic agenda. With only such a Europe can we have a full give-and-take between equals, an equal sharing of responsibilities, and an equal level of sacrifice.[8]

In this view, generally shared by Kennedy's successors, the Atlantic relationship was analogous to a multinational industrial corporation in which influence is apportioned in relation to the responsibilities assumed. The trouble with this idea of burden sharing as the motivating force of the Atlantic Alliance is that it confuses the operation of a partnership with its purpose. Europe, whether it functions as a collection of nation-states or as the European Union, will share America's burden only if its objectives parallel America's own and if it believes that, without its contribution, the common purposes will not be achieved. This has not been the case. During the Cold War, there was indeed a common purpose, but America's allies were convinced at every step that America would carry out its global responsibilities even when its allies fell short. Today the nature of the common purposes is so much in dispute that the question of burden sharing is rarely reached.

The ultimate issue is not technical but philosophical: Will Europe's emerging identity leave room for an Atlantic partnership? Will America's triumphalism over winning the Cold War veer toward hegemony? French Foreign Minister Hubert Védrine has left no doubt that, in his view, the purpose of achieving a European identity is to reduce the dominance of the United States:

> American supremacy today is . . . felt in the economy, in monetary affairs, in technology and in military fields, as well as in lifestyles, language and the mass culture products that are swamping the world, shaping the ways of thinking, and exercising a fascination that even works on adversaries of the United States. . . .

In keeping with America's view both of itself and the rest of the world over the last two centuries, most great American leaders and thinkers have never doubted for an instant that the United States was chosen by providence as the "indispensable nation" and that it must remain dominant for the sake of humankind. . . . Americans have no doubts and the more forthright amongst them are quick to remind us that the contemporary world is the direct outcome of Europe's complete failure to manage its own and the world's affairs in the first half of the twentieth century.[9]

Védrine's analysis is not without merit. For much of the 1990s, America's Atlantic policies oscillated between imperiousness and indifference, between treating Europe as an auxiliary or as a photo opportunity. A serious strategic dialogue did not materialize, in part because the United States never paused long enough to conduct such a strategic dialogue with itself. A series of initiatives was undertaken unilaterally and made the subject of consultation—if at all—only after a decision had already been taken.

Whereas American unilateralism has resulted from policy decisions which can be modified, the challenge of European integration to America is structural, involving three key issues: the European Union's image of itself; the impact of European integration on Atlantic relationships; and American attitudes toward the different options for European integration.

In defining their identity, the European states are importantly the products—perhaps even the prisoners—of their historical experience. Centuries of operating a system of competing state sovereignties have taught them that persuasiveness in negotiations depends importantly on the options the negotiator has available or is perceived to have at his or her disposal. Europeans historically associated diplomacy with a balancing of rewards and costs; they have little use for an abstract concept of universal goodwill as a facilitator of diplomacy. Still, European societies are not shaped by uniform historic experience. This is reflected in the different attitudes of Britain, France, and Germany toward the idea of Atlantic partnership and European integration.

During the Cold War, Britain was comfortable with American predominance in NATO because its historical experience differed so significantly from that of its neighbors on the continent. For continental nations, the nightmare has always been hegemony by a powerful neighbor. For Britain, the threat to independence has been associated with a hegemonical power on the continent of Europe; salvation in two world wars arrived from across the sea. In British eyes, the role of the United States in the postwar world appeared on the whole benevolent, and friendship with the United States has been the central theme of British foreign policy ever since the end of the Second World War, perhaps even since the First. This "special relationship" was not a primarily sentimental gesture; Britain had survived the centuries as an island outpost off the coast of Europe by never losing sight of its national interest. In pursuit of that interest, it built an independent nuclear force a decade before France did, a clear implication that there were limits to British reliance on the special relationship.

France, lacking the advantages of a common language with a rationalist system of education, conducts a less pragmatic foreign policy. Its leaders strive to create the impression that French (or European) policy has extracted from the United States what America might, in fact, have been quite willing to concede without pressure. Britain pursues its interests by making itself so much a part of the decision-making process that to disregard its views is almost embarrassing. France has pursued its interests by making it too painful to ignore them. Britain has treated Atlantic relations as a common enterprise; French leaders, flaunting their independence, conduct them as a zero sum game in which one side of the Atlantic or the other is bound to have the upper hand.

It is not that France does not understand the United States' role as the ultimate safety net for French (and European) autonomous policy. Nor do French leaders have any illusions about the relative power position of the two countries. In the major crises of the Cold War—the challenges to Berlin between 1957 and 1962, the Cuban Missile Crisis in 1962, the Gulf War in 1990–1991—France proved a staunch ally; deployment of intermediate-range missiles in Germany in 1983 would not have been possible without the eloquent support of French President François Mitterrand.

But the Cartesian, ultrarationalist education of French policymakers causes them to believe that the United States will understand their somewhat cynical applications of *raison d'état,* and will always respect the motivations which induce France to define European identity as a challenge to the United States, even while relying on it as guarantor of France's security. This high-wire act, tolerable when an overriding danger set limits to the game, threatens to undermine the cooperation of last resort on which French leaders still count even when opposition to the United States has become standard operating procedure on many contemporary issues. The policy of seeking a European identity by challenging the United States works best when only one party resorts to it. If the United States retaliated systematically, as sooner or later it will, the strain with the European Union and, even more within it, could become severe.

Germany navigates uneasily between these two poles. It supports the European Union but, unlike Britain and France, it is not in a position to invoke a successful tradition of diplomacy based on the national interest. Even were it to sympathize with the goals of French policy in the abstract, it lacks the self-confidence to conduct the brazen policy of simultaneously challenging and relying on the United States—or perhaps has too great a sense of realism to attempt it.

The United States has watched the various options being proposed for integrating Europe with a benevolence toward the objective and a delicate neutrality that does not declare itself on the kind of Europe being built. The Cold War orthodoxy that European integration would lead automatically to a strong Europe and a more vital Atlantic partnership is still dominant.

But the time has come to take another look at this core assumption of American policy. For at least two other outcomes are possible: a Europe shrinking from global responsibilities, assuming the status of a mini–United Nations and delivering moral homilies while concentrating on economic competition with the United

States; or, alternatively, there could emerge a Europe challenging the United States and constructing a foreign policy of mediating between America and the rest of the world, rather like what India attempted during the Cold War. With domestic politics reigning supreme and no looming security threat, Europe may feel in no hurry to choose between these options. It may thus wind up merging the two approaches, either of which would, step by step, erode the Atlantic partnership.

The first issue to be dealt with is why the Atlantic partnership needs to be revitalized. What is to be the purpose of such an exercise?

Despite the absence of a commonly perceived unifying threat, geopolitics has not disappeared as an element of international politics. NATO still remains as an insurance policy against a new Russian imperialism. Without the United States, Europe would be a peninsular extension, even a hostage, of Eurasia, drawn into the vortex of its conflicts and a prime target of the radical and revolutionary currents sweeping so many adjacent regions. Without the United States, Germany would lack an anchor to restrain national impulses (even as a member of the European Union); both Germany and Russia would be tempted to view each other as their best foreign policy option.

At the same time, the United States, separated from Europe would become, geopolitically, an island off the shores of Eurasia resembling nineteenth-century Britain vis-à-vis Europe. It would become obliged to conduct the kind of balance-of-power strategy toward Europe that it has traditionally rejected. America lacks neither the means nor the opportunity for such a policy, but adopting it would require a psychological wrench and a huge adjustment in its national mode of operation which should be undertaken only as a last resort.

The test will be the ability of the Atlantic nations to work together on issues more immediate than geopolitical theory. At least three issues confront especially Europe, the outcomes of which will determine the future of all nations bordering the Atlantic. As democracies and practitioners of market economics, the Atlantic nations have a stake in preventing economic recessions—the stability of their institutions depends on it. They really have no choice except to coordinate their policies to reduce the dangers of a global economic crisis, which is the major threat to contemporary democracy.

The economic challenge is compounded by a demographic one. In almost all European countries, the birthrate will not sustain the present population, which is already inadequate to meet the needs for labor in a globalized economy. With the improvements in medicine, the percentage of those having to be supported by a shrinking labor force will rise dramatically; the overall population of most European states will drop precipitously—and this in the face of mounting demographic pressures from the poor countries at the fringes of Europe to the east and the south.

Then there is the future of the vast region to the east of the borders of NATO and the European Union. The arrangements that followed the collapse of the Soviet Union were, in their nature, transitory, with respect to both the internal arrangements and the foreign relationships. In many of them—the Baltic states excepted—the generation that inherited power was almost invariably drawn from the previous Soviet leadership group, albeit with nationalist credentials. This generation is now passing from the scene.

Confronted on the one side by skillful, persistent, and insistent Russian pressures to draw them back into some sort of organic relationship with Moscow and, on the other, by the prospects of Europe and even of NATO, these successor states of the Soviet Union will be obliged to make some fundamental choices. Chaos beckons in that vast region unless Europe and the United States define a common task and not appear on the scene as potential rivals. Much depends on the future of Russia, its internal evolution and its relationship to the international order, which will be discussed later in this chapter.

The future of the Mediterranean basin is no less a challenge. The pressures of globalization, of demographic growth in all non-European countries of the region, are ushering in a period of adjustment and potential turmoil comparable to the post-Communist adjustments in Eastern Europe. Most Atlantic nations, while paying lip service to the problem, avoid dealing with it on a systematic basis or approach it on a country-by-country basis, usually when a crisis is already at hand.

Finally, in the globalized world, the quality of life is taking on increasing urgency for peoples and leaders alike. The advocates of such issues have often isolated themselves by presenting their cause as an alternative to traditional foreign policy and by seeking to vindicate it through confrontational methods. But they have a case even when they stultify themselves by exaggerated, self-righteous rhetoric. Representing only 15 percent of the world's population but more than 50 percent of its GDP, the nations of the North Atlantic do indeed have an obligation to help alleviate global problems for which much of the world has neither the material nor the technological resources. It is in the nature of the subject that they need to do so collaboratively, requiring institutions and procedures without which there can be no successful pursuit of the kinds of nonmilitary goals that have heretofore not figured prominently on the Atlantic agenda.

But what if the cooperative course suffers shipwreck because of the European apprehension that any emphasis on Atlantic partnership will dissolve the prospects for identity? Those who seek identity via confrontation with America must not delude themselves into believing that the United States will remain forever passive when its policies are being challenged as a matter of principle. Sooner or later, it will be driven to defend its interests. Then the nations of the West will be back on the course that nearly destroyed them twice in a generation—this time not by war but by an exhausting national rivalry. Ironically, the upshot of such an evolution could well be a weakening of European integration, because, in the end, some key members of the European Union are bound to reject the risks of growing estrangement from the United States.

A consistent pattern of European opposition to American policies cannot be explained away indefinitely as part of the inevitable growing pains of the European Union, or obscured by ritual protestations of allied unity at highly publicized, essentially ceremonial meetings. The United States owes it to its values and its interests to make every effort to revitalize the Atlantic relationship and to help it achieve a new set of common purposes, to treat Europe as a close partner, and to consult with it carefully in advance of major decisions. But, ultimately, Europe must be judged, and the American policy toward Europe adjusted, according to the same criteria as apply to other great powers—on the degree to which European policies and American national interests are able to reinforce each other. Future generations must not be able to ask themselves how it was possible for the nations bordering the Atlantic to spend their energies on abstruse debates of identity *against* cooperation when all around them fundamental problems were threatening the very framework of their societies, and the option of cooperation was always open.

EUROPEAN INTEGRATION AND
ATLANTIC COOPERATION

One of the obstacles to addressing the core issue of Atlantic relationships is largely bureaucratic: it is the time European leaders are obliged to devote to elaborating the process of integration itself. The complex discussion about enlarging the European Union, adapting its institutions, and devising common legislation imposes its own priorities and schedule. Projects for Atlantic cooperation—or other long-range issues—seem less urgent and, in the absence of an immediate crisis, less important. Day-to-day routine thus takes its toll on the habits of Atlantic cooperation, if only because the United States is excluded—by definition, as it were—from those activities which demand the greatest attention of Europe's leaders.

But even with respect to issues where the European Union and the United States interact, the new structures and the methods by which they operate are themselves becoming obstacles to closer cooperation. As the European Union moves toward a greater identity, the existing pattern of Atlantic consultations will inevitably change. This is a fact of life, and the United States needs to accept it.

The kind of European integration that evolves will importantly affect the process of Atlantic consultation. Three possible approaches are under discussion:

The first is the supranational one publicly put forward by German Foreign Minister Joschka Fischer. It implies moving ahead with creating European federal institutions and endowing them with legislative powers. Fischer's proposal of European-wide elections leading to a European executive and legislature is the most far-reaching concept put forward thus far.[10]

Such a scheme runs up against the contradiction—in the words of French Foreign Minister Hubert Védrine—between "enlarging Europe and strengthening it."[11] Enlargement seeks to expand the European Union to the Russian border (and, in some scenarios, it includes Russia as well). Further integration—"deepening," to use the technical jargon—is, in some respects, incompatible with expansion. This is because not every member of the projected European Union will be prepared to subordinate its sovereignty to the extent required by complete political integration.

The second is the proposal for a "multispeed Europe." It would encourage the European Union, with its present core of fifteen nations, to proceed toward political and economic integration while permitting other European nations to associate with it on a less rigid set of procedures. A multispeed Europe would allow plural associations with the integrated core: some could be economic, others military, and all the members of the Union might participate together with the integrated core on some agreed decisions in a specified manner.[12]

Finally, British Prime Minister Tony Blair has proposed a variation on the theme of a multispeed Europe.[13] Because British public opinion would never accept a supranational outcome, and because Blair wants Britain neither to be left at the fringe of such a Europe nor to give up its close relationship with the United States, the Prime Minister has proposed a confederal Europe without a core group. Its members would be free to form various, more integrated, groupings within it for a variety of specified purposes.

The United States should not intervene directly in European

constitutional debates. On one level, they represent the internal matters of Europe. But since each involves some form of integrated European position, they raise what is evolving into the key issue of Atlantic cooperation. For the process by which the European Union, even in its present form, negotiates with the United States leaves little scope for a creative American contribution. When the United States deals with the nations of Europe individually, it has the possibility of consulting at many levels and to have its view heard well before a decision is taken. In dealing with the European Union, by contrast, the United States is excluded from the decision-making process and interacts only after the event, with spokesmen for decisions taken by ministers at meetings in which the United States has not participated at any level. When America encounters spokesmen for the unified Europe, it discovers that its interlocutors have very little flexibility, because decisions taken by the Council of Ministers can be altered only by going through the entire internal European process again. Traditional channels of U.S.-European cooperation are drying up with respect to economic matters. Analogous procedures are now being proposed as well for foreign and security policy. Growing estrangement between America and Europe thus is being institutionally fostered. In some respects, America's possibilities of consultation with the European Union are less substantial than with other friendly, nonallied countries. A balance must be found between the United States insisting on its views as if it were a member of European institutions and its being so marginalized as to be able to participate in European deliberations only after they are, in effect, concluded.

Many advocates of the supranational Europe argue that the real American interest is to keep Europe divided into national states so as to enhance America's ability to dominate by exploiting European rivalries. This is a misconception. Hegemony is not in the American interest for reasons I will discuss in the concluding chapter. But neither is isolation. A wise American policy will seek to navigate between a Europe abdicating from international responsibilities and a Europe striving for a global role in rivalry with the United States.

Whatever the direction of European unification, a new approach to Atlantic cooperation has become imperative. NATO can no longer serve as the sole institution for Atlantic cooperation; its functions are too limited, its core membership too small, and its associated membership too large to deal with the tasks ahead, including even some in the field of security.

STRATEGIC DOCTRINE: EUROPEAN MILITARY CRISIS MANAGEMENT

The subject that most immediately demonstrates the relationship between Atlantic cooperation and European integration is the so-called European Security and Defense Policy, which has led to the creation of a European Force with command structure and political direction formally independent of NATO. Advanced first at the Saint-Malo summit of December 1998 between British and French leaders, the European Force proposal was accelerated immediately after Kosovo at a European summit in Cologne in June 1999. On November 21, 2000, at a meeting of European defense ministers in Brussels, a formal plan for it was announced. According to the Military Capabilities Commitment Declaration, the European Force is slated to reach by 2003 a strength of one hundred thousand persons, four hundred combat aircraft, and one hundred vessels, capable of sustaining a mission of sixty thousand combat personnel for a period of a year. The stress is on the "European Union's autonomy in decision-making," though there is a provision for an exchange of information with NATO which is to be negotiated.

From a long-range point of view, a European military capacity is a logical parallel to the emergence of a European political identity. And such a force is bound to have a certain capacity for autonomous action, much as the various national forces do, whether or not they are technically assigned to NATO. The worrisome aspect of the European Force is that its autonomy seems to be treated as its distinguishing feature, and cooperation with NATO appears to be conceived as a special case.

Kosovo, so the proponents of the European Force argue,

demonstrated the vast disparity in military capabilities between the two sides of the Atlantic. And heavy-handed American conduct verging on the domineering contributed to the decision to speed up the creation of an independent force to regain some means for vindicating strictly European interests.

But the emphasis of the European Force so far has been on autonomy rather than on increasing military capabilities. If one of the motivations for the European Force is to reduce the sense of relative impotence inspired by the high-tech American military establishment, how can that be reconciled with the shrinking defense budgets of almost all the European countries? If existing defense budgets are maintained or reduced, funds for the European Force will necessarily have to come out of projected NATO budgets. Thus the European Force would be a net contribution to allied defense only if it leads to an overall increase in European defense budgets or if it is linked in some organic manner to NATO.

More important, what exactly are the autonomous interests being served? Where precisely would the European Force operate? Since European spokesmen have so far rejected the defense of European territory as a mission, its major utility would be for minor actions at the periphery of Europe in which no major power is involved, or outside the area of NATO responsibilities. Even then, only a very rash group of European leaders would dare to mobilize the European Force without American logistics and intelligence support or assurances of American goodwill. In practice, the European Force is not so much autonomous as it is designed for such symbolic efforts as peacekeeping or special missions involving few risks.

The independent European Force will, in most foreseeable circumstances, have to be coordinated with NATO. And its plan indeed involves an arrangement to use the NATO logistics system. But Javier Solana, the European Union High Representative for Common Foreign and Security Policy, has spoken as if the European Force would be an organizationally distinct group that would negotiate with NATO in much the same way it would with non-NATO countries: "It remains to be seen . . . how to institutionalize the EU's relation with NATO on the one hand and how to institutionalize relations between the EU and other non-NATO countries."[14]

In Eurospeak language, it has been repeatedly affirmed that "the EU will only launch and conduct military operations where NATO as a whole is not engaged."[15] In practice, this can mean only one of two situations. Either the United States favors the projected operation but, for reasons of its own, chooses not to participate—in short, a kind of agreed division of labor. This might work, though the American dissociation must not reach a point where it tempts pressure on Europe from powerful countries like Russia. But what if the European Union undertakes a military action with which the United States disagrees? How should one interpret the extraordinary situation in which all members of the Alliance save America and Canada go to war while the strongest member and ultimate guarantor of security stands aloof? Would the European Force then have access to NATO logistics assets, which are, in the main, American? Would the United States come rushing to the rescue if things went wrong?

Behind these military questions looms a political one. Any crisis in which using the European Force is to be contemplated would require a meeting of Europe's Council of Ministers before NATO meets. The American NATO ambassador (or Secretary of State) would then encounter colleagues who have already reached a collective decision and could not participate in the discussion in their individual capacity, thereby creating a European caucus within NATO and imposing on NATO the procedures which already blight America's relations with the European Union. The United States is nevertheless put at risk because of its security guarantees and need for its logistics support. Leaders who question national missile defense for the United States because it might lead to the decoupling of America from Europe should respect American concern about new structures based institutionally on precisely such a decoupling.

The dispute being generated by the European Force bears some analogy to the controversy produced by President de Gaulle's decision to proceed with a French nuclear *force de frappe*. Like the European Force, it was designed to be free-standing and independent of NATO; as now, it was justified as a possible alternative to—really a last resort against—an American failure to fulfill its Alliance obligations, or for the ultimate defense of French interests not shared by the United States. But there are important differences. The *force de frappe* applied only to the nearly inconceivable contingency in which a NATO country would risk nuclear annihilation without American support. The European Force, by contrast, is designed for contingencies most likely to arise—low-level conventional conflicts at the periphery of Europe or controversial peacekeeping missions on distant continents. The *force de frappe* was designed for the solitary action of a single ally. The European Force is designed for actions endorsed by *all* allies without the United States—symbolically a much more fateful step.

I supported the independent European nuclear forces at the time because I was convinced that, in the end, they would provide the basis for a more balanced partnership. In time, the European Force might play a similar role provided it can be related to an agreed political framework. The key issue raised by the European Force beyond the diversion of resources is the need for political coordination between the United States and the European Union, and between NATO and the European Force. This cannot be achieved by reassurances at meetings of heads of government that can only be tested when it is too late. A separate European military force can work only if the political coordination between the two sides of the Atlantic is enhanced. That, however, is the issue the advocates of the European Force are deliberately evading. Absent such an agreement, the so-called autonomous European Force could produce the worst of all worlds: disruption of NATO procedures and impairment of allied cooperation without any added allied military capability and without meaningful European autonomy.[16] If an organic relationship can be established, the European Force could provide a new political flexibility for the Atlantic Alliance, including especially a link between NATO and the non-NATO members of the European Union.

For the membership of the European Union includes states

which are not members of NATO—today Ireland, Austria, Sweden, and Finland, tomorrow several countries of Eastern and Central Europe. This reality confers a new dimension to the debate over further expansion of NATO. A properly conceived plan of interaction between the European Union and NATO might be able to achieve security guarantees for countries whose independence and territorial integrity are a vital interest of all the Western democracies but whose formal membership in an integrated NATO military command might prove too inflammatory. It could do so by elaborating a distinction between a guarantee of territorial integrity without membership in the integrated military command. This applies especially to the Baltic states. Were Russia to restore its rule, or even its dominance, in those countries, it would signal a return to the imperialism with which it threatened Europe for centuries and an unacceptable shift in both the European and the global equilibrium. On the other hand, the border of Estonia is thirty miles from St. Petersburg. Advancing the NATO integrated command this close to key centers of Russia might mortgage the possibilities of relating Russia to the emerging world order as a constructive member.

If the European Union aspires to be treated as a unit, it follows that some link must be established between the security of those of its members that are not part of NATO and the military structure of the European Union. If there is one region for the defense of which the European Force envisaged by the European Defense Initiative is organically appropriate, it would be precisely in such states. Nor is it possible in a well-conceived Atlantic partnership for NATO to ignore security threats to member states of the European Union, whether or not they are formally members of the Alliance. Strangely, in view of the frequent affirmations of European identity, the European Union insists that membership in it involves no security guarantees. But is Europe really prepared to claim that it has two categories of members, one category of which it is willing to expose to military attack? What then becomes of the oft-invoked European identity? Or of a security and defense policy that does not aspire to defend its own territory?

The European Union, to be truly worthy of its name, must in

time be prepared to resist by force attacks on the security of any of its members, much as its national states do today. And if the European Union is obliged to defend one of its members, whether or not it belongs to NATO, the United States will not be able to stand by.

The argument that the European Union would decouple from NATO were it to assume some responsibility for the defense of its own territory is, with all respect, nonsense. If that were true, the national forces maintained by members of the Alliance would also decouple their countries from NATO. If Europe becomes serious about defense, the expansion of the European Union and of NATO merge to some extent. These steps are needed: The European Union must affirm its determination to safeguard its territorial integrity. NATO needs to affirm that the territorial integrity of the European Union is a vital NATO interest. Then it will be possible to design security guarantees without forward deployments. An indispensable component of such a policy would be rapid membership of the Baltic states in the European Union even if they do not meet all the technical criteria; a union of three hundred million people should be able to make exceptions for the eight million in the Baltic region if the European and Atlantic interest requires it.

STRATEGIC DOCTRINE: MISSILE DEFENSE AND THE ATLANTIC ALLIANCE

Every two decades, a debate about nuclear strategy seems to break out in the Alliance. The subject varies: in the 1960s, it concerned American opposition to national nuclear forces in Europe; in the 1980s, it was about deploying American nuclear missiles in Europe; at this writing, the subject is the American proposal to develop a missile defense system.

The current debate is turning into a test case about whether a serious strategic dialogue within the Alliance is still possible, or whether it will be submerged by domestic politics. The American President's first obligation is to provide for the safety of the American people by deterring attacks on the homeland, on American forces abroad, on America's allies, and to reduce the impact of such attacks should deterrence fail. A bipartisan commission headed by Donald Rumsfeld—now President George W. Bush's Secretary of Defense—was set up in 1998 to study the danger of missile attack. The commission concluded unanimously that the threat posed by a number of hostile emerging states "is broader, more mature and evolving more rapidly than has been reported in estimates and reports by the Intelligence community." [17] Furthermore, the commission argued, "the U.S. might well have little or no warning before operational deployment" of missiles capable of reaching U.S. territory with biological, chemical, or nuclear warheads. [18]

Despite such warnings, national missile defense has become one of those symbolic issues against which elite opinion has rallied for decades, taking little account of the intervening political and technological changes. Five arguments are generally put forward in opposition to a national missile defense:

1. that a workable system cannot be designed;
2. that if it were, it would undermine the strategic doctrine of Mutual Assured Destruction;
3. that it violates the 1972 ABM Treaty and would jeopardize the entire gamut of Russo-American relations;
4. that an anti-missile program would decouple the defense of Europe from America, because the United States might be perceived as withdrawing into a Fortress America (interestingly, this argument is never heard from America's Asian allies); and
5. that an American missile defense would promote nuclear proliferation—an argument put forward jointly by President Chirac of France and President Putin of Russia.

Without claiming to be a technical expert, I have been exposed to enough briefings to be convinced that the prospects of missile defense are promising. This view of America's potential is obviously shared by Russia and China, as is shown by their persistent opposition to any American missile defense system. Most of the technical doubts in the West have concentrated on the system developed in the Clinton administration in an effort to remain compatible with the ABM Treaty. It is designed to shoot down a nuclear warhead in the final phase of its trajectory when it is small, traveling extremely fast, possibly maneuverable, and very hard to detect. This is why most missile defense thinking now concentrates on shooting down the missile during the boost phase when the missile is moving slowly, cannot be maneuvered, and, because of its fuel load, is large and easier to detect.

As for the argument that national missile defense runs counter to the long-standing strategic concept of Mutual Assured Destruction, a reassessment of that doctrine is long overdue, whatever the view regarding missile defense. Advocates of the doctrine argue that nuclear war is best prevented by guaranteeing that the failure of deterrence will produce the most cataclysmic outcome. They therefore oppose any strategy based on discriminating targeting and any attempt to construct defensive systems. Security is sought in an essentially nihilistic insistence on leaving the civilian population, one's own as well as of potential adversaries, totally vulnerable to nuclear attack. In these terms, defense policy turns on itself; in seeking to guarantee the total vulnerability of the population, a doctrine of defense becomes explicitly anti-defense.

This theory emerged out of academic seminars and from theoreticians who would never be required to make the fateful decisions they were urging. It is one thing to theorize about mutual deterrence based on the threat of mutual suicide, quite another to implement such a concept in an actual crisis. Who, in fact, would be prepared to assume the moral responsibility for resorting to a strategy that guarantees the deaths of tens of millions, if not hundreds of millions, on both sides in a matter of days? How can such a strategy be made credible? How can democratic governments implement such a course? It is impossible to believe that democratic governments in Europe, priding themselves on their humanitarian impulses, would in fact carry out their retaliatory threats.

The diplomacy appropriate for such a strategy would have to be designed to demonstrate that, when security is involved, normal calculations do not apply. Leaders would have to display a high propensity for recklessness to make such a strategy credible. But, in both Europe and the United States, the Mutual Assured Destruction theory is being advocated most passionately by those who started their public life in demonstrations attacking *any* reliance on nuclear weapons.

Whatever tenuous plausibility the MAD theory may have had in a two-power world evaporates when eight nations have tested nuclear weapons and many rogue regimes are working feverishly on the development of nuclear, chemical, and biological weapons of mass destruction, as well as on the ballistic missiles with which to deliver them. If one of these weapons destroyed an American or European city by accident or design, how would democratic leaders explain to their publics their refusal—not inability, but refusal—to protect them against even limited missile attacks?

The contrast between the security situation of 1972, when the ABM Treaty was signed, and of today is stark. One signatory, the Soviet Union, has disappeared as a legal entity. Missile technologies have evolved in sophistication and proliferated into nations (North Korea, Iran, Iraq, India, Pakistan) not considered likely candidates for advanced military technology when the agreement was concluded.

Since I have held and published these views for four decades, it is appropriate to ask why an ABM Treaty was signed by President Richard Nixon in 1972, when I served as National Security Adviser. The blunt answer is that, while the Nixon administration started its term in office determined to move away from the MAD concept, it was partially forced back into its framework by congressional and bureaucratic pressures. Early in his first term, Nixon ordered the Pentagon to develop a strategy concentrating on military rather than civilian targets. In 1969, he also submitted to Congress a missile defense program providing for twelve sites to protect missile silos and the population against limited attacks from the Soviet Union, against attacks from emerging nuclear powers, and against accidental and unauthorized launches from any source.

Nixon's ABM program was criticized with precisely the same arguments being deployed against the contemporary programs for missile defense: that it would not work; that it would work so well as to be destabilizing; that it would weaken the Atlantic Alliance by decoupling the defense of the United States from that of Europe; that it would drive the Soviet Union into intransigence and an arms race.

Amid the passions of the Vietnam protest and in a Congress dominated by the opposition party, these criticisms merged with the prevailing assaults on the entire defense budget. The initial authorization for the ABM passed the Senate by one vote, the Vice President's. In subsequent years, Congress used the appropriations process to destroy what it had narrowly failed to defeat in the original authorization. Each year, the number of ABM sites was reduced by Congress until, by late 1971, only two remained. And the Soviets, aware of these domestic pressures, were stonewalling discussions on limiting their offensive buildup, proceeding then at the rate of two hundred long-range missile launchers a year. In this atmosphere, the Defense Department, acting through Deputy Secretary of Defense David Packard, wrote to President Nixon in late spring of 1970 that a strategic arms control agreement should be negotiated as soon as possible. Failing that, the Soviets might soon outstrip the United States in strategic forces.

Nixon was far from converted to the MAD theory but, faced with a Congress determined to gut missile defense, decided to freeze—and thereby to preserve—a nucleus ABM deployment in return for equivalent limits on the Soviets' own missile defense, and to use that decision to put a ceiling on the Soviet offensive buildup. At the Moscow summit of 1972, the Soviets accepted the American insistence that offensive weapons be limited simultaneously with defensive weapons. This history is relevant because many who treat the ABM Treaty as the cornerstone of arms control misunderstand the original impetus for it.

In assessing Europe's reactions to contemporary missile defense, it must be kept in mind that the arguments largely recycle what European opponents of American defense policy have been alleging about every major new American weapons program or strategic doctrine for the past thirty years—from Kennedy's "flexible response" in the 1960s, to Reagan's Strategic Defense Initiative (SDI) and intermediate-range missiles in the 1980s. Opposing new offensive weapons placed in Europe in the 1980s and new defensive weapons based in the United States in this century, these critics—often the same personalities—have charged on each occasion that the new programs would decouple America from Europe and torpedo important negotiations with Moscow.

In each case, the critics have been proven wrong. In the Nixon administration, the United States ABM program broke the deadlock in U.S.-Soviet strategic arms control negotiations. In the Reagan administration, SDI and intermediate-range missiles in Europe brought the Soviets back to the conference table. The same outcome is likely today—indeed at this writing there are already indications of a Russian willingness to explore some kind of missile defense. Russia has thousands of nuclear weapons in its arsenal. Therefore it will be many decades, if ever, before an American missile defense program precludes an ultimate Russian nuclear safety net, even as it constrains many of the more limited ones. Every opportunity exists, therefore, for continuing a diplomacy designed to make a nuclear conflict between the two largest nuclear powers ever less probable.

Finally, once European critics disenthrall themselves from outdated slogans, they will recognize the absurdity of the proposition that an America totally vulnerable to nuclear attack from any direction is the best guarantee for Europe's security. Common sense suggests that the opposite must be true. A United States that is totally vulnerable to nuclear attack is much more likely to shrink from fulfilling Alliance obligations. And these arguments apply as well to the defense of European territory against missile attack.

The argument that an American missile defense system spurs nuclear proliferation makes no more sense. Why should countries not now possessing nuclear missiles be more likely to acquire them because penetrating American territory has become more difficult? Large countries seeking or possessing nuclear missiles and weapons may indeed add to their numbers to defeat American defenses. But even if they are able to sustain that race—which for the so-called rogue states is highly improbable—it would leave America's population no worse off against an all-out attack than it is today, and it would have to be at the sacrifice of an adversary's other military options. Without an American missile defense, the calculations of a country seeking to blackmail the United States are limited only by the reliability of its weapons. With a missile defense, the calculations become more complicated. The adversary cannot know which warheads will get through even if he calculates some will. Or else it would require a scale of attack that verges on all-out war.

Many countries, including China, which is not a signatory to the ABM Treaty, have joined the chorus of opposition to missile defense. So long as there is uncertainty about America's decision, that chorus can only grow in intensity. An early American commitment to a program is therefore essential. Within that context, there should be consultation with allies, especially about giving them an opportunity to participate in the defense system and to extend its coverage to Europe.

But, with all respect for the views of allies and other important countries, the United States cannot condemn its population to permanent vulnerability. All this implies the urgent need to clarify the purpose of missile defense, its technology, and the diplomacy associated with it. Partly for domestic reasons, the purpose of missile defense has been defined exclusively as resisting attacks from rogue states, sparking a debate about what a rogue state is or whether the threat is real. But it is important to avow that the missile defense is needed as well against established nonrogue nuclear powers. Given the cataclysmic consequences of even a single explosion, the United States must protect itself to the extent possible against accidental launches, unauthorized attacks, or limited attacks for whatever purpose. Or, to put it another way, the United States needs to raise the admission price of any nuclear attack as high as possible. In this concept, missile defense may be effective against small nuclear powers or reduce the options of large countries to efforts of a scale that they are not prepared to risk, because the consequences would be too unpredictable.

The decision on missile defense having been made, an open-minded study should seek to determine the most appropriate technology. This had been inhibited by efforts of the Clinton administration to develop a technology that might fit into the ABM Treaty. But were this possible, what would be the relevance of the treaty? At any rate, it has become clear that the most studied technology is probably the least suitable for effective defense. An urgent decision is needed on this issue, unimpeded by those whose vested opposition to defense causes them to demand criteria the fewest new weapons have ever met. Only when the United States has defined its necessities can it conduct a serious dialogue on whether to amend or to withdraw from the treaty. It will also be the most meaningful basis for a negotiation on agreed limits to missile defense and an arrangement on nuclear stockpiles appropriate to the contemporary technology and political environment.

RELATIONS WITH RUSSIA

The West's relations with Russia have always been laced with ambivalence. For Europe, Russia was a relative latecomer on the international scene. Backward, mysterious, elemental, enormous, it exploded on Europe's consciousness only in the eighteenth century. In the first quarter of that century, Russia was still fighting Swedish invaders deep inside what is present-day Ukraine. Less than fifty years later, during the Seven Years' War, Russian armies stood on the outskirts of Berlin. Another generation later, after the defeat of Napoleon, Russian troops occupied Paris.

More autocratic than any of the European states, Russia practiced a mystical and nationalistic form of the Christian religion in Russian orthodoxy—a state church which endowed Russia's quest for prestige and expansion with legitimacy. Though Russia participated in the diplomacy of the European balance of power, it did not apply its principles to neighboring countries. It proclaimed a zone of special influence in the Balkans, where it advocated both Pan-Slavism and the right to protect Orthodox Christianity against the Muslim Ottoman Empire, as well as in Central Asia, where it pursued both a colonialist and a religious mission.

Russia has always been sui generis—especially when compared to its European neighbors. Extending over eleven time zones, Russia (even in its present, post-Soviet form) contains the largest landmass of any contemporary state. St. Petersburg is closer to New York than it is to Vladivostok, which is in turn closer to Seattle than it is to Moscow. A country of that size ought not to suffer from claustrophobia. Yet creeping expansionism has been the recurring theme of Russian history. For four centuries, Russia has subordinated the well-being of its own population to this relentless outward thrust threatening all its neighbors. In the Russian mind, the centuries of sacrifice have been transmuted into a mission, partly on behalf of security, partly in the service of a claimed superior Russian morality.

Throughout history, Russia's achievements and ambitions have kept pace with its physical dimensions. On two occasions, Russia's vastness and its peoples' capacity for endurance prevented a conqueror from dominating Europe: Napoleon in the nineteenth century, Hitler in the twentieth. But, in the aftermath of each stupendous national effort, Russia identified peace with imposing its autocratic domestic principles everywhere within the reach of its armies: in the name of conservatism through the Holy Alliance in the nineteenth century, and in the name of Communism in the twentieth century.

On both occasions, Russia overextended itself and suffered a shipwreck: in the Crimean War in the nineteenth century, and when the Soviet Union collapsed in the twentieth. Throughout its history, with all its ups and downs, Russia has conducted a persistent, patient, and skillful diplomacy: with Prussia and Austria against the specter of French domination; with France against Imperial Germany; with England, France, and Hitler's Germany to avoid isolation; with the United States and Britain to avoid disaster during World War II; and, during the Cold War, by trying to split Europe from the United States through a combination of nuclear blackmail and the support of movements that portrayed the United States as the greater threat to nuclear peace.

Russia's history has left Europe with a legacy of romantic nostalgia for the periods of cooperation but also with a vague dread of Russia's vastness and inscrutability. Many in Germany identify national disasters with the abandonment of Bismarck's legacy of always keeping open a diplomatic option to Russia; France recalls having been saved in two world wars by alliance with Russia. Britain's historical memory is more sober and less sentimental; too much of its history is bound up with resisting Russian threats to the Bosporus and on the approaches to India.

The historical memories of all these countries are reinforced by the pressure of public opinion urging their governments to act as a pivot between Russia and the United States. This is why some European leaders talk of inviting Russia, at some point in the future, to join the European Union. It also is the impetus behind the efforts of all the major nations of Europe to establish a special relationship with Russia, both to prevent a recurrence of historic pressures and as a hedge against their neighbors doing the same thing.

The American historical experience with Russia has been less direct. In the nineteenth century, Russia was treated as the epitome of European autocracy; after the Bolshevik Revolution in 1917, it became for many the incarnation of radical evil. The United States did not establish diplomatic relations with the Soviet Union until the beginning of 1934. In the 1930s, some small groups, spurred by the rise of Nazism, saw in Communism the best barrier to Fascism and the harbinger of a new and more just world order. Germany's invasion of the Soviet Union gave rise to a feeling of goodwill toward the victim together with a sentimentalization of Soviet reality. President Franklin Roosevelt treated the Soviet Union as one of the pillars of an incipient world order, apparently convinced that neither centuries of tsarist autocracy and imperialism nor a generation of Stalinism would pose an insuperable obstacle to postwar Soviet-American collaboration.

The honeymoon proved to be short-lived. Stalin's intransigence, Communist ideology, and the Soviet occupation of Europe up to the Elbe River and dividing Germany produced a reaction of suspicious hostility. International relations became essentially bipolar as the two superpowers confronted each other across a dividing line running through the center of Europe and multiplied their nuclear armaments on both sides of it.

During these forty years of confrontation, a minority in the United States—and somewhat larger groups in Europe—challenged the underlying premises of Atlantic Cold War policy. Sometimes exploited by Communist peace offensives even when independent of them, the advocates of a return to the Soviet-American camaraderie of the war years blamed the United States for excessive preoccupation with nuclear strategy and power politics. During the last two decades of the Cold War, a series of negotiations was conducted with the Soviet Union, mostly dealing with arms control but motivated in good part by the consciousness that, whatever the parties' ideological and geopolitical differences, nuclear weapons posed the risk of a cataclysm threatening the very survival of civilization, and that the two nuclear superpowers had a duty to limit or, if possible, to eliminate it altogether.

These negotiations led to a three-way split of American opinion: a group that believed that the Soviet system would be transformed by the very process of negotiations (or had indeed already transformed itself); a group that viewed Communism as the principal, if not the only, challenge to peace in the world and held that permanent peace could be achieved only by a crusade to bring about the collapse of Communism; and a third group that sought to contain the Soviet Union by a combination of diplomacy and strategy until exhaustion eroded Communist ideological fervor and changed the Soviet Union from an ideological cause to a state pursuing traditional national interests.

The debate among these three groups came to an end with the end of the Cold War itself. But because the first two groups had based their views on the same premise, namely that the Russian challenge was almost exclusively the consequence of the Communist ideology and structure, post–Cold War American thinking about Russia became increasingly preoccupied with the internal changes taking place in Moscow. As Communism unravelled, the relations of the Atlantic nations with Russia were based less on geopolitical considerations than on assumptions regarding Russia's internal situation. And that, in turn, became identified with the personality of the Russian leader, Boris Yeltsin.

The Western democracies began to act as if Russia's domestic re-form were the major, if not the sole, key to a stable relationship. Russia was treated not as a serious power but as the subject of occasionally condescending disquisitions on the state of its internal domestic reform.

Acting as if they were themselves a party to Russian domestic politics, Western leaders during Boris Yeltsin's term in office showered him with accolades, attesting to his commitment to reform. President Clinton, on the occasion of Yeltsin's resignation, spoke of Russia as having become "a pluralist political system and civil society competing in the world markets and plugged into the Internet." He explained Yeltsin's leaving office as "rooted in his core belief in the right and ability of the Russian people to choose their own leader."[19] Almost every other observer viewed Yeltsin's resignation as a skillful manipulation of the Russian constitution in order to entrench as his successor a KGB-trained protégé practically unknown six months earlier, and to protect his own and his family's post-presidential existence.

Equating foreign policy with Russian domestic politics tended to identify the United States in the minds of many Russians with the weird Yeltsin-era hybrid of black markets, reckless speculation, outright criminal activity, and state capitalism in which huge industrial combines were run by their erstwhile Communist managers, all in the guise of privatization. This state of affairs enabled Russian nationalists and Communists to claim that the entire system was a fraud perpetrated by the West to keep Russia weak.

As a general proposition, when foreign policy toward Russia is identified with shaping Russian domestic politics, the ability to influence the external conduct of the Russian state is weakened. Yet it is precisely the external actions of Russia that have historically presented the greatest challenge to international stability. Indeed, the Western democracies, by making themselves so much a party to Russia's domestic drama, provided an incentive for Russia's leaders to escape present-day frustrations by evoking visions of a glorious past.

Whatever the merit of these views during Russia's precarious transition from Communism and however considerable Yeltsin's achievement in navigating it without catastrophe, the world is now dealing with a new type of Russian leader. Unlike his predecessor, who cut his political teeth in the power struggles of the Communist Party, Putin emerged from the world of the secret police. Advancement in that shadowy world presupposes a strong nationalist commitment and a cool, analytical streak. It leads to a foreign policy comparable to that during the tsarist centuries, grounding popular support in a sense of Russian mission and seeking to dominate neighbors where they cannot be subjugated. With respect to other powers, it involves a combination of pressures and inducements, the proportion between which is reached by careful, patient, and cautious manipulations of the balance of power.

On December 31, 1999, the day before his elevation to the presidency, then Prime Minister Putin wrote: "It will not happen, if it ever happens at all, that Russia will become the second edition of, say, the United States or Great Britain. . . . For Russians, a strong state is not an anomaly, which should be got rid of. Quite the contrary, they see it as a guarantor of order and the initiator and the main driving force of any change."[20] Putin explicitly reaffirmed Russia's imperial tradition in his inaugural address in May 2000: "We must know our history, know it as it really is, draw lessons from it and always remember those who created the Russian state, championed its dignity and made it a great, powerful and mighty state."[21]

Both Russia and the United States have historically asserted a global vocation for their societies. But while America's idealism derives from the concept of liberty, Russia's developed from a sense of shared suffering and common submission to authority. Everyone is eligible to share in America's values; Russia's have been reserved for the Russian nation, excluding even the subject nationalities of the empire. American idealism tempts isolationism; Russian idealism has prompted expansionism and nationalism.

This attitude was reflected in a Russian national security policy document adopted on October 3, 1999, when Putin was Prime Minister, and signed into law as one of his first official acts upon assuming the acting presidency in January 2000: "to create a single economic domain with the members of the Commonwealth of Independent States"—that is, all the former constituent republics of the Soviet Union (with the exception of the Baltic states, which are not members of the Commonwealth but which are nevertheless facing constant Russian pressure).[22]

The document does not define what is meant by a "single domain," or how such an ambition could be confined to the economic field. Faced with almost unanimous resistance to these designs, Russian policy under Yeltsin, and even more so under Putin, has sought to render independence so painful for the former constituent republics of the Soviet Union—through the presence of Russian troops, the encouragement of civil wars or economic pressure—that a return to the Russian womb appears as the lesser of these evils.

This policy is making significant progress. In Moldova, the Communist Party has won the most recent election. Georgia faces unremitting Russian pressures: economic, in the manipulation of Russian energy exports; military; and political, in Russian support for dissident groups. Azerbaijan and Uzbekistan face similar pressures. Belarus is already a de facto satellite of Russia. And Ukraine is rent by domestic divisions, of which Russia is partly the cause but also appears to some as the solution to the besieged government (which is responsible for some of its difficulties). And throughout its former empire, Russia is extending its domestic influence by skillfully using the process of privatization to buy up industries in former republics of the Soviet Union, thereby magnifying its economic influence.

One of the key challenges to the relations of the Atlantic nations with Russia is whether Russia can be induced to modify its traditional definition of security. Given its historical experiences, Russia is bound to have a special concern for security around its vast periphery and, as discussed earlier, the West needs to be careful not to extend its integrated military system too close to Russia's borders. But, equally, the West has an obligation to induce Russia to abandon its quest for the domination of its neighbors. If Russia becomes comfortable in its present borders, its relations with the outside world should rapidly improve. But if reform produces a strengthened Russia returning to a policy of hegemony—as, in effect, most of its neighbors fear—Cold War-style tensions would inevitably reappear.

The United States and its allies need to define two priorities in their Russia policy. One is to see to it that Russia's voice is respectfully heard in the emerging international system—and great care must be taken to give Russia a feeling of participation in international decisions, especially those affecting its security. At the same time, the United States and its allies must stress—against all their inclinations—that their concerns with the balance of power did not end with the Cold War. The United States must do more than remonstrate about Russia's support of Iran's nuclear program, its systematic attack on American policies in the Gulf, especially in Iraq, and its eagerness to foster groupings whose proclaimed aim is to dismantle what Russian leaders persist in describing as American hegemony. The United States should respect legitimate Russian security interests. But this presupposes that the Russian definition of "legitimate" be compatible with the independence of Russia's neighbors and that it takes seriously such American concerns as limiting proliferation of nuclear and missile technology.

Russia's internal evolution cannot be treated as the principal answer to the foreign policy challenge with which it has always confronted its neighbors. The relationship between market economics and democracy—and between democracy and a peaceful foreign policy—is not nearly so automatic as conventional wisdom proclaims. In Western Europe, it took centuries for the process of democratization to come to fruition and did not preclude a series of catastrophic wars. In Russia, lacking a vital tradition of capitalism or democracy and which participated in neither the Reformation, the Enlightenment, nor the Age of Discovery, this evolution is likely to prove particularly complicated. Indeed, in the early stages, the process may provide an incentive for Russian leaders to mobilize domestic support by appealing to nationalism.

With all these reservations, the United States and the Atlantic nations have no small stake in a Russia which develops economically and becomes democratic, a Russia which, for the first time in its history, gives priority to its domestic growth rather than seeking security through foreign adventures. They should be patient, but they cannot mortgage the security of Russia's neighbors, or their own, to this quest. For its part, Russia should have every incentive to reverse its historic priorities. Its large armory of nuclear weapons, even if technologically less useful for offensive operations—and perhaps precisely because of that—provides a safety net against Napoleonic or Hitlerian designs on its territory. And even nonnuclear weapons have become so powerful and accurate that old-style wars between major powers grow less and less conceivable.

For well-disposed foreign countries, the thorniest foreign policy challenge posed by Russia is how a potentially powerful country with a turbulent history can develop a stable relationship with the rest of the world. Now reduced to the boundaries of Peter the Great in Europe, Russia must adjust to the loss of its empire even as it builds historically unfamiliar domestic institutions.

The Atlantic allies owe it to Russia to acknowledge that it is undertaking a historic transition and to be helpful where they can. But however sympathetic the Atlantic nations are to this effort, they do themselves no favor by pretending that Russia has already accomplished a process of reform that is only in its infancy, or by celebrating Russian leaders for qualities they have yet to demonstrate. Whether Russia enters the international trading system as a reliable partner will depend to a large extent on its ability to introduce a transparent legal system, a predictable governmental structure, and genuine, rather than oligarchic, market economics. As these goals are approached, Russia's natural resources and its large pool of trained manpower will surely produce a substantial flow of foreign investment.

Some imagine that Europe can assist Russia in its integration into the international community by acting as the middleman between Russia and the United States. Prime Minister Tony Blair has claimed a role for Britain as "pivot," applying it to the contentious issue of missile defense. Others hint at Russian membership in NATO as an ultimate goal. Still others speculate on Russia's eventual membership in the European Union as a counterweight to either the United States or Germany.

But neither course represents a meaningful option for the next two decades. Russian membership in NATO would turn the Atlantic Alliance into a mini–United Nations type of security instrument or, alternatively, into an anti-Asian—especially anti-Chinese —alliance of the Western industrial democracies. Russian membership in the European Union, on the other hand, would split the two sides of the Atlantic. Such a move would inevitably drive Europe further toward seeking to define itself by its distinction from the United States and would oblige Washington to conduct a comparable policy in the rest of the world. An institutional relationship between Russia and Europe that is closer than that of Europe with the United States, or even comparable to it, would spark a revolution in Atlantic relations—the reason why Putin is so assiduously courting some of America's allies.

Every serious student of history recognizes the importance of a significant role for Russia in the building of a new international order without encouraging it into its historic patterns. At the end of the Napoleonic wars, Europe had faced a similar dilemma. Despite the fear of a resurgence of French militarism, Europe nevertheless succeeded in integrating France into the international system. The Quadruple Alliance—of Russia, Britain, Austria, and Prussia—protected Europe against a militarily resurgent France. At the same time, France was made an equal participant with the members of the Quadruple Alliance in the so-called Concert of Europe, which dealt with the political issues affecting the political stability of Europe.

Some analogous solution is needed for the contemporary international order. NATO must be maintained as a hedge against a reimperializing Russia. Coincidentally, the industrial democracies should design a responsible system of cooperation with Russia. The political consultative mechanisms within the Organization for Security and Cooperation in Europe (OSCE) should be strengthened, raised to a head-of-state level, and meet periodically to review the international situation. Russia is already participating in the G-8 heads of state meetings. In this manner, a new order in Europe will be built from west to east and not, as some are urging, from east to west.

TOWARD A NEW STRUCTURE IN ATLANTIC RELATIONS

NATO will no longer prove adequate as the sole institutional framework for Atlantic cooperation. A vehicle for Atlantic cooperation going beyond security is needed to embrace all the nations of the European Union, including those which are not members of NATO, the various institutions of the European Union, and the North American members of the Atlantic Alliance—the United States, Canada, and, in time, Mexico.

A Trans-Atlantic Free Trade Area (TAFTA) would serve such a purpose. Initially designed for manufactured goods and services, with negotiations regarding agriculture to follow, TAFTA would accelerate the movement toward free trade to which all the nations of the North Atlantic region are committed. It would also counter the centrifugal forces weakening North Atlantic cooperation and give a new impetus to a sense of common destiny among the nations bordering the North Atlantic.

The conditions are propitious. Labor standards, wage scales, and environmental concerns on the two sides of the Atlantic are comparable. In time, NAFTA (the North American Free Trade Agreement including the United States, Mexico, and Canada) and TAFTA could be merged. At that point, new consultative machinery in the political and social fields would need to be developed to forge closer links between the Western Hemisphere and the European Union. As Russia's economy develops and its internal policy becomes more constitutional, associate membership for it in such a free trade area would become a distinct possibility.

The realm of political consultation requires the greatest burst of creativity. The central issue is just how much unity the Atlantic democracies need to manage their future, and how much diversity they can stand. It is in America's interest that Europe become a more active participant in world affairs. But it is not in America's interest that this identity be defined in opposition to the United States. An Atlantic Steering Group representing the various components of the Atlantic area should be formed, composed of the United States, the integrated European Union, the European nations not part of the politically integrated Europe, the NATO Secretary General, and the European Union High Representative for Common Foreign and Security Policy. It should meet at stated intervals, backed by a secretariat, to develop parallel approaches to world affairs but also to manage differences as they arise. The membership of this group could also participate in the mechanism for consultation with Russia under the auspices of the OSCE described earlier.

The Atlantic region would, in this conception, be characterized by a series of overlapping circles. On the military side, there would be NATO, together with whatever military force the European Union generates and which, in practice, would have to be integrated with NATO in some manner. On the security side, all members of the European Union must have some kind of NATO guarantee even when they are not part of the integrated command. Whatever the adaptations, NATO would remain as the key security organization. On the economic side, there would be the Trans-Atlantic Free Trade Area. Political issues would be dealt with by the Atlantic Steering Group.

It is not an exaggeration to say that the future of democratic government as we understand it depends on whether the democracies bordering the North Atlantic manage to revitalize their relations in a world without Cold War and whether they can live up to the challenges of a global world order. If the Atlantic relationship gradually degenerates into the sort of rivalry that, amidst all its great achievements, spelled the end of Europe's preeminence in world affairs, the resulting crisis would undermine those values the Western societies have cherished in common.

While many pay lip service to the importance of this goal, there has been no real urgency in dealing with it. The disputes within the Atlantic area are real enough, and many of them—especially in the economic field—involve significant competing constituencies on both sides of the Atlantic. The desire of Europe for a greater identity is valid and, in the long run, also in the interest of the United States. The difficulty is to find a definition of identity that is something other than almost congenital opposition to the United States. A relationship of genuine cooperation implies that the two sides of the Atlantic are willing to modify their immediate short-term interests for the long-term necessities of a broader vision. But as Western democracies are ever more driven internally by short-term considerations, the constituencies for the long term shrink; the political rewards are for actions either which demonstrate immediate benefits or reward short-term passions. It therefore comes down to a question of leadership on both sides of the Atlantic.

While many of these pages have deplored trends within Europe, anyone concerned with the future of Atlantic relationships must recognize that overbearing American triumphalism bears its own share of responsibility. There has been too great a tendency to identify cooperation with concurrence with an American agenda; too much American domestic legislation being applied to close allies in their own countries; too little understanding of the needs of societies adjusting to the loss of their previous preeminence. A more sensitive American policy is essential. But so is a less doctrinaire European one. After all, the task of leaders is to take their societies from where they are to where they have never been.

◇ ◇ ◇ ◇ ◇ ◇ ◇ ◇ ◇ ◇ THREE

The Western Hemisphere: The World of Democracies II

REVOLUTION IN THE REGION

To the extent that political and economic institutions determine the nature of a region's international role, Latin America is comparable to the nations bordering the North Atlantic. Its political systems are democratic; its economies are increasingly market-oriented; disputes between its nations are settled by negotiation or arbitration. Wars between the countries of Latin America are, to all practical purposes, excluded. Occasional border confrontations, such as those between Peru and Ecuador in the 1980s, stand out as throwbacks to an earlier age, unlikely to be repeated in any significant way in the years to come. Arms expenditures as a proportion of the domestic product are lower in Latin America than in any other region of the world. From these perspectives, Latin America—especially Argentina, Brazil, and Mexico—is entering the globalized world and marks a success story for the principles of democracy and free markets. When President Clinton, at the Western Hemisphere summit in Miami in December 1994, proposed a Free Trade Area of the Americas (FTAA), he was appealing to this Latin American world.

But there is also another Latin American world that is underdeveloped and a long way from sharing in advanced technology and the Internet. In that Latin America, the gap between the political and the economic worlds is flagrant. There the chasm between rich and poor is growing. In some countries—Venezuela, for example—populist, in essence authoritarian, movements are challenging democratic institutions. In others—Colombia being the most flagrant case—leftist guerrillas, backed by resources from the narcotics trade, are undermining national cohesion. A new form of nationalism may emerge, seeking national or regional identity by confronting the United States. In its deepest sense, the challenge of Western Hemisphere policy for the United States is whether it can help bring about the world envisioned by the Free Trade Area of the Americas, or whether the Western Hemisphere, for the first time in its history, will break up into competing blocs; whether democracy and free markets will remain the dominant institutions, or whether there is a gradual relapse into populist authoritarianism, at least in some countries.

This challenge is all the more serious because, at least since the Monroe Doctrine, the United States has thought of itself as having a special role in the Western Hemisphere. Fot its part, Latin America has gone along with the convenient principle of a Pan-American community, though it has far from agreed to the U.S. definition of the responsibilities and inhibitions it implied. In any event, the nature of that special role is undergoing a profound change because, starting in the 1980s, a political and economic transformation took place in Latin America no less far-reaching than the one which occurred at about the same moment in Eastern Europe and the Soviet Union.

As it emerged from World War II, and for three decades thereafter, Latin America was a region of authoritarian regimes—many of them military, some of them maintaining their power by repressive methods. Only Costa Rica and Colombia had, to a degree, an uninterrupted record of civilian governance.

Starting in the 1980s, civilians elected by votes based on wide suffrage replaced military leaders; human rights began to enjoy protection from those in authority; legislatures regained the power of initiative. The fact of some backsliding—and of the egregious long-standing exception of Cuba—does not gainsay the remarkable choice of the democratic alternative throughout Latin America.

The triumph of the ballot has been matched by equally impressive advances on the economic front. Until the watershed events of the 1980s, virtually all the nations of Latin America were afflicted by profligate public sector deficits, unemployment (sometimes disguised by bloated public payrolls), inefficient state-owned enterprises, protective tariffs, and uncompetitive economies. Starting in the 1980s, led by Argentina, Brazil, Mexico, and Chile, central governments and provinces throughout the hemisphere began shedding businesses suited to private enterprise and potentially subject to the disciplines of the marketplace. Inflation has been greatly reduced. Global competitiveness is improving. Free trade throughout the hemisphere has become, at least formally, the objective of all the nations of the region.

In their relations with one another, the nations of Latin America have undergone equally profound transformations. Argentina and Brazil have opted out of what, for a time, seemed ominously to be the beginning of a nuclear arms race. Both have formally promised to abandon any aspiration to build nuclear devices or delivery systems. In this, they have joined Mexico, which declared its commitment to forgo a nuclear capability a decade earlier. The rest of Latin America has followed suit. There is no competitive military buildup in the region nor any prospect of one. In short, the key nations of Latin America exhibit a host of traits likely to make them prime candidates for full-fledged membership in the group of developed nations: a growing tradition of representative government and open societies, a commitment to universal education, and equal and efficient administration of justice.

NEW CHALLENGES

At this writing, these hopeful prospects describe a vision, but not yet a reality; to achieve it, a second stage of domestic change and reform is necessary. The rudiments of democracy are everywhere (again, except in Cuba). But in no country is it beyond challenge—as recent events in Peru and Venezuela demonstrate, not to speak of Haiti where even the pretense of democracy is vanishing. The first phase of privatization, fiscal reform and tariff reduction, has taken place. But the hard work of rooting out corruption, establishing judicial security, and delivering public services efficiently and equitably has only begun. In several countries, notoriously Colombia but also Mexico and several of the Caribbean ministates, the commercialization of the narcotics industry has brought official corruption to new heights. Indeed, in Colombia, the central government has formally ceded public control of specific territory to radical guerrillas. Similarly, Peru and Ecuador are unable or unwilling to assert sovereignty over significant parts of their territory. Violence is mounting nearly everywhere in Latin America, and public security has become a growing problem.

Public services, most conspicuously education and public health, rank far below the standards of other Western nations—and not primarily because of inadequate funding. In several countries, expenditures per public school student are equal to Europe's. If Latin America is to maintain and enhance its global competitive position, a thorough reform and modernization of educational policies and practices are imperative.

Equally vital to modernization is the reform of the systems of justice and of the legal codes. In some countries, justice is for sale and heavily influenced by the political leadership. Property titles are insecure. Dispute resolution by the courts is idiosyncratic and unpredictable, giving rise to the sense that the legal system is inadequate to the challenge of protecting persons or property.

All these shortcomings are thrown into sharp relief by the process of globalization. As industrialization moves people from the countryside to the cities, traditional support systems are weakened and gradually evaporate. Income gaps that were bearable in rural societies turn into challenges to the political order. Whatever the gains from productivity and export earnings, if they are not translated into economic benefits for the majority of the population and if the fiscal prudence demanded by the international financial markets is perceived to be bearing most heavily on the disadvantaged, the political system becomes vulnerable to challenge.

The gap between the economic and the political worlds is the Achilles' heel of the process of globalization. As I shall describe in Chapter 6, globalization carries with it the risk that developing countries evolve into two-tiered economies. Perhaps 20 percent of their economies will be part of the international system, typically as components of large multinationals. The rest—and perhaps the majority of their populations—could be left behind, without access to the income, jobs, and opportunities generated by globalization. This dichotomy produces a potential for resentment, backlash against the United States, and social unrest, especially if, in a recession, the American economy has a harder landing than generally forecast.

Moreover, domestic savings cannot be expected to provide the investment required to take the region to the next stage of growth. As a result, many of the most productive assets in Latin America are likely, sooner or later, to be owned by foreigners. Economists may react with enthusiasm to this demonstration of the efficiency of the market, but some Latin American political leaders will be tempted to exploit the public perception of de facto erosion of national sovereignty and merge it with the assault on the market-oriented political system.

Such has been the case in the Andean countries. In each of them, the military has assumed a new prominence. Presidents have concentrated power in their hands at the expense of the elected legislatures. Individual liberties and press freedoms have been curtailed, and institutional crisis is rife. This is particularly ominous in Venezuela, where a populist former army officer, Hugo Chávez, has exploited the public resentment with corruption and inequality and tried to channel it into a challenge to United States policies and prescriptions to remarkable demagogic advantage. Chávez has abolished many of the constitutional and democratic restraints of the Venezuelan political system; the laudable objective of eliminating corruption and nepotism has been turned into a platform for a populist military autocracy. The rise in the price of oil, Venezuela's principal export, has enabled Chávez to avoid the consequences of his flirtation with Fidel Castro and his anti-American and, to some extent, anti-capitalist slogans of a kind that seemed to be transcended by the transformations of the 1980s.

As part of the same process, Peru is emerging from Alberto Fujimori's combination of personal autocracy, nepotism, and market economics to an as yet undefined alternative. Alan García, whose statist approach ruined Peru's economy and paved the way for Fujimori, has returned from exile, and other contestants will watch the evolution in neighboring countries closely before they choose their own course.

Similarly, Ecuador has experimented with, and rejected, more chiefs of state in recent years than its bewildered citizens care to remember—and, in the midst of the crisis, decided to abandon its currency and dollarize the country's financial system. Neither globalization nor democracy has brought stability to the Andes.

Is Chávez a relic of a bygone era or the augury of a new style in Latin American politics? Is he inheriting Castro's mantle, or is he a passing phenomenon? Does the globalized economy provide enough psychological and political fulfillment to sustain democratic institutions, or does it create a vacuum for a new cycle of semi-authoritarian populism? Will the upcoming generation of young political leaders seek to follow the radical populist style of Chávez or of Brazil's Fernando Henrique Cardoso's emphasis on democracy and free markets? The answers to these questions, and America's role in dealing with them, will shape the future of Latin America.

The United States cannot directly affect internal developments in Peru, Venezuela, and Ecuador. The attempts by the Clinton administration to do so usually occurred when a governmental crisis was already in full train and was arguably made, if anything, worse by heavy-handed American pronouncements. In the short term, the best option for the United States is to push the emergence of the Free Trade Area of the Americas proclaimed at the Miami summit of 1994 as the underpinning for the democratic market-oriented alternative.

Is There a Road Out of Chaos?
Plan Colombia

Colombia is a country rife with ambiguity. It has a long history of uninterrupted democracy; for much of the last half-century, its leaders have been impeccably civilian and emerged from periodic elections though, for much of the period, the political parties have conspired to alternate in the exercise of power. Colombia also largely avoided the cycle of boom and bust afflicting its neighbors. Through prudent fiscal management, it essentially escaped the Latin American debt crisis of the 1980s and required no restructuring of its international debt.

But Colombia also has a tradition of extreme violence. For the past half-century, it has found itself torn by a vicious civil war. Part of the reason for the endemic violence is that Colombia is highly heterogeneous. Different cultures in various parts of the country amount, in fact, to different societies: the highlands, where most of the people of European origin live; the coastal plains, inhabited by many of the descendants of slaves brought to the country in the nineteenth century; and the forested regions, where vestiges of the original Indian culture survive.

The civil war, originally started by radical Marxist groups, has merged with the narcotics industry, supplying much of the illegal drugs consumed in the United States. The narcotics producers finance the guerrillas who, in return for the weapons they are thus able to acquire, supply safe havens for narcotics production. As a result, the guerrillas are, in many respects, better financed than the government. The government has thus far been unable to break the resulting military stalemate; its frustrations have reached a point where it has granted the guerrillas safe havens. Parts of the country are thus, in effect, governed by radical groups determined to overthrow the central government and by narcotics producers openly flouting the national legislation.

In the process, Colombia finds itself trapped in the classic dilemma of guerrilla warfare. The guerrillas do not have to fight except when they are fairly sure they have the upper hand—especially when they operate out of safe havens. And they do not have to win battles; their goal is to inflict casualties that will cumulatively sap the government's staying power and its base of political consent. Guerrillas generally win so long as they do not lose and, conversely, the government loses if it does not win—that is, if it does not destroy the guerrillas.

Historically, guerrilla wars, like civil wars, have ended either in total victory for one side or in the utter exhaustion of both sides. Negotiations between the parties almost never conclude in compromise—though they continue to rank as a favorite prescription of North American advisors urging "political" outcomes. Nor have they succeeded in Colombia despite the government's strenuous attempts and the extraordinary step of ceding substantial territory to the two major guerrilla bands.

All this has turned Colombia into the most menacing foreign policy challenge in Latin America for the United States. A collapse of governance threatens. Self-appointed paramilitaries are conducting open warfare against the guerrillas, and law and order is well on the way to a total breakdown. For the United States, the consequences of such an outcome would be grave. National disintegration in Colombia would be a body blow to the economic progress of the region, would generate a wave of refugees that would inevitably reach the shores of Colombia's neighbors and the United States, and would end even the limited measures of drug trafficking control that presently exist in the country. It would leave a radical Marxist government backed, at least for the moment, by narcotics money in the largest and most traditional nation in the Andes. This crisis is several orders of magnitude more serious than the instability in Haiti, which precipitated the Clinton administration's maladroit intervention, or in Panama, which triggered a military response by the George H. W. Bush administration.

There can be little question that the United States has an interest in the reestablishment of stability in Colombia. It should do what it can to help build a government there capable of enforcing its own laws against poppy and coca production, against drug processing plants, and against the elaborate transport systems devised to move drugs from Colombia for distribution and consumption in the United States. This is why, in its last months, the Clinton administration put forward, under the slogan "Plan Colombia," a program of major assistance. A projected $1.2 billion is to be spent for advanced helicopters and other equipment, with American advisors training Colombian officers for fighting the guerrilla war. The purpose is to destroy the drug segment of the guerrilla movement, leaving the guerrillas either to wither away or negotiate their way out.

Unfortunately, the almost exclusive emphasis of Plan Colombia on a military solution virtually invites failure. To assist the Colombian government to assert its own authority over the drug-producing guerrilla areas, to control the processing and transport systems, and to win the triangular war with the guerrillas and the paramilitary forces, much more is needed than attack helicopters and a handful of battalions of troops subjected to a short course of American instruction. The drug growers, largely small dirt farmers, must be given wider opportunities for alternative crops. United States assistance to Colombia for alternative agriculture has been pitifully small compared to the military aid. Yet it is the economic desperation of the Colombian farmer that makes him an easy target for the drug producers.

Then, too, the right-wing paramilitary organizations must be brought to heel. The human rights of those living in the zones of violence must be protected not only from the guerrillas but also from the self-appointed private security forces that justify their existence by the ineffectiveness of governmental policing and security forces. Wholesale reform of the institutions of criminal justice is essential.

In these circumstances, Plan Colombia bears within it the same fateful momentum which drove America's engagement in Vietnam first to stalemate and then to frustration: at the outset, the United States limits its involvement to training and the provision of vital military equipment—in this case, large attack helicopters. But once the effort goes beyond a certain point, the United States, to avoid the collapse of the local forces in which it has invested such prestige and treasure, will be driven to take the field itself.

When the stakes are this high, it is dangerous to undertake the enterprise without the support of at least some of the major Latin American countries. Hemispheric cooperation, however, has been sorely lacking with respect to Plan Colombia. Under Hugo Chávez, Venezuela, which has a long frontier with Colombia, sympathizes with the radical guerrillas and opposes even an indirect American presence near its borders. Brazil, with another long border, has so far been noncommittal with respect to the U.S. role. Peru and Ecuador are too preoccupied with their domestic problems to lend active assistance. Colombia's neighbors generally fear the plan's success almost as much as its failure. They are concerned that, if the narcotics industry is pushed out of Colombia, it will move into Ecuador, Peru, and Brazil and protect the coca crops with its own armed forces which then will turn into guerrilla movements. Many of them fear a leftist government in Bogotá more tolerant of the drug cartel less than they do narcotics centers on their own soil.

As an alibi for their reluctance to cooperate, the Latin American governments tend to cite U.S. hypocrisy, claiming that the United States is more prepared to fight the drug war on foreign soil than to curb its domestic consumption. Latin America's criticisms of the U.S. emphasis on the problem of supply have merit, as does its emphasis on the shortcomings of the United States's domestic war on drugs. Yet this does not alter the reality that the effect of the drug culture is even more corrosive in Latin America than in the United States. In highly centralized systems like those of Latin America, corruption associated with the drug trade inevitably reaches high government officials and the criminal justice system. In a decentralized system like that of the United States, corruption focuses on the local level. In Latin America, the trade in illegal drugs is politically destabilizing; in the United States, it is a political embarrassment and a social crisis. Nevertheless, both regions will pay an enormous price—not the least of which will be the corrosive influence on the bilateral relationship—if the problem is not dealt with cooperatively.

The new administration has no more important task than to obtain Latin American cooperation for a program which combines the military aspects of Plan Colombia with a farsighted social program of agricultural and judicial reform. An important first step is the expanded cooperation between Mexico and the United States in stemming the flow of drugs from Colombia through Mexico to the United States. As Mexican President Vicente Fox has stated, this program of cooperative control could be extended to Central America and Colombia. The other countries, especially Colombia's neighbors, should grasp the fact that they will not be able to avoid the growing danger of the Colombian government disintegrating or losing control over more and more of its countryside. At some point, it may conclude that it has no alternative but to negotiate an agreement with the guerrillas that will become the final step on the road to losing control altogether. And the impact of such a collapse and the emergence of a radical government financed by drug money would prove devastating to other countries in the region.

The decision of the Clinton administration to resist such an outcome, unilaterally if necessary, is understandable. But so is the concern of those who see the same danger looming at the end of a prolonged and inconclusive anti-guerrilla/anti-drug effort. As someone who served in an administration which inherited a stalemated war in Vietnam, begun as an effort to use American technology to defeat indigenous guerrillas, I am perhaps excessively sensitive to the prospect of a conflict launched with noble motives but likely to end in stalemate, disillusionment, and an even greater threat to stability and security.

The military aspect of Plan Colombia and its unilateral execution by the United States is at best a way to buy time for a hemispheric, multilateral social and political program. But what if the Latin American countries refuse to go along? Given the importance of Colombia and the dangers associated with its collapse, a substantial assistance program is appropriate. But the United States must not cross the line to an advisory effort that makes it a participant in the conflict. Training of Colombian military personnel should take place in the United States or at nearby bases, for example, in Panama. The purposes and equally the limits of such a program need to be clearly defined. And the inevitable national debate must be conducted with some understanding of local realities, especially since guerrilla groups have learned to exploit Western human rights concerns to trigger intervention (as in Kosovo) or to induce withdrawal (as in Vietnam).

Before the United States becomes too deeply enmeshed unilaterally, the new administration should define its objectives: Are they stabilization of the military situation or victory? And what is the difference? What is the danger that military stabilization is the prelude to a prolonged defeat? If victory is the objective, what is its definition, how long will it take, and what effort will it require? How far can the United States go alone? Above all, the administration must explain to the public what it faces, lest America drift into decisions on a largely tactical basis that permit neither success nor extrication.

THE PROMISE OF THE WESTERN HEMISPHERE

Ironically, President Clinton, whose frantic quest for a foreign policy legacy shadowed his last months in office, may well have created his most enduring legacy in the early months of his presidency when he gave his support to free trade in the Americas. In 1993, Clinton shepherded through Congress the ratification of NAFTA —the North American Free Trade Agreement embracing Canada, Mexico, and the United States—that had been negotiated during the terms of his predecessors.

NAFTA has proved to be of lasting benefit to each of the partners. United States trade with Mexico exceeds trade with Japan and with all of Europe. Over 70 percent of Mexico's exports goes to the United States. The access to the North American market that NAFTA guaranteed has encouraged a substantial influx of fresh capital into the country. This trend would surely be repeated elsewhere if free trade between the NAFTA countries and Latin America were implemented. NAFTA was a crowning achievement of foreign policy, especially if its principles can now be extended to embrace the rest of the hemisphere.

In a seminal speech to the December 1994 Miami summit, Pres-

ident Clinton proposed precisely such a step by transforming unilateral proposals similar to those of Presidents Ronald Reagan and
George H. W. Bush for free trade in the Americas into a formal undertaking by all the heads of state of the hemisphere. Clinton described NAFTA as the vital first step for a new kind of community
of nations, built on a common base of democratic values, drawn together by the free exchange of goods, services, and capital, dedicated to human rights, and committed to the preservation of their
common environment.

A Western Hemisphere Free Trade Area is important for economic reasons as well. The FTAA would be an incentive for other
nations to move forward with the global effort to expand free trade
in the agricultural, communications, and service sectors while
strengthening the bargaining position of the Western Hemisphere
vis-à-vis other regions. The issue is not theoretical; a series of tight
deadlines are driving the trade negotiations. The next summit of
the Americas is, at this writing, scheduled for Quebec City on April
20–22, 2001, and will be followed by the FTAA negotiations slated
for November 2002 and co-chaired by Brazil and the United
States. These are planned to be concluded by 2005. Mercosur, a
Latin American trading bloc, has opened negotiations on free trade
with the European Union with a target date of 2004–2005. If the
United States fails to pursue a clear and forward-looking policy, the
nations of the Western Hemisphere will negotiate competitively
with other regional groupings or organize themselves in smaller
groups to the exclusion of the United States. Both these options are
contrary to the U.S. national interest.

Yet this is what has been happening since the Clinton administration defaulted on its own farsighted vision. It failed to implement its promise to Chile for early access to NAFTA, and it
ignored feelers from Argentina in the same direction during Carlos
Menem's presidency. The practical expression of this retreat from
its own initiatives was the Clinton administration's refusal to ask
Congress for renewal of the fast-track authority which lapsed in
1994. That authority, under which U.S. trade negotiations had
been conducted since 1974, enabled the president to negotiate an

agreement and submit it to Congress for approval or rejection without the possibility of amendment.

The Clinton administration recoiled from acting on its convictions because it found both U.S. political parties split between groups rejecting an institutional connection with the rest of the world and others seeking to impose U.S. standards unilaterally (especially labor and environmental criteria). As a result, a U.S. president lacked the authority for the first time in more than two decades to pursue either the expansion of NAFTA beyond Canada and Mexico or negotiations with the other regional groupings. In the absence of fast-track authority, interlocutors know that negotiations would be unending and burdened with the risk that any deal reached might be amended by Congress and then need to be renegotiated.

This paralysis is all the more debilitating because it occurred simultaneously with the emergence of Mercosur, linking Brazil, Argentina, Paraguay, and Uruguay in a South American free trade area under the leadership of Brazil. Chile, tired of waiting for the long-promised access to NAFTA, has become an associate member of Mercosur, as has Bolivia; Venezuela and Peru have expressed strong interest. Like every new trading bloc, Mercosur affirms that its intentions are nondiscriminatory; the reality is otherwise. It is the defining characteristic of a trading bloc that its internal barriers are lower than its external ones; its bargaining position depends on its ability to grant or withhold benefits that its own members enjoy as of right.

It is precisely with this siren song that Europe beckons beyond the Atlantic. On a visit to Latin America in March 1997, French President Jacques Chirac urged on his hosts that the future of Latin America was not to the "North," meaning NAFTA and the United States, but with Europe. Other self-proclaimed European anti-hegemonists—the code word for those in favor of reducing American power and influence—have elaborated the same theme. A good example is an interview in December 2000 with the then president of the Council of the European Union (of foreign ministers)—the Portuguese António Guterres—defending an agricultural European agreement on the ground that its impact would reduce the influence of the United States:

> The strengthening of ties with Mercosur is of strategic importance and must, in case of a country that has a global vision as France does, prevail over other considerations (e.g., differences in agricultural policy). Because when it comes to building a new multipolar order that can limit the United States' natural hegemony, Europe will have to make some concessions.[1]

Some Latin American proponents of Mercosur have not hesitated to associate themselves with this sentiment.

With the prospects of the FTAA stalled, trade negotiations in the hemisphere have languished, submerged by bureaucratic disputes which occasionally serve as a proxy for an incipient contest between NAFTA and Mercosur. The danger of continued drift is that Latin America's integration will evolve its own rhythm without reference to, and perhaps even inimically toward, a larger hemisphere structure. This would not be simply a setback to U.S. economic prospects in a market of four hundred million people, which accounts for 20 percent of its overseas trade, but, above all, to its hopes for a world order based on a growing community of democracies in the Americas and Europe.

NAFTA AND MERCOSUR

In the absence of a dynamic and forward-looking United States policy, Mercosur may turn into a replica of those trends in the European Union that define Europe's political identity in distinction to the United States, if not in outright opposition to it. Especially in Brazil, there are leaders attracted by the prospect of a politically unified Latin America confronting the United States and NAFTA. "Mercosur is a destiny for us," Brazil's President Cardoso has said, "while the FTAA is an option."[2]

But if the leaders of the Western Hemisphere do not find a way to reconcile the "destiny" and the "option"—even more, if they are treated as incompatible—societies with comparable histories and free institutions would be repeating in the twenty-first century the same self-destructive course that depleted their substance in the twentieth. At this writing, Brazil and the United States find themselves in tacit competition, obscured by the reluctance to make it explicit and the realization that open conflict would run counter to their economic necessities. For its part, the United States has no reason to be the first to abandon the road to partnership. It has everything to gain from strengthening its bilateral relations with its neighbors to the south, especially with the principal nations of Mexico, Brazil, and Argentina, while at the same time carrying out an intensive diplomacy to bring both NAFTA and Mercosur into a Western Hemisphere free trade area.

Mexico already enjoys a special relationship with the United States and is its second largest trading partner. NAFTA, attacked at the time of its creation on both sides of the Rio Grande as an impossible marriage of the rich and poor, has turned into an astonishing success. As a result, Mexico has been dramatically reinventing itself. In the old Mexico, business—including the business of government—was dominated by a self-perpetuating political elite; newcomers were distinctly unwelcome. The old Mexico, more concerned with past grievances than future opportunities, was self-absorbed and locked into cycles of boom and bust, of progress and corruption. It looked northward with a mixture of envy and fear, congenitally opposed to whatever the United States advocated in international affairs and, at the same time, comfortable in the knowledge that any security challenge to the Western Hemisphere would, in the end, be dealt with by the "Colossus of the North."

Today competition and transparency have replaced monopoly and secret dealings in almost every aspect of life, and most Mexicans appear eager to embrace reform. In part, this reflects the enormous historical, economic, technological, and cultural forces that are reshaping societies everywhere. But, to a considerable extent, the transformation reflects experiences unique to Mexico. President Carlos Salinas de Gortari, who came to power in 1988 in a tainted election, fostered economic liberalization that gave freer play to competitive forces and tempered the state's domination of the economy. This in turn made possible the negotiation of the North American Free Trade Agreement.

Salinas and his technocrats ultimately suffered shipwreck because they failed to adapt the Mexican political system to the economic changes they had brought about. President Ernesto Zedillo —emergency substitute candidate in 1994 after Luis Donaldo Colosio was assassinated—took the historic step of installing an electoral system that assured a fair and free election. When Vicente Fox took office in December 2000, he was the first modern Mexican president chosen in a free election and governing in a genuine multiparty system.

Fox has inherited massive challenges as well: the monarchical style of government prevalent before the July 2, 2000, election needs to be adapted to a separation of powers and a legislative branch in which the president lacks a majority. Fox is the first Mexican president in seven decades not to have at his bidding the apparatus of a governing party with a majority in Congress and whose nominees dominate the judiciary.

One of the positive contributions of the previous governing party, the Institutional Revolutionary Party (known by its Spanish acronym PRI), had been its skill in absorbing and mitigating the extremes of the right and left. No longer a governing party, the PRI is likely to shed this attribute.

Moreover, many Mexicans supported Fox not necessarily because they agreed with his moderate center-right positions but because they wanted to break the PRI's monopoly on government. As the new Mexican system settles down, they are likely to drift toward their standard preferences, and Mexico may well be heading toward a right-left alignment similar to that in many of Europe's parliamentary systems. This creates the need for coalition-building in the process of government—a new experience for the Mexican political system.

Many tasks await Fox. Wealth is still badly skewed in favor of the relatively few. Real wages are too low to provide much of the population with a decent income. Drug money corrupts the police and judicial system. The country's physical infrastructure has not kept up with the new economic opportunities. And the Mexican educational system is inadequate for the needs of the twenty-first century.

At the same time, Mexico is uniquely positioned to benefit from its ties with the United States. No other country with such a large population shares as long a border with such a rich neighbor. But if geography were enough, Mexico would long since have been an economic success. Two changes have presented it with a new window of opportunity: NAFTA and globalization.

NAFTA has generated trade and investment exceeding the most optimistic forecasts due, in part, to the record growth in the United States. But it is also because Mexico is well positioned to take advantage of globalization. For the tools of the new globalized economy arrive in Mexico nearly at the same time and almost at the same cost as they do in the industrialized countries. With technology the key to growth, any country prepared to learn to use it can succeed, especially when, as in Mexico, there is a preponderance of young people who have grown up with computers and the Internet. With 65 percent of the Mexican population under thirty years of age, Mexico could emerge as a major factor in the world economy, provided it radically transforms its educational system, reforms its public finance, and manages to control the narcotics trade—goals Fox has made prime priorities.

Mexican realities thus mesh with early evidence of the priorities of the George W. Bush administration. As a former governor of Texas, President Bush has personally experienced the importance to the United States of a healthy, creative, and productive Mexico. And he has responded by acknowledging Mexico's priority on his foreign policy agenda, which includes as a major item joint efforts with Canada to integrate NAFTA into a hemispheric Free Trade Area by 2005.

Reaching that goal will depend to a large extent on another quite different special relationship—that between the United States and Brazil. The evolution of Brazil's foreign policy has been, in many respects, the opposite of Mexico's. The greater part of Mexico's history was marked by a mixture of suspicion and resentment of the

United States even while geographic propinquity and economic reality imposed close cooperation. It is only lately that a special friendship has emerged. By contrast, until very recently, Brazil was by tradition the closest ally of the United States in the Americas. Geographic remoteness kept the two countries from impinging on each other until the last half-century and then not in a manner that encroached on Brazil's perception of its sovereignty.

Moreover, unlike the other Latin American states, Brazil is of continental dimensions. To be sure, its people did not, until the second half of the last century, develop the country by exploring its interior, as the settlers of North America did, but instead clung to a strip of the coast as if determined to keep open the link to the Old World.

Nevertheless, Brazil's vastness has conferred on its institutions and policy a self-assurance that freed it from the self-assertiveness imposed by the compulsion to propitiate a restive national consciousness. Prior to its national independence, Brazil was not so much a colony as the largest part of the single kingdom of Portugal. For nearly a generation, while Napoleon occupied Portugal and for some time afterward, Rio de Janeiro was the capital of the Portuguese empire. This history has spawned Latin America's most effective foreign service—well trained, multilingual, pursuing the Brazilian national interest with a combination of charm, persistence, and a careful assessment of international realities. Once when I described a certain group of countries to a Brazilian foreign minister as respecting only strength, my interlocutor replied: "Yes, especially in those who are strong."

Thus, for the greater part of its history as a sovereign state, Brazil insisted on a special relationship with the United States and was accorded as much. It acted as the same kind of ally of the United States that Britain became in Europe after the Second World War. A Brazilian division fought in Italy at the side of the Allies in World War II; Brazilian troops joined U.S. forces in the occupation of the Dominican Republic in 1965, and the entire force was ostensibly led by a Brazilian general.

Throughout Brazil viewed its relationship with the United

States as similar to the twin-pillars concept put forward by President Kennedy for the Atlantic partnership. Brazil saw itself as organizing Latin America while the United States performed the same task in North America, the two enterprises to work in harmony through frequent exchanges aimed at articulating a common set of purposes. The theoretical sovereign equality of each Latin American nation postulated by the inter-American system was not part of Brazil's foreign policy vocabulary.

As late as 1976, during the presidency of Gerald Ford, the United States accorded Brazil a special consultative status. Asked by the chairman of the House Foreign Affairs Committee, Thomas "Doc" Morgan, whether the United States was thereby elevating Brazil to the status of a world power, I replied:

> Mr. Chairman, this agreement does not make Brazil a world power. Brazil has a population of 100 million, vast economic resources, a very rapid rate of economic development. Brazil is becoming a world power, and it does not need our approval to become one, and it is our obligation in the conduct of foreign policy to deal with the realities that exist.

The special relationship then established did not prosper, however. The existence of a military regime in Brazil after 1964, growing concerns about its authoritarian tendencies, and U.S. trade legislation produced a series of irritations which intensified during the Carter administration. A hiatus in United States–Brazil intimacy of nearly a decade followed, and Brazil began to look elsewhere. By the 1980s, it had, in effect, decided that the vagaries of U.S. domestic politics and its own growing strength and self-confidence made it inappropriate to rely on a special honorific status in essence bestowed by the United States. Brazil replaced the policy of exclusive reliance on the United States with a deliberate effort to multiply its diplomatic and economic options and to influence the United States through the richness of its alternatives. Brazil henceforth would seek to forge a dominant position in Latin America on its own, relying on the vibrancy of its economy, the size of its population (upward of 150 million at the turn of the century), and the partners it could enlist in Mercosur.

As this policy has evolved, Brazil has become increasingly sensitive to real or perceived slights from the United States. Leading personalities are suspicious that the FTAA is designed to the unilateral benefit of the United States; that concerns about environmental conditions are a subterfuge for diminishing Brazilian sovereignty over the Amazon; and that the United States uses antidumping and labor standards as a pretext for protectionism. Progress toward the FTAA requires a major effort to put relations with Brazil on a new basis.[3]

Such an effort is all the more important because, in the 1990s, Brazil joined the wave of political and economic restructuring that had started with Mexico and Chile. Under the leadership of a remarkable president, Fernando Henrique Cardoso, Brazil reduced its hyperinflation of as much as 40 percent a month to well below 10 percent a year. As a result, groups with fixed incomes, previously the victims of inflation, were rising into the middle class and contributing not only to economic growth but to political stability. State-owned enterprises were systematically privatized; trade barriers were reduced, if not always at a pace desired by U.S. trade negotiators; foreign investment was encouraged; government was confined to sectors governments are uniquely equipped to handle; economic growth was increasingly left to market forces.

Brazilian industry, which had been parochial and protectionist, became more and more international. With a growth rate of 4 percent, financial stability, a large internal market, and a stable government, Brazil was being transformed into one of the major economic and political countries of the twentieth century. From that position of strength, Brazil—with its adroit diplomatic style cushioning a purposeful policy—has set about to extract from the United States something of the same preeminence in hemispheric affairs it had sought to achieve through the special consultative arrangement which had aborted two decades earlier.

Perceiving existing inter-American institutions as a means to buttress United States domination, Brazil has also tried to slow down the hemisphere-wide free trade idea in order to solidify Mercosur; bind Argentina, Paraguay, and Uruguay to it; and oblige the United States to deal with a regional bloc rather than with individual countries.

From a strictly geographical perspective, Mercosur makes sense. But as long as the monetary systems of its two largest members, Brazil and Argentina, are at odds with Brazil having a floating currency and Argentina tying the peso to the dollar, significant institutional integration will be slow and tensions inevitable. In any event, Brazil's neighbors are unlikely to subordinate their eagerness for close relations with the United States to theories of Latin American solidarity.

The United States has no reason to oppose Mercosur so long as it functions as a partner to NAFTA in the process of creating a Free Trade Area of the Americas. But it is another matter if Mercosur, even before it is fully formed, is turned into an effort to exclude the United States from bilateral dealings with traditional friends or if it were to pursue internal arrangements similar to some of those developing in the European Union which, in the economic and political fields, tend to confront the United States with a series of faits accomplis. This would introduce a rigidity and a confrontational style into the Western Hemisphere relationships inimical to the fulfillment of its historic promise and practices.

If matters are allowed to drift, all this has the makings of a potential contest between Brazil and the United States over the future of the Southern cone of the Western Hemisphere. Such an outcome would be an indictment of statesmanship on both sides. It should be possible to restore a large degree of the traditional intimacy between the two countries once both realize that a conflict between them can have no winners. The United States, in its dealings with Brazil, needs to display greater sensitivity to the sense of dignity of a society on the verge of becoming a major power. This means restraint in hortatory diplomacy and in the attempt to impose every American preference via sanctions. It also requires a commitment to resolve the existing bitter trade disputes over Brazilian sugar, citrus, and steel exports. For its part, Brazil should remember that its traditional diplomatic style works better with Americans than the French method of faits accomplis. Given the differences between Europe and Latin America over agricultural policy, the European option is a negotiating ploy rather than a long-range policy.

The United States should pay no heed to the advocates of delaying the building of the FTAA until Mercosur is fully elaborated. Rather, the two efforts should proceed in tandem. Hemisphere-wide trade should not be made dependent on the pace of integration of either regional grouping. Pending the completion of the FTAA, the United States should remain open to bilateral trade arrangements between appropriate Latin American countries and NAFTA as the best way to accelerate the momentum toward an overall Western Hemisphere system and as a major step toward a new international order. The ultimate compromise would be an arrangement in which Brazil goes along with the FTAA while the United States places no obstacles in the way of Mercosur.

In many respects, the role of Argentina will be crucial in shaping this evolution. That Argentina should play so important a part in Western Hemisphere relations would have seemed inconceivable a few decades ago. For most of its history, Argentina did not look north but east toward Europe. Blessed with vast resources and a talented population, it had, before the advent of the Perón dictatorship, the sixth largest per capita income in the world. Within the Western Hemisphere, it emphasized its distinctiveness, disdainful of its neighbors to the north and resentful of the United States's dominant role without, however, going beyond an attitude of condescending aloofness.

The advent of the dictatorship of Juan Perón ended Argentina's claim to uniqueness. For the last half-century, Argentina has been a land of paradoxes. For a long time, the richest country of Latin America with the highest literacy rate and the most substantial middle class, it has also generated the most bizarre forms of governance under the influence of the first Mrs. Perón and the governance of the second. As if afraid of stability, it has thrown itself into turmoil repeatedly just when success was in sight. A sophisticated governing class was nevertheless unable to keep successive governments from thwarting the prospects opened up by its vast riches.

Perón placed the dominant sectors of the economy under government control, saddled the nation with an unsustainable program of social welfare for the workers to ensure his own popularity, and proclaimed a foreign policy defined by strident anti-Americanism. Overturned by the military and exiled to Spain in 1955, Perón was swept back into power in 1973 as a result of the inability of his successors to manage the country. But he died in 1975 and left the ruins to his utterly unprepared second wife. Even after Perón's death, Peronism commanded the loyalties of at least 40 percent of the population, effectively precluding reform. Peronista governments would not, and non-Peronista governments could not, move toward democracy and reform. By the mid-1970s, Argentina was essentially without government. The military finally invited Señora Perón to leave in 1976, to be replaced by a directory of generals and admirals also unequal to the challenge. They intensified the state's grip on economic activity, ran up vast budget deficits, and then, in an act of desperation, invaded the Falkland Islands.

The humiliating defeat of the Argentine forces provided, ultimately, a national catharsis. The military retired to barracks, and elections were held for a civilian government. President Raúl Alfonsín, however, proved unable to turn the economy around; inflation hit new heights and employment new lows. When Carlos Menem came to office as head of the Peronista party, the nation was ready for strong medicine though, given Menem's Peronist background, few expected him to be the one to prescribe it. As it turned out, Menem's courage and uncanny instincts surprised the nation. Early in his administration, with the advice and counsel of one of the towering figures of the Latin American economic revolution, Domingo Cavallo, Menem turned Argentine history on its head, tied the peso to the dollar, dismantled state-owned enterprises, and brought the public sector budget under control and inflation to its knees. He created a new Argentina, utterly different from the historic experience of all Argentines. In the process, by the mid-1990s, he had made the country a major leader of the movement toward democracy in the region, allied his nation with the United States in international peacekeeping efforts, and abandoned every element of Peronism except its name.

Had the United States at that moment possessed fast-track authority and invited Argentina either into NAFTA or into a bilateral trade agreement, chances are that Menem would have eagerly accepted, and a new impetus would have been given both to the Argentine economy and to the FTAA. But with the Clinton administration stalling on implementing its own proposals, Argentina concentrated on membership in Mercosur without, however, endowing it with the political character Brazil sought.

Events gave Argentina no rest. Menem's bid for a third term as president was broadly unpopular, and the election in 2000 went to Fernando de la Rua, an impeccably honest, able, decent democratic leader without Menem's boldness. And just as de la Rua took office, the international environment turned bleak. The dollar, to which the Argentine peso and therefore Argentine exports were tied, rose. Brazil, Argentina's major export market, ran into economic difficulties and devalued its currency, reducing at a single stroke Argentina's export earnings. After the Miami summit, the move toward free trade for the hemisphere had been submerged in seemingly endless technical negotiations of a complexity which only passionate bureaucrats could tolerate. Argentina's political and economic progress stalled.

As of this writing, Argentina is seeking to pull itself out of this tailspin. Domingo Cavallo has been entrusted with another opportunity to rescue the Argentine economy on the basis of a program of national unity. His record alone inspires confidence, and there are also long-term factors favoring Argentina's recovery. The dollar is weakening, and dollar-obligation interest rates have gone down while Brazil's import prospects are improving as the Brazilian economy once again gains momentum. Export prices for Argentina have gone up. If the national unity program manages to bring about fiscal reform, Argentina's potential should spark a substantial re-covery. The United States should do its utmost to help overcome the short-term crisis.

In the long term, the most important issue before Argentina, as for all the nations of the hemisphere, is the prospect for Western Hemisphere free trade. Argentina is, in a sense, a proxy for the rest of the region. More sharply than most, it illustrates the conse-quences and potential benefits which would accrue from the com-mercial integration of Latin America and North America. Argentina's export opportunities in the United States and Canada would be greatly enhanced. It would become, as Mexico did when it joined NAFTA, vastly more attractive to direct foreign investment. This would relieve Argentina of its presently excessive reliance on external borrowings. Finally, a successful free trade arrangement for the Americas might in turn be the key with which to unlock the European market to Argentine agricultural products, particularly beef and grain, which are now turned aside by the European Union's Common Agricultural Policy.

But, by the same token, this opportunity for Argentina presents a political dilemma. To opt for the FTAA without qualification might put Mercosur at risk and, with it, the significant benefits Argentina enjoys through access to the Brazilian market. It could, in a broader sense, be a body blow to its political links with Brazil, now at a level of cordiality unprecedented between the two superpowers of South America.

The challenge to the statesmen of the hemisphere: to build a free trade system in a way which benefits all the nations without a confrontation between NAFTA and Mercosur. There is no point in a competition for preeminence between Brazil and the United States. The United States has no reason to oppose a Mercosur that represents a regional trading unit. And Brazil does not need con-frontation with the United States to define its eminence, nor should it seek the role to which its qualities entitle it by dividing the Western Hemisphere into rival groupings. Argentina and the other nations of the region should be able to participate in the general Western Hemisphere free trade arrangement and, at the same time, preserve special trading arrangements with their neighbors in Mercosur. The nations of the hemisphere should resist the temptation of reversing the dictum of British Foreign Secretary George Canning, who welcomed the Monroe Doctrine by stating that the New World had been called into being to redress the balance of the old. Is the European Union now to be called into being to encourage and then exploit a rivalry between Western Hemisphere blocs? Rather than using Europe as a counterweight to NAFTA, the goal should be to unite NAFTA, Mercosur, and the European Union in an Atlantic free trade area.

The Western Hemisphere thus represents a microcosm of the international challenges facing the United States. It illustrates the opportunities of a global economy based on market forces, but also the need to close the gap between the economic and the political structures of globalization. There is the reality that economic growth requires reform and that reform presupposes a stable, legitimate, and democratic political structure with transparent institutions and an independent judicial system. There have emerged new threats to security and to the stability of societies in the narcotics industry, terrorism, and guerrilla movements. But there is also the prospect of a regional structure embracing the entire Western Hemisphere to usher in a new period of growth and democracy. And, beyond it, there is the prospect of an Atlantic free trade area. Much depends on whether the United States can provide the statesmanship this opportunity demands.

FOUR ◇ ◇ ◇ ◇ ◇ ◇ ◇ ◇ ◇ ◇ ◇

Asia: The World of Equilibrium

ASIA'S GEOPOLITICAL COMPLEXITY

In the first half of the twentieth century, the United States fought two wars to prevent the domination of Europe by a potential adversary. After the Second World War, no Western European country was strong enough to dominate Europe or was any longer prepared to resort to war as an instrument of policy against its neighbors. Threats to security came from outside.

In the second half of the twentieth century (in fact, starting in 1941), the United States went on to fight three wars to vindicate the same principle in Asia—against Japan, in Korea, and in Vietnam. But the aftermath in Asia has not evolved as it did in Europe. The nations of Asia view one another as strategic rivals even as they co-operate on many economic matters. Wars between them are not likely, but neither are they excluded. The international order of Asia therefore resembles that of nineteenth-century Europe more than that of the twenty-first-century North Atlantic.

A look at the political and economic map of Asia illustrates the region's vast importance and complexity. It comprises an advanced industrial country in Japan, with an economy larger than that of any of the historic states of Europe; three countries of continental scale in India, China, and Russia; two countries—South Korea and Singapore—approaching the economic and technological capacity of the advanced industrial states; two large archipelagoes—the Philippines and Indonesia—composed of thousands of islands and controlling some of the major sea lanes; Thailand and Burma, two ancient nations with populations approximating those of France or Italy; and North Korea, a rogue nation developing nuclear weapons and long-range missiles. A largely Muslim population is spread across the peninsular and insular expanses of Malaysia and Indonesia, the latter having the largest Muslim population of any country in the world. Finally, there is Vietnam, which has demonstrated its military prowess and fierce nationalism in wars against France, the United States, and China, and its two neighbors, Laos and Cambodia, over which it exercises a kind of dominion.

Asia's economy is becoming ever more important for that of the United States and the world. In 1996, Asia accounted for 68 percent of U.S. trade with the entire world; U.S. exports to China grew at an average rate of 13 percent in the 1990s; and U.S. investment there tripled in that same period. However, while Asia is tied into the global economy, it lacks a regional structure to mitigate that economy's turbulence or any financial firewall other than the strength of its various national economies. Asia's financial crisis of 1997 demonstrated the vulnerability of especially its small- and medium-sized economies to changes in interest rates, currency valuations, and flows of speculative capital over which those countries had little or no control. An Asian economic bloc has not yet emerged though some Japanese proposals tend in that direction, and there are even incipient moves toward an Asian Free Trade Area, backed by China and Japan. Mutual national suspicions are still too great and the levels of development too varied to permit the Asian equivalent of a European Union in the middle-term future. But this does not mean that the nations of Asia, large and small, accept their vulnerability. Another significant financial crisis in Asia or in the industrial democracies would surely accelerate efforts by

Asian countries to gain greater control over their economic and political destinies by the creation of an Asian counterpart to the existing regional systems.

A hostile Asian bloc combining the most populous nations of the
world and vast resources with some of the most industrious peoples
would be incompatible with the American national interest. For
this reason, America must retain a presence in Asia, and its geopolitical objective must remain to prevent Asia's coalescence into
an unfriendly bloc (which is most likely to happen under the tutelage of one of its major powers). America's relationship to Asia is
thus comparable to that of Britain toward the continent of Europe
for four centuries. Winston Churchill described that situation elo-
quently:

> For four hundred years the foreign policy of England has been to
> oppose the strongest, most aggressive, most dominating Power
> on the Continent. . . . These four centuries of consistent purpose
> amid so many changes of names and facts, of circumstances and
> conditions, must rank as one of the most remarkable episodes
> which the records of any race, nation, state, or people can show.
> Moreover, on all occasions England took the more difficult
> course. Faced by Philip II of Spain, against Louis XIV under
> William III and Marlborough, against Napoleon, against
> William II of Germany, it would have been easy and must have
> been very tempting to join with the stronger and share the fruits
> of his conquest. However, we always took the harder course,
> joined with the less strong Powers, made a combination among
> them, and thus defeated and frustrated the Continental military
> tyrant whoever he was, whatever nation he led. Thus we pre-
> served the liberties of Europe, protected the growth of its viva-
> cious and varied society. . . . It is a law of public policy which we
> are following, and not a mere expedient dictated by accidental
> circumstances, or likes and dislikes, or any other sentiment.[1]

In the twenty-first century, an analogous objective for the
United States in Asia poses a more complex challenge. The European balance of power was sustained by nation-states of substan-

tially homogeneous ethnic composition (with the exception of Russia); many of the major Asian states (China, Russia, India, Indonesia) are continental in size and multiethnic in composition. The European equilibrium was seamless in the sense that all major states were part of it—that is, the interplay of their alliances constituted the balance of power; thus a crisis over Serbia in the Balkans escalated into the First World War. The Asian balance of power is more differentiated and therefore more complex.

In Europe, two world wars and the insufficient scale of the European nation-state in the face of global challenges have made the nineteenth-century balance of power irrelevant. The nations of Europe no longer treat one another as strategic threats; threats from outside Europe have been dealt with by the alliance with the United States.

By contrast, the nations of Asia have never acknowledged a common danger, having quite differing views about what threatens their security. Some have historically feared Russia; others worry mostly about China; still others are concerned about a resurgent Japan; some in Southeast Asia consider Vietnam the principal danger. India and Pakistan are each obsessed with the threat of the other.

With respect to regional disputes, the nations of Asia have shown themselves far readier to use force than have those of Europe, chastened by the carnage of two world wars. Any increase in strength by one country therefore produces compensatory adjustments by all others able to attend to their own security. This is why defense expenditures throughout Asia have been steadily rising despite the end of the Cold War. According to estimates by British Aerospace, by 2010, the military expenditures of Asian nations will exceed those of Western Europe and reach a level two-thirds of that of the United States.[2]

In contrast to nineteenth-century Europe, there exists no single homogeneous equilibrium in Asia; the vastness of the region and the differences in culture and history have combined to produce two strategic balances: in Northeast Asia, China, Japan, Russia, and the United States interact with a potential flashpoint on the volatile

Korean peninsula; in Southeast Asia, China, India, Japan, the United States, and Indonesia are the principal actors whose interests must be reconciled with those of Vietnam, Thailand, Australia, and the Philippines.

Moreover, the roles played by most Asian nations are themselves in flux. As Japan evolves in the direction of a more overtly national policy, its activism in both strategic balances is likely to grow and will be primarily directed at containing the influence of China. Similarly, India is emerging as a major power and will become increasingly active in Southeast Asia, emulating the traditional policy of the British raj, which aimed for dominance from Singapore to Aden. China will insist on a political role commensurate with its growing economic power.

All this explains why the U.S. security system in Asia is quite different from that which exists in Europe. In the Atlantic Alliance, a large American military presence, integrated military command, and permanent council of ambassadors underscore America's commitment. The U.S. mutual security treaty with Japan is buttressed by no formal machinery; it is closer to being a unilateral guarantee than a reflection of an overarching Asian strategy. The American military presence in the Philippines, which formally ended in 1992, did not preclude that country's participation in the Nonaligned Movement. Only in South Korea are the lines drawn as they were in Europe, though with much greater reliance on indigenous forces than was the case along the Iron Curtain during the Cold War. Close bilateral cooperation with Australia at the fringe of Asia backs up these arrangements.

From a security point of view, the nations of Asia coexist in two different worlds simultaneously. With respect to the global balance of power, they shelter under America's protection of the global equilibrium. Yet many define their contribution to that equilibrium by a doctrine of nonalignment which avoids formal political ties with the United States and leaves them free to participate even in policies designed to weaken America's alleged dominance.

The confluence of these elements prevents the United States from adopting any uniform approach to the construction of an international order for Asia. In Europe, the United States pursued a dual military and political strategy: the creation of a military alliance to face down the threat of Soviet invasion, coupled with the systematic fostering of democratic institutions by supporting European economic recovery and, later, European integration. Neither of these strategies has ever been fully applicable in Asia—except in America's bilateral relations with Japan and Korea. The wars in Korea and in Vietnam were not fought on behalf of a regional alliance. In the Korean War, those countries which fought at America's side, most of them European, did so to reinforce their own claim for American engagement in Europe and not in the name of an Asian security system. A technically multilateral defense of South Korea became possible because, during the decisive vote in the U.N. Security Council, the Soviet representative happened to be boycotting that body in protest over the exclusion of Communist China from the United Nations. The Korean War turned into a U.N. mission juridically although it was in fact orchestrated primarily by the United States.

In Vietnam, no NATO ally supported the United States even politically; they only differed in the degree of their aloofness. South Korea, Thailand, Australia, and the Philippines did extend various kinds of direct and indirect assistance; Korea, in fact, dispatched two combat divisions. And perhaps some sort of Asian security system might have emerged had America pursued the war to a successful outcome. But after it became apparent that the United States was looking for a way out, SEATO (Southeast Asia Treaty Organization), the potential nucleus of any security alliance, fell apart, and its place was taken by ASEAN (Association of Southeast Asian Nations)—a regional grouping for economic and political cooperation devoid of security functions.

This history needs to be kept in mind by those who argue that America's Asia policy should be designed in direct analogy to the Cold War, with China replacing the Soviet Union as the organizing threat. But, in Asia, the political and strategic conditions simply do not exist for drawing a dividing line and grouping all the nations on one side of it—barring some major Chinese provocation. The attempt to do so—overtly or tacitly—would have quite the opposite effect from what is intended. Friendly countries would, in all probability, choose conspicuous dissociation. They would position themselves somewhere in the middle, bringing about the progressive isolation of the United States in the region while inciting Asian nationalism and neutralism.

Nor will Wilsonian appeals to democracy provide a rallying point. Though most Asian countries have adopted some sort of electoral system, democracy has not been their defining national experience, except possibly in the Philippines—though, even there, the Spanish colonial rule of some three hundred fifty years is still a powerful influence. In any event, no country of the region—not even strongly democratic Australia—would run the risk of initiating confrontation with China or any other major power in the name of democracy. Japan's democratic institutions originated as an adaptation of long-standing conventions to the convictions of its occupation forces in the wake of the Second World War. However firmly these institutions are now established, no Japanese party or leader is prepared to spread them to other parts of Asia if only because such a course would be treated by the other nations of Asia as an example of new Japanese imperialism.

The Republic of Korea sees in its alliance with the United States a way both to preserve its independence and to promote Korean reunification. Despite its democratic domestic institutions, of which it has every reason to be proud, Korea's foreign policy is not driven by Wilsonian principles. More afraid of democratic Japan than of autocratic China, South Korea will not participate in crusades to alter the domestic structure of any Asian state, least of all China, which it needs to balance its relations with North Korea, Japan, and Russia.

Nor do Thailand and the Philippines regard their domestic institutions as guides to foreign policy. Indonesia, even as it struggles to build democracy, does not consider that process relevant to its own diplomacy; it has maintained friendly relations with Iraq, Iran, Libya, and Cuba—all under American sanctions—and has justified them as being necessary for satisfying important domestic constituencies. And India, the most democratic of the Asian states, has never permitted its domestic structure to determine its foreign policy; throughout much of the Cold War, its relations with the Soviet Union were friendlier than those with the United States.

That the experiences of the Atlantic Alliance are not readily applicable to Asia should not, however, prevent the United States from fulfilling its geopolitical and strategic objectives there. If anything, conditions for it are more favorable in Asia than they were in Europe in the early days of the Cold War. No Asian nation—not even China—is in a position to threaten all its neighbors simultaneously, as the Soviet Union was able to do until the very end of the Cold War. India, Japan, China, and Russia are individually strong enough to resist attacks from any one neighbor and surely in combination with other threatened Asian states. Besides, South Korea, Vietnam, or Australia would not exactly be pushovers for any potential aggressor.

The geopolitical challenge of every major Asian nation, including China, is not so much how to conquer neighbors as how to prevent these neighbors from combining against it. Japan's nightmare is the consolidation of the Chinese giant. China's own concerns regarding Japanese and Russian designs are based on a century of experience. The frontier between China and India has been in dispute for over half a century and, before that, was contested by Imperial China and the British rulers in India.

This reality is sometimes obscured by meetings between Asian leaders—especially of China and Russia—proclaiming a strategic partnership against the specter of American hegemony. However genuine their expressed concerns over American dominance, summit meetings between heads of state cannot abolish long-standing geographic and strategic realities. Russia's long border with China, only sparsely populated along the Russian side, is inherently porous and has been so throughout recorded history. Neither country will entrust the security of these borders to the continued goodwill of the other, whatever its current irritation with an allegedly hegemonic United States. Only the unlikely prospect of relentless American bullying of both could drive them to a deeper partnership.

A comparable analysis could be made of every other Asian nation's relationship with the United States. None, not even Vietnam's, could benefit by establishing with any Asian adversary of the United States closer relations than it has with Washington. Therein lies America's comparative advantage and the key to preserving the various balances in Asia.

America's preference should be to maintain cooperative relations with all the nations of Asia and to avoid a policy geared to the assumption of inherent hostility by any major Asian power until there is a clear demonstration of it. In this way, the United States will be in a position to make its support decisive when it is, in fact, needed and to avoid tempting other states into passivity or into playing America off against an adversary of its own making. At the same time, the United States must turn implacable when the balance of power or America's national interests are, in fact, threatened.

Concern for human rights will, of course, remain an important feature of American foreign policy, whoever is president. It reflects the sort of people Americans are. And it will affect governmental decisions where there exists scope for discretion. Wise Asian leaders will take America's values seriously and avoid endangering a relationship on which so much of Asia's stability as well as the peace of the world depend.

RELATIONS WITH JAPAN

The key relationship for the United States in Asia is with Japan. Japan is an ally; American military bases are located on its soil; it has by far the largest economy in Asia, and it will retain this position for at least the next quarter of a century. It is also a country with intangibles of culture that America is ill-prepared to understand fully. American leaders treat Japanese democracy as if it were an indigenous phenomenon, as if its leaders were motivated by the same imperatives as are those of America, and as if it were in perpetual need of instruction alternating with reassurance. American economists rail against the shortcomings of the Japanese economy, and, to the bafflement of their American critics, the Japanese have so far stubbornly failed to adopt America's insistent prescriptions.

With respect to the common security, Japan is invited to share burdens based on concepts devised in Washington and transmitted to Tokyo as received truth. This approach has generated fewer overt challenges to American dominance than it has in Europe because it has served Japanese purposes to acquiesce in the suggested military buildup and enhanced strategic role. For it enables the country to move toward a more assertive international role and to extend its strategic and political reach without exposing itself to opprobrium for pursuing a forward national policy. Strategic dialogue—even to the extent that it takes place with Europe—has been intermittent, if that, partly because, for nearly half a century after its defeat in the Second World War, Japan has concentrated on its economic revival, leaving security policy largely to the United States, and also because of the Japanese national style, which seeks decisions via consensus rather than confrontation.

Japan's culture does not so much seek to beguile foreigners—as does China's—as to surround them with its pervasive distinctiveness so that they have no choice but to adjust to its requirements. The institutions are singular and explicitly marked "not for export." China, at the center of a continent, has been obliged to protect its essence and independence by manipulating the foreigners along its borders and, when necessary, taming them by conversion to Chinese culture. Island Japan chose the opposite course.

For four hundred years before it was forcibly opened to the West by Commodore Matthew Perry in 1854, Japan dealt with the outside world by sealing itself off. It elaborated its military tradition in feudal conflicts and grounded its domestic structure on pride in its singularity. Japan, in fact, had so much confidence in its uniqueness that, after Perry's arrival, it did not fear adapting its institutions to Western ways because it was so confident that it would nevertheless maintain its special character.

On a crowded island, no strategic or psychological depth is available for domestic conflict. Thus, over the centuries, Japanese society developed the supple and subtle formalities which cushion disagreement and permit decisions to emerge from consensus without declaring winners or losers. This required an elaborate sense of hierarchy in which the lower orders could participate by being given a sense of being looked after, much as a family looks after its offspring. Even in the modern period, the distinction between rich and poor has been smaller—or at least less conspicuous—in Japan than in any other advanced industrial country and has been so throughout Japanese history.

Japan went from feudalism to an amalgam of aspects of West European parliamentary systems, Prussian military institutions, and British naval practices, all of it held together by the divine figure of the emperor and a hierarchical feudal sense so unique that it came to rank as yet another feature of Japanese exceptionalism. After its defeat in 1945, Japan once more adjusted its institutions while preserving their unique character. It adopted a parliamentary political system and a constitution, much of it drafted at the headquarters of the American occupation forces, renouncing war as an instrument of policy. Japan was able to undertake these changes because the Japanese sense of cultural identity was so strong that it actually transformed what would have been a revolutionary upheaval in other countries into an aspect of the essential continuity of Japanese culture.

Thus any resemblance between Japanese and Western political institutions is usually largely superficial. Japanese elections since 1945 have, with one brief exception, confirmed the ruling party in office, and the Liberal Democratic Party (LDP) has governed with only the briefest interruption for some fifty years. Elections determine not the designation of the prime minister—as they do in Western parliamentary systems—but the relative position of the four or five factions into which the ruling party is divided. Each is headed by a leader who, having risen to eminence by seniority, controls the votes of his faction and is appointed as faction leader by his predecessor. Japanese prime ministers are invariably drawn from the same limited circle—of either faction leader or his designee—and can usually be predicted a decade beforehand with only the occasional scandal or premature death upsetting the sequence.

As a result, Japanese foreign policy cannot be understood in terms of the decisions of individual leaders. It is much more accurate to view it as a family enterprise which considers itself in rivalry with a world of impersonal, potentially hostile corporate competitors perceived as forever remote and ultimately perhaps incomprehensible.

This cultural abyss produces a strange and sometimes frustrating pattern in negotiations between Japanese and American leaders. The American president functions not only as head of government but also as head of state; having paramount authority within the executive branch, he is expected to make decisions, overrule subordinates, and, if necessary, dismiss them. The Japanese prime minister emerges from a complicated negotiation that takes place every two years among the various factions; in practice, he is eligible to be reelected to the established two-year term only once (and can therefore not serve more than four years). Parliamentary elections play only a subsidiary role in this process. The prime minister is almost invariably already in place when they occur and, short of an upheaval that replaces the Liberal Democratic Party, remains in office afterward. By the next election, he has been replaced through the internal processes of the LDP. Japanese Cabinet ministers cannot be dismissed by the prime minister unless their faction agrees, nor can they be ordered to carry out measures their faction chooses to oppose.

Thus Japanese leaders march to drummers quite different from those of Western democracies. The Japanese elite is trained to avoid direct confrontation and is uncomfortable with procedures that reach decisions by personal fiat. A course of action emerges from a long process of consultation designed to avoid the impression that winners are being separated from losers—the very essence of the way status is established in Washington. High office in Japan is not an entitlement to issue orders, much less to rule by decree; it basically confers the privilege of taking the lead in persuading one's colleagues.

A Japanese prime minister is the custodian of national consensus, not the creator of it. Faced with American negotiators seeking to sway him on a personal level through the insistent reiteration of arguments or personal charm—as if the failure to agree were the result of incomprehension—the Japanese leader takes refuge in obscure evasions or, if pressed to the wall, implies the promise of something he cannot implement, hoping that some turn of events will come to his rescue. Some of this conduct, of course, may also be a deliberate strategy meant to wear down impatient American interlocutors.

Summits between American presidents and Japanese prime ministers therefore all too frequently end in frustration. The American president asks for a decision—that is, an act of will to be imposed on reluctant colleagues or on a resistant bureaucracy. Since no modern Japanese prime minister has—or has ever had—that much authority, any acquiescence expresses at best a commitment to make an effort to persuade, not to command. Until the group relevant to the consensus (usually those who have to implement the decision) agrees that there is no alternative, the promise cannot be fulfilled. The single-mindedness of the consensus process is purchased at the cost of a seeming imperviousness to the sensibilities and views of foreigners and a languid pace in reaching decisions.

A comparable cultural gap exists in the economic field. The necessity for Japanese structural reform has been a staple of American economic advice and pressures on Japan for more than a decade. Structural reform is said to be needed to restore growth to a stagnant economy for a vibrant Japanese economy is believed to lend momentum to world economic growth. This American missionary effort is backed by generally unexceptionable economic competence. But it has had little immediate effect. The reason cannot be that the Japanese do not understand the American advice. A society that has shown such remarkable discipline and dedication in overcoming its crises for a century and a half is unlikely to fail for lack of comprehension. If it ignores the advice, it must be because the Japanese leaders do not feel the same urgency, either because they make decisions at a different pace from America's, or because the short-term impact of accepting American advice is too unsettling to established cultural patterns.

For Japan, helping the world economy is not a sufficient motive to change its way of doing business or to undermine its political cohesion, especially as the Japanese public does not feel poor, whatever American warnings. Indeed, American lectures and pressures may compound a sense of insecurity among the Japanese that causes them to increase their savings, thereby magnifying the problem of insufficient demand of which economists complain (though the upper limit for refrigerators and appliances in small Japanese houses may play a role). If history is any guide, Japan will move only when it feels the pressures of the lack of competitiveness affecting its population directly, and not before. Even then it will do so via the traditional consensus system by which the various groups affected are brought along as a group rather than by the Western method of a decision imposed either by the chief executive or by legislation.

The major transformations in Japan—the Meiji Restoration or the industrialization after the Second World War—took fifteen years to get started, after which the consensus system implemented them with extraordinary speed. It is, of course, possible that the Japanese system has ossified and is no longer capable of adaptation. The next decade will show whether an aging population and rigid bureaucracy have prevented Japan from dealing with what is for it a whole new world, or whether Japan is like the marathon runner whose speed cannot be judged by his progress per mile but only after the course has been run. Whatever the outcome, Japan will, for the next decades, remain economically the strongest country in Asia by a considerable margin.

Understanding these cultural issues is becoming more important today because Japanese-American political relations are on the verge of a sea change. Under the impact of defeat and the dangers of the Cold War, Japan accepted to nestle under the protection of the United States and to abandon its historic self-reliance. A determined economic competitor, it nevertheless subordinated its foreign and security policies to those of the United States. So long as Japan faced only one principal threat to its security—the Soviet Union—Japanese and American views on security ran on parallel tracks.

That attitude is unlikely to persist. South Korea and China are gaining in political influence, economic potential, and military strength; North Korea is emerging as a significant player as a result of actions by Seoul, Washington, and Beijing, about which Japan was not consulted before the event, if indeed it was even informed. The most intact portion of Russian military power is situated in Siberia. Under post–Cold War conditions, Japanese long-range planners will not believe that they can always rely on the United States to view the resultant interplay of forces entirely from their perspective. Washington will deny this vociferously, and it is sincere in doing so. But reassurances lose a great deal of their persuasiveness when every incoming American administration starts out proclaiming a reassessment of existing policies, when trade quarrels mount, and when major decisions regarding Asia are taken unilaterally by Washington—not infrequently under domestic political pressure. It is no accident that the Japanese defense budget has been creeping steadily upward, making it already the second largest in the world. In the political realm, Japan is certain to try to reclaim a considerable degree of freedom of action.

The extent of Japanese autonomy from American security and foreign policies and the eventual nature of that autonomy will depend on the ability of both countries to bring about a more balanced political and strategic dialogue. It will make a major difference whether Japan increases its freedom of action—which implies a certain distancing from the United States—gradually or suddenly, and whether it seeks its autonomy as an expression of renewed nationalism or shapes it as a contribution to a cooperative world order, a difficult concept in a society built on hierarchy. A key objective of American foreign policy must be to draw Japan into broader political relationships *before* its political and military strength develop a momentum of their own.

This imposes two requirements on the United States: to continue American engagement in Asia—symbolized by the American military presence—and to redefine the Japanese-American alliance. Without an American military presence in Asia, Japan will be increasingly drawn to security and foreign policies based on national impulses. When Japan and the United States formulate their policies in concert, Japan's buildup of an autonomous military power will be both limited and defined by a strategic context, and the impact of such buildup on the rest of Asia will be far less disturbing. A new dimension must therefore be given to bilateral political dialogue and to the coordination of foreign policies, especially in Asia.

American relations with China will importantly affect Japanese-American relations. Sino-Japanese relations are dominated by ambivalence on both sides. Until the emergence of modern Japan in the late nineteenth century, China had not encountered an Asian state capable of contesting Chinese preeminence in Asia. China was not then concerned with the equilibrium in Asia, for it was the equilibrium by itself.

Until China was unified by Mao Zedong, modern Japan had never encountered another Asian country it needed to treat as a permanent competitor. But China's emergence has awakened Japanese fears, conferring an entirely new impetus to its considerations of strategy. During the late 1990s, an eminent Japanese explained to me that Japan's strategy must allow for two contradictory contingencies: the disintegration of China as a result of its inability to absorb the consequences of modernization, and the growing power of China if modernization succeeds. In either case, so the argument went, Japan must begin the task of building barriers to possible Chinese hegemonic aspirations or else avoid being a mere bystander to an internal Chinese catastrophe which would surely draw in outside powers. The importance Japan attaches to these objectives is demonstrated by the patterns of its investment in Asia, which trace a line around China's periphery from Taiwan to Vietnam to Uzbekistan, from which Chinese power can be contained or influenced depending on circumstances. Such considerations probably also shaped Japan's decision to lend money to Southeast Asia during the financial crisis of 1997 despite its own economic stagnation.

Whichever of these contingencies arises, Japan will insist on handling relations with China at a pace it is able to influence. Given the close cultural link to the mainland from which it borrowed many of the principal elements of its own culture, Japan will resist having its options toward China foreclosed by any other country, however closely allied. If an American confrontation with China is perceived in Japan as having been provoked by the United States, the Japanese-American alliance will come under severe strain; Japan will do its utmost to find a way out. Good relations with China—or at least a relationship in which America is not perceived as the cause of crisis—is a prerequisite for the vitality of the Japanese-American alliance.

Another key challenge is policy toward Korea. Few subjects are more sensitive for Japan. All too conscious of Korean resentments over the Japanese occupation which lasted for forty years, Japanese leaders are well aware that Korean foreign policy is inevitably directed at preventing a recurrence of Japanese domination of Northeast Asia. At the same time, Japan considers it essential for its security that Korea not be tied to another major Asian power. And it is also uneasy about South Korea's emergence as an economic competitor, not to speak of its increasingly assertive diplomacy and even—though this is rarely admitted—its American ties.

Thus Japan's dual-track policy: it wants American troops to stay in Korea as a key element in the Asian equilibrium, all the more so as their withdrawal would make it domestically difficult to maintain American bases in Japan and thereby create an entire new set of security problems for both Japan and the rest of Asia. But Japan also seeks to maintain an influence of its own on the Korean peninsula. Ambivalent about Korean unification because a unified Korea would eventually become an even more assertive competitor, politically and economically (and presumably would base its foreign policy on suspicions of Japanese motives), Japan helps North Korea to survive economically by permitting remittances from the Korean diaspora in Japan. But the North Korean nuclear and missile capability—together with the prospect that, in case of unification, they might be added to the arsenal of a unified Korea—acts as a spur to Japanese rearmament, to the development of a missile defense for Japan, and to maintaining the option of building nuclear weapons of its own.

In 1993, then Prime Minister Kiichi Miyazawa was asked by a journalist whether Japan could accept a North Korean nuclear capability. He answered in a very un-Japanese way with the single lapidary word, "No." What did this mean? That Japan would launch a diplomatic offensive? That it might take countermeasures and, if so, what kind? That it would develop its own nuclear capability if all else failed? Probably these questions have not yet been answered in Japan's internal councils or in any agreement with the United States. But it is clear that, in due course, they will be answered either within the context of a United States–Japan joint strategy or by Japan deciding to chart its own autonomous course.

RELATIONS WITH KOREA

Korea has been a focal point of Asian crises for the last hundred years. In 1904–1905, the Russo-Japanese War was fought over which country would control Korea. In 1908, Japan extinguished Korea's independence. After the Japanese occupation ended in 1945, Korea was partitioned along the 38th parallel when the Soviets brought in Kim Il Sung to establish what turned into the world's most repressive Communist regime. In 1950, that regime unleashed another brutal war in which the United States and its South Korean allies, together with token U.N. forces, prevented a Communist takeover of South Korea. Since then, the 38th parallel has demarcated one of the most absolute dividing lines in the world—ideologically, politically, militarily, and economically.

In the last year of the Clinton administration, the future of the Korean peninsula suddenly moved to center stage. South Korean President Kim Dae Jung was invited to visit Pyongyang, the capital of North Korea. The second highest-ranking North Korean military officer was invited to Washington, and Secretary of State Madeleine Albright paid a return visit to Pyongyang.

These dramatic events must not obscure the reality that the tensions on the Korean peninsula reflect a series of complex and interlocked issues not resolvable by dramatic gestures. These involve the relative roles of Seoul and Pyongyang, specifically the responsibility of each for the process of unification (if it takes place at all); the possible scenarios for the evolution of North Korea; the role of the interested outside powers, which include Japan, China, Russia, and the United States; and the continued presence of American troops in South Korea, which has profound consequences for the future military and political position of the United States in Asia, since the future of American bases in Japan may well depend on it.

After South Korea emerged from the devastation of the Korean War, it gradually evolved into a genuine democracy and has reached the threshold of being an advanced industrial country with a growing capacity to compete in the world markets. In the same period, the North turned into a caricature of a Stalinist state, being arguably the most absolute police state in the world today. Its economy is a shambles; the difference in the standard of living between the North and South avoids being a domestic challenge to the North Korean dictatorship only because that regime has succeeded in sealing its population off and because its security agencies are among the most brutal and ruthless in the world. North Korea's obsolescent industry is incapable of competing in world markets, and its agriculture has collapsed to the point of producing near permanent starvation, estimated to lead to the deaths of tens of thousands annually and malnutrition among the rest of the population.

By devoting an unprecedented proportion of its gross national product to military purposes, North Korea has created large tank forces and masses of artillery deployed within range of South Korea's capital of Seoul and capable of inflicting vast devastation and hundreds of thousands of casualties without warning. It has turned the manufacture of nuclear weapons and missiles into a successful vehicle for international blackmail. North Korea gains foreign exchange through the sale of missiles to countries hostile to the United States and by blackmailing the United States, Japan, and South Korea into giving it modern technology with the threat of building nuclear weapons or long-range missiles.

The long-term objective has not been war, which North Korea could not sustain, but to demoralize South Korea and undermine its relations with the United States by discussing the future of the Korean peninsula directly with Washington. If North Korea succeeds in establishing itself as the legitimate representative of the Korean national interest, Seoul would be marginalized as an American auxiliary.

For a while, this policy was not without success. In 1994, the United States conducted separate negotiations with North Korea on the basis of which Japan and South Korea agreed to build two heavy water nuclear reactors for North Korea and the United States agreed to supply oil for North Korea's power plants in return for a suspension (but not abandonment) of its nuclear program. Though the deal was put forward as a contribution to nonproliferation, it probably had the opposite effect. For it may have encouraged other rogue states to initiate nuclear weapons programs to generate a comparable buyout.

The deal may also have accelerated other aspects of the North Korean proliferation problem. For shortly afterward, North Korea tested a long-range missile that flew over Japan under the pretext of space exploration. This set off another negotiation that brought Secretary of State Madeleine Albright to Pyongyang to explore the price of stopping that program. The aborted visit of President Clinton in his last month in office, which apparently was intended to follow the pattern of the nuclear deal of offering so-called scientific missile technology in return for abandoning the program labeled "military," would have been part of that political price.

Negotiations with North Korea did achieve a suspension of North Korean plutonium production but at the price of implying that the future of Korea might be settled directly between Washington and Pyongyang, excluding Seoul. Two events arrested the trend. The first was the death in 1994 of North Korea's dictator

Kim Il Sung, which limited Pyongyang's maneuvering room. The second was the election of Kim Dae Jung to the South Korean presidency, which increased Seoul's diplomatic scope. Kim Dae Jung's so-called "sunshine policy" of encouraging economic cooperation, family reunification, and other exchanges reestablished the balance with the United States in contacts with the North.

But it did not settle the issue of the content of these contacts. For when the North Korean ruler, Kim Jong Il, invited South Korean President Kim Dae Jung to Pyongyang in the summer of 2000, the floodgates opened. Though Kim Dae Jung received little more than promises of a return visit by Kim Jong Il to Seoul and an extremely limited opportunity for family reunification, the outside world greeted the change in North Korean tone euphorically as the harbinger of a new era. The second highest-ranking North Korean military officer was warmly received in the Oval Office and hosted at a formal State Department dinner. These Washington meetings were followed a few weeks later by Secretary of State Albright's visit to Pyongyang, where she attended a mass rally celebrating the fifty-fifth anniversary of the Korean Workers Party. Other nations eager not to be left behind were straining to beat the path to Pyongyang.

The collective rush for direct talks with Pyongyang may have the ironical consequence of tempting Kim Jong Il to return to the previous policy of isolating Seoul because he could draw the conclusion that he no longer needs direct talks with South Korea to solve his internal problems. In March 2001, the European Union heads of government announced a diplomatic mission to help fill the alleged gap left by "America's hard-line policy," in the words of the Swedish foreign minister, whose country held the EU's rotating presidency. They should ponder whether, in taking this course, they are not bringing about the exact opposite of their proclaimed intentions. Will diplomatic contact for its own sake move the most brutal Communist regime to a conciliatory policy? Or will Pyongyang be tempted to extract economic help by a change of tone and, if it succeeds, then lose interest in talks with Seoul over Korean unification and with America over missiles?

Thus there is a need for the close coordination of American and

South Korean strategies. Neither America nor South Korea—and least of all the European Union—can want, simply on the basis of a gentler tone, to support Pyongyang's control system or to encourage its military blackmail. Progress in relations with Pyongyang must be based on clear standards by which progress can be measured—much as was done between the United States and the Federal Republic of Germany when the process of reconciliation between East and West Germany, begun in 1969, was linked successfully to guarantees for the status of Berlin.

These should include a much fuller exchange of human contacts than the largely token ones now permitted. There should be as well a thinning out of military forces along the 38th parallel and an unambiguous renunciation of nuclear weapons by both sides. The pattern of the nuclear deal of offering so-called scientific technology for so-called weapons technology should be abandoned, because these technologies are really dual in use and offer an incentive for rogue states to pursue the same blackmail route. At the same time, Seoul and Washington should be receptive if North Korean actions provide evidence that it is seeking to evolve from the status of a rogue state. In that effort, procedure merges with substance.

Successive American administrations have held firmly to two principles: that the American alliance with South Korea is the key to stability on the Korean peninsula, and that the key to an improvement in relations with Pyongyang is progress in North Korea's relations with the South through bilateral talks.

In the new atmosphere in Korea, the overwhelming interest of the United States remains to encourage South Korea to play the leading role in inter-Korean negotiations and not to substitute itself. Pyongyang must be convinced that the road to Washington leads through Seoul and not the other way around. If these priorities are reversed, South Korea will gradually be marginalized. North Korea may receive the economic assistance it needs not from—or via—South Korea but from outside countries jockeying for a preferred position in Pyongyang. An American (or European) reconciliation with Pyongyang not preceded by reconciliation of the two Koreas would be achieved at the risk of gradual toughening of Pyongyang's stance toward South Korea and eventual demoralization in Seoul—even when the short-term requirements of the Korean electoral cycle suggest a more impetuous course.

But American deference to South Korea in matters affecting political and economic relations and human contacts with North Korea can bring lasting progress only if Seoul shows understanding for Washington's global responsibilities. South Korea's leaders should neither appoint themselves as spokesmen for the transfer of military or dual-use technology to the North, nor attack major American military programs such as missile defense.

In the process, America must not lose sight of the fact that Korea is where the interests of several major powers intersect. Neither China nor Japan is eager for a rapid unification of Korea—especially were a unified Korea to inherit North Korea's nuclear and missile technology. Both have vivid historical memories of invasions launched against their territories from Korean soil. Beijing is concerned about the impact of Korean nationalism on the Korean minorities in Manchuria. For its part, Japan has permitted American bases on its soil largely to defend the status quo in Korea, and it fears that a unified Korea might seek to rally its public by appealing to the long-standing antipathies toward Japan. Thus China and Japan favor a deliberate pace of Korean diplomacy—though not necessarily the regime in Pyongyang.

For all these reasons, Washington needs to stay in close touch on Korean prospects with all the interested parties, especially Japan, but also with China and Russia. No neighbor of Korea can benefit from military turmoil on the peninsula even if there are differences about the nature and pace of a desirable evolution. None can want to be surprised by sudden eruptions. An important beginning would be cooperation among the four powers most interested in Korea's future to end Pyongyang's blackmailing tactics with respect to weapons of mass destruction. For, whatever their differences, none of the interested powers can wish to be drawn into a conflict by proliferation measures that could have been avoided by joint action.

Consultation is necessary also because other outcomes are possible than the continuation of the repressive Pyongyang regime or its collapse. Countries uneasy about Korean unification may well be prepared to encourage a more benign government in Pyongyang while favoring its remaining separate from Seoul. But, in the real world, such options are limited. Any democratic government in North Korea will seek unification. Any authoritarian government will repeat the existing dilemmas. In the end, it will be no more possible to keep Korea divided by the actions of outside powers than proved to be the case in Germany.

Of course, the North Korean regime may collapse, as East Germany did, because Kim Jong Il loses control over events. In many respects, this is probably Seoul's nightmare. A rapid unification process for Korea would dwarf the monumental problems Germany faced for a decade. The ratio of the population of West to East Germany was about three to one; in Korea, it is closer to two to one. The ratio of the per capita GDP in Germany was approximately two to one; the ratio in Korea is closer to ten to one—meaning that the economic challenge of unifying Korea is far more daunting than in Germany.

At that point, the four outside powers—the United States, Russia, Japan, and China—would have to discuss the international status of Korea while the two Koreas settle the internal arrangements, a procedure similar to the one preceding German unification.

As for the United States, it has no reason to oppose Korean unification and every motive to support it. But far more is at stake for America than the future of Korea, for the future of Asia will importantly depend on what happens to American forces now stationed along the 38th parallel.

While Kim Jong Il has been quoted by South Korean President Kim Dae Jung as favoring the continued presence of American troops, regardless of what happens in the inter-Korean talks, this is not an assurance on which long-range policy can be built. Nor will the future of American troops in Korea depend entirely on the leaders of the two Koreas. Were tensions to ease dramatically, the presence of American troops could become highly controversial within South Korea, regardless of the wishes of the incumbent president. In turn, with the departure of these forces, the future of American bases in Japan would become problematical. And if American troops leave the rim of Asia, an entirely new security and, above all, political situation would arise all over the continent. Were this to happen, even a positive evolution on the Korean peninsula could lead to a quest for autonomous defense policies in Seoul and Tokyo and to a growth of nationalism in Japan, China, and Korea. The United States may not be able to arrest such trends, but it should not slide into them through preoccupation with the tactics and headlines of the moment.

RELATIONS WITH CHINA: THE HISTORICAL CONTEXT

At the beginning of a new American administration, two schools of thought dominate the American debate:

The view of the Clinton administration was summed up in the slogans "engagement" and "strategic partnership." Based on the Wilsonian premise that a world composed of democracies can hold no enemies—at least none prepared to vindicate their views with force—the multiplication of contacts on trade, environment, science, and technology is believed to strengthen the forces favoring international cooperation and internal pluralism.

The opposing point of view regards China as a morally flawed inevitable adversary—at the moment with respect to Taiwan, eventually the Western Pacific, and, in time, the global equilibrium. According to this school of thought, the United States should therefore act toward China not as a strategic partner but as it treated the Soviet Union during the Cold War: as a rival and a challenge, reducing trade wherever possible to nonstrategic items, creating an alliance of Asian states to contain China or, failing that, building up Japan to help America share the burden for the defense of Asia and the containment of China. Advocates of this point of view would treat Taiwan as an independent country and a military outpost and, in practice, scrap the "one-China" policy on which

Sino-American relations have been based since diplomatic contacts were reestablished in 1971.

The fundamental question the new administration must answer for itself is whether either of these approaches really meets America's contemporary needs. The approach of the Clinton administration avoided the geopolitical challenge of the relationship with China. But it is one thing to reject a strategic partnership that never functioned; it is another to treat China as a permanent adversary. The conditions of Asia are not analogous to the Cold War. Then, a single ideological adversary threatened all the nations of Western Europe, which eagerly sought American assistance. In Asia, barring major Chinese provocation, the United States would have to conduct a containment policy alone and over an indefinite period of time.

Unless their own survival is directly and clearly threatened, the Asian nations will not be prepared to join a crusade that groups them together as were the nations of Europe in opposition to a single threat. An Asian version of the containment policy of the 1980s will find few, if any, takers except perhaps in Vietnam, thus turning history on its head; much more likely, it will cause the Asian nations to move away from the United States. America's ability to influence Japan would decline. Korea would turn into a tinderbox. Nations with ambitions or territorial claims would sense new opportunities. America's European allies would eagerly step into the economic and political vacuum. A policy that is perceived as having designated China as the enemy primarily because its economy is growing and its ideology is distasteful would end up isolating the United States.

To be sure, it is in the American national interest to resist the effort of *any* power to dominate Asia—and, in the extreme, the United States should be prepared to do so without allies. But a wise American policy would strive to prevent such an outcome. It would nurture cooperative relations with all the significant nations of Asia to keep open the possibility of joint action should circumstances require it. But it would also seek to convey to China that opposition to hegemony is coupled with a preference for a constructive relationship and that America will facilitate and not obstruct China's participation in a stable international order. Confrontation with China should be the ultimate recourse, not the strategic choice.

The inadequacy of both the dominant schools of thought was brought home by the incident of the American reconnaissance plane that, in April 2001, landed on Chinese soil where its crew was detained for eleven days. The prospects of "engagement" were overwhelmed by the realities of Chinese domestic politics. But the ideological interpretations of the challenge provided no guide to the Bush administration either. For Chinese conduct was shaped much more by nineteenth-century ideas of nationalism than by nineteenth-century Marxism. Long-range surveillance from just outside the territorial limits, while consistent with international law, is a challenge to traditional notions of sovereignty based on the premise of the impermeability of frontiers and now made irrelevant by modern technology. This was compounded by Chinese obsessions regarding perceived colonial conduct. This is why the challenge to America did not come from the ideological part of Chinese society, the Communist party, but—by all accounts—from students and the military.

It is important to get this conjunction of motives straight if one wishes to analyze the relevance of the incident to future Sino-American relations. Chinese conduct was shaped primarily by an attempt to navigate the shoals of Chinese domestic politics on the part of a government whose ideological element is in decline and which is facing a succession decision within two years. The challenge to American foreign policy is how to deal with Chinese nationalism without inflaming it while standing firm when it turns to threats. The challenge to Chinese leaders is to learn to assess the constraints of American values and public opinion.

In a mood of fatalism, the emergence of China is often compared to that of Germany in the nineteenth century, which ultimately led to World War I. But there was nothing foreordained about that war. History has recorded it above all as a failure of statesmanship, a blunder that produced costs out of proportion to any conceivable gains for all the parties. Which of the statesmen who went to war in 1914 would not have jumped at the chance to revisit their decision when they looked back a few years later and saw the catastrophe they had inflicted on their societies, on European civilization, and on the long-term prospects of the entire world?

Of course, the choice is not entirely up to the United States. Faced with a threat of hegemony in Asia—whatever the regime— America would resist as it did Japan's in the Second World War and the Soviet Union's in the Cold War. But insofar as the choice depends on American action, it should be made with great care. It cannot be settled by hairsplitting disputes over the term by which to characterize Sino-American relations. Nor should the issue be decided by the domestic imperatives of budgetary battles.

Defining the national interest regarding China is complicated by the vast cultural differences between the Chinese and American approaches to foreign policy and the changes in the international environment since American emissaries first visited Beijing in 1971. American leaders emphasize personal goodwill and personal relationships. In its continuous history spanning five millennia, China has witnessed too many upheavals and tragedies to rely on the goodwill of individuals who, in the context of history, are by definition transient. The United States, in its national experience of two hundred years, has been able to overcome its challenges by a combination of idealism, willpower, organization, and a benign geography. China has many great achievements to its credit, but it has also frequently encountered problems that could be overcome only by endurance. China's approach to policy is skeptical and prudent, America's optimistic and missionary. China's sense of time beats to a different rhythm from America's. When an American is asked to date a historical event, he refers to a specific day on the calendar; when a Chinese describes an event, he places it within a dynasty. And of the fourteen imperial dynasties, ten have each lasted longer than the entire history of the United States.

Americans think in terms of concrete solutions to specific problems. The Chinese think in terms of stages in a process that has no precise culmination. Americans believe that international disputes result either from misunderstandings or ill will; the remedy for the former is persuasion—occasionally quite insistent—and, for the latter, defeat or destruction of the evildoer. The Chinese approach is impersonal, patient, and aloof; the Middle Kingdom has a horror of appearing to be a supplicant. Where Washington looks to good faith and goodwill as the lubricant of international relations, Beijing assumes that statesmen have done their homework and will understand subtle indirections; insistence is therefore treated as a sign of weakness, and good personal relations are not themselves considered a lubricant of serious dialogue. To Americans, Chinese leaders seem polite but aloof and condescending. To the Chinese, Americans appear erratic and somewhat frivolous.

Partly because of the difficulty the two sides have had in understanding each other's culture and code of conduct, they have rarely succeeded in getting Sino-American relationships into a stable balance for any extended period. In the early 1900s, America's approach to China was heavily influenced by missionaries and traders, both largely oblivious to the humiliation Chinese society felt when subjected to the colonialist pressures of the European powers. In the 1930s and during the Second World War, China was idealized as a victim of Japanese aggression and as a heroic democratic ally. After the Communist victory in the civil war, China was transformed in the American public mind into the incarnation of ideological and strategic hostility. A combination of Maoist militant ideology, China's intervention in the Korean War, American distaste for Beijing's domestic institutions, and the interposition of the American Seventh Fleet in the Taiwan Strait produced a period of nearly a quarter-century in which the two countries had no diplomatic relations and very little contact of any kind.

After diplomatic contact was restored in 1971, five American administrations of both parties went on to pursue a broadly bipartisan policy based on Sino-American cooperation. It was only in the 1990s that the idea of confrontation between the two countries gained momentum again, threatening to return the relationship to the tensions of half a century before. At this point, a digression tracing that evolution may help to define the nature of the existing choices.

In 1971 and 1972, President Richard Nixon and Chairman Mao Zedong reestablished diplomatic contact, not because American and Communist ideologies had become more compatible but because of their respective geopolitical necessities. During the early period of renewed contacts, much innocent nonsense was disseminated about how "unnatural" the estrangement between the American and Chinese peoples had been, as if rapprochement had fulfilled some deep emotional need on both sides. The facts were far more prosaic. China, in its long history, has rarely had the experience of dealing with other societies on the basis of equality. For the greatest part, it was dominant in its region; in the nineteenth century and the first half of the twentieth, it was humiliated by the imperial powers. Before that, it had felt most comfortable when it was able to stand aloof and self-contained, as a culture whose uniqueness placed it beyond the reach of outsiders—and, until approximately 1500, also as the most advanced nation in science and technology. For China, there was nothing unnatural about living apart from the United States.

Nor can it be said that, in 1971, there was any groundswell of demand in the United States for an opening to China. Whatever public pressures for it existed derived not from geopolitics but from a general idea that "good relations" were their own reward and that the Cold War could best be ended by overcoming the hostility as a kind of psychological exercise.

What brought the two nations together was their leaders' awareness of a common threat. The Chinese leaders saw an awesome buildup of Soviet military power along their border, including nuclear missiles and forty modern combat divisions—over a million men. By 1969, it was obvious to China that Marxist theory not only did not shield it from Soviet military pressures but provided a pretext for them. For the newly promulgated Brezhnev Doctrine claimed for the Kremlin the special right to use military power within the Communist world to enforce its unity.

For the United States, opportunity was merging with necessity.

Under the impact of the Vietnam War, the United States—or, to be more specific, Richard Nixon—recognized the role China might play in establishing a new Asian balance of power. In geopolitical terms, there were powerful reasons for a rapprochement with China to balance the Soviet Union—either to restrain it or to induce it to negotiate seriously; to isolate Hanoi and thereby spur an end to the Vietnam War; to maintain America's self-confidence amidst the painful withdrawal from Indochina; and, finally, to demonstrate America's undiminished capacity to master an international environment that was turning multipolar.

The new links between China and the United States flourished so long as the two sides were in a position to concentrate on the common objective of resisting what their communiqués came to describe as "hegemony." Simply put, this meant resisting Soviet attempts to upset the global or Asian balance of power and some tacit agreement on an appropriate strategy to achieve this end.

Even then, the different histories and geopolitical situations of the two sides produced disagreements on tactics. Beijing, being directly threatened, favored resolute confrontation with Moscow. Washington, having allies and a restive public opinion to consider, emphasized tactics that would give Moscow an opportunity to settle or shift to it the onus for confrontation. China was suspicious of any negotiation between Washington and Moscow—explicitly concerned that the appearance of progress would undermine the West's willingness to stand up to the Soviet Union, implicitly fearful that it might lead to some unspecified U.S.-Soviet arrangement at China's expense, if only by permitting the Soviet Union to direct its attention to Asia. For its part, Beijing tended to compete with Moscow in the developing world by appealing to radical movements, and this often caused it to back leaders or causes that were hardly America's favorites.

The weakening of executive authority in the United States due to Watergate and its aftermath reduced Beijing's confidence in America's ability to resist Soviet pressures and blandishments, complicating America's ability to navigate the complex triangular passage of the relationship among Washington, Moscow, and Beijing.

The challenge for the United States was to make sure that it always had more options than either of the other two parties within the triangle. This obliged the United States to stay closer to both Moscow and Beijing than they were to each other, with a tilt toward Beijing since it was the Soviet Union which represented the more immediate and by far the more powerful threat.

Despite its complexity, this balancing act was carried out successfully for twenty years by five presidents of both parties—an extraordinary bipartisan achievement. Some of these presidents justified the triangular policy on an explicitly conceptual basis, others in a more pragmatic case-to-case manner. Despite differences, an unusual coordination of strategies and, on the whole, of policies was achieved. High-level Chinese-American meetings rarely dealt with technical or day-to-day issues (in those days, there was little, if any, commercial contact); most of the dialogue involved sharing long-term global geopolitical assessments, projections, and strategies.

This bipartisan consensus was shattered by two events: the first was the collapse of Communism, starting in 1989 with revolutions in Eastern Europe and culminating two years later in the disintegration of the Soviet Union. The second was the bloody repression of the students in Tiananmen Square. The collapse in Moscow destroyed the common fear while the domestic upheaval in Beijing undermined domestic American support for a policy based on common purposes. The anti-Communist right, always uncomfortable with close ties with a Communist country, began to treat the Beijing government as the new evil to be extirpated. And the American left, always uncomfortable with a policy based on geopolitics, returned to its emphasis on human rights and the promotion of democracy as the main priorities in American foreign relations.

The events in Tiananmen Square had been more complex than a simple anti-Communist revolt, having at least three causes: the revolt of students based on Western principles of democracy; workers rebelling to remove, or at least to alleviate, the inequities, abuses, and dislocations generated by economic reform; and the internal struggle within the Communist Party largely about the political consequences of the reform of the economy.

For Deng Xiaoping, who ruled China at the time and for the decade preceding it and who was excoriated by the Western media, the Tiananmen Square uprising represented an ironic reversal. Mao had imprisoned him for a decade as a "capitalist roader," and history is likely to treat him as a reformer who launched China on the road to modernization. The Deng reforms initiated in 1979 sent tens of thousands of Chinese students to Western countries, where they were exposed to values for which they shed their blood in Tiananmen Square. Deng abolished the agricultural communes and made China nearly self-sufficient in food. He industrialized the drab, gray, fearful China of the Cultural Revolution by emphasizing consumer goods.

What Deng and his associates did not foresee—or thought they could avoid—was the political consequences of overcoming the economic stagnation of Mao's China, which had fallen prey to the inevitable diseases of mature Communism. Its incentives rewarded stagnation and discouraged initiative. In a centrally planned economy, capital goods and services are allocated by bureaucratic decision. Over a period of time, prices established by administrative fiat lose their relationship to costs. So long as the system is run as a police state, the pricing system becomes a means of extorting resources from the population. However, as soon as terror eases, prices turn into subsidies and are transformed into a method of gaining public support for the Communist party. In the end, everything from food to housing is subsidized without any criterion for efficiency and hence turns into an obstacle to a rising standard of living.

Placing wide discretionary authority in the hands of bureaucrats leads to corruption. Jobs, education, and most perquisites depend on some kind of personal relationship. It is one of history's ironies that Communism, which claimed to be the harbinger of a classless future, in the end generated a privileged class comparable to that of traditional feudalism.

When Deng and his associates chose to overcome this trend by embracing market economics and decentralized decision making, they combined—in the initial stages of reform—the problems of central planning with those of a free market. The attempt to make prices reflect real costs leads to price increases, at least in the short term. A burst of inflation was one of the triggers of the unrest.

The shift to a market economy actually magnified opportunities for corruption, at least initially. Because the shrinking but still very large public sector coexisted with a growing market economy, two sets of prices resulted. Unscrupulous bureaucrats and entrepreneurs were thus in a position to shift assets and commodities back and forth between the two sectors for personal gain. In short, the beginning of reform can—and, in China, did—produce severe short-term dislocations among the constituencies at the core of the discontent.

Deng had been perhaps too daring in his economic reforms and surely too cautious in the political reforms his policies made inevitable—ironically, the opposite mistake of his contemporary, Mikhail Gorbachev. His task was made all the more difficult by the ambivalence of many in the ruling Communist elite. In most countries undergoing comparable economic transitions, innovative managers at lower levels must overcome resistance from a more conservative senior leadership. In China, the opposite occurred. The top leadership's emphasis on incentives and market forces had to be implemented by executives without experience for such measures and no enthusiasm for the process of reform. Deng had to fight, therefore, on two fronts: against the corruption tempted by reform, and against the survivors of Maoism insisting on their version of a Communist economy. While he won the battle in the economic field, he settled for continued Communist dominance in the political arena. Deng opted to live with the paradox of insisting on political stability in order to complete an economic and social revolution. In his mind, he was fighting chaos, not democracy. "I am still a reformer," Deng said to me six months after the suppression of the Tiananmen Square revolt, "but if stability had been lost, it would have taken a generation to restore it."

I have sketched the circumstances surrounding the upheavals of Tiananmen Square because they marked the turning point at which China began to be perceived by many as an ideological and geopolitical adversary. In fact, they grew out of the dilemmas of reform as much as out of Communist ideology. They were almost totally dominated by considerations of Chinese domestic politics and did not represent a philosophy meant to be applicable elsewhere.[3]

But whatever Deng's motives, the brutality of the repression at Tiananmen Square witnessed on television by the entire world stigmatized China as a repressive regime. This coincided with a period (beginning in the mid-1970s) of increased emphasis on human rights in the industrial democracies and especially in the United States where the human rights issue was on home ground and quickly became the dominant theme of America's relations with China. All other issues were both submerged by the concern with China's domestic structure and distorted by it because disagreements that before that time had been considered the normal by-product of relations between great powers now came to be treated in much of American public discussion as conflicts with a totalitarian evil.

At the same time, China's military modernization, which had been postponed during the first decade of Deng's reforms, attracted growing attention. Chinese moves were increasingly interpreted in terms of a geopolitical and ideological design on its neighbors. A cycle of self-fulfilling prophecies followed, accelerated not a little by occasionally heavy-handed Chinese tactics.

During the George H. W. Bush and Clinton administrations, the political and psychological basis for constructive Sino-American relations was gradually weakening. President Bush, who, in the mid-1970s before the establishment of diplomatic relations had served as head of the United States Liaison Office in Beijing, sought to keep the relationship on some sort of even keel even after the events in Tiananmen Square. Bill Clinton began his term with rhetoric that made improvement in Chinese human rights practices the key to Sino-American ties even in the economic field. By 1995, his administration had, however, returned to the pattern of regular dialogue established by predecessors even while justifying it with slogans that evoked a more Wilsonian theme.

While the Clinton administration did consolidate the economic relationship with China by supporting World Trade Organization membership for China and normal United States–China trade relations, it never did settle on a convincing geopolitical rationale. Applying to China policy its domestic tactics of co-opting the goals of critics while claiming it had a better way of accomplishing them, the Clinton administration proclaimed a policy of "engagement." It asserted that it would bring China over to the American perception of human rights and domestic governance by multiplying contacts in all fields but especially in trade.

In Clinton's second term, the slogan of engagement was raised to "strategic partnership," which implied some kind of global cooperation—a proposition which proved politically controversial and substantively empty in the face of continuing crises and the absence of any sustained political dialogue (for example, during President Clinton's entire nine-day visit to China in June 1998, there were only four hours of discussion at the summit level—reduced further by the need for translation).

As a result, at the end of the Clinton administration, China policy remained hostage to domestic politics. What has been lacking is a definition of the national interest that gives the relationship some geopolitical content. Trade and other New Age issues such as the environment and narcotics are not enough to distill a sense of direction or to overcome the mixture of cooperation, suspicion, mutual misunderstanding, and stagnation that characterize Sino-American relations at the turn of the century. This potentially combustible combination must not be left in its present state for the sake of the stability of Asia and the peace of the world.

RELATIONS WITH CHINA: THE STRATEGIC CONTEXT

We thus return to the original questions: Should the United States use all the means at its disposal to delay as long as possible the emergence of China as a major power? Or should it attempt to bring about an Asian structure open to cooperation with all states, a structure based not on the assumption of any one country's inherent aggressiveness yet supple enough to resist any country's hegemonic aspirations?

While these questions apply to some degree in every part of the world, they are particularly relevant to relations between the world's most powerful industrial nation and the world's most populous nation. China has the longest uninterrupted history of any country in the world and is controlled by the last major government to call itself Communist. It is the state with the greatest potential to become a rival of the United States at some point in the new century—though, in my view, not in the first quarter.

The answer to these questions will resolve not some theoretical debate but the shape of the twenty-first century world. And that world has few analogies to the Cold War. Soviet ideology had insisted on its universal applicability, and every Soviet leader until Mikhail Gorbachev proclaimed the worldwide triumph of Communism as the ultimate goal. Soviet armies occupied Eastern Europe. The Brezhnev Doctrine affirmed Soviet determination to maintain Communist parties in power, by force if necessary, and the Soviet Union intervened militarily in Hungary and Czechoslovakia and threatened to do so in Poland and—indirectly—in China. The Chinese Communist leadership conducts no such policies abroad and makes no such universal claims; it does not have at its beck and call a worldwide network of Communist parties or radical organizations proclaiming their loyalty to Beijing. Nor does China challenge the domestic structure of other states on ideological grounds.

It is nationalism, not Communism, which could lead to confrontation with the United States and then not over the issue of global hegemony but over Taiwan. In the first two decades of its rule, the legitimacy of the Chinese Communist party was based on having unified the country and expelled the colonialists (Japanese and Western). For two decades after the catastrophe of the Cultural Revolution, the party's legitimacy was based on its ability to produce stunning economic progress (which had the unintended effect of weakening its political monopoly). Now that a so-called socialist market economy has been established and is growing, the governing group may be tempted to rest its claim to a monopoly of power on nationalism. As this claim evolves, it may inflame the issue of Taiwan's future, but it does not necessarily translate into a quest for hegemony in Asia.

China's foreign policy is patient and long-range. Viewed from Beijing, the geopolitical challenge is likely to be perceived not as the conquest of neighboring countries but as preventing a combination of them against China. Least of all can it be in the interest of China's leaders to provoke the United States, the most distant country, which historically has never threatened China's unity and integrity. To be sure, Chinese public statements often criticize American military alliances in Asia, giving credence to the view that China's long-term objective is to undermine the American role and presence in the region. Yet one need not postulate Chinese goodwill or permanent peaceful intentions to conclude that prudent Chinese leaders will not lightly risk confrontation with the world's dominant military power at this stage of China's evolution. In addition, modern China has a huge stake in the international economic system—more than the Soviet Union ever had—generating powerful incentives not to challenge the status quo in Asia.

Conflict with the United States would free all the countries around the vast Chinese periphery to pursue their various ambitions and claims. A far more prudent course for China would be to implement the basic maxim of its traditional statecraft—of pitting the far-off barbarians against those close by. In such a context, the United States is cast in the role of a geopolitical option for China—even as a potential safety net—rather than an innate adversary. On the whole—and despite some ups and downs, largely over Taiwan—this has, in fact, been the thrust of Chinese policy.

Some perspective is also called for with respect to the Chinese military capacity to challenge the United States directly. The Soviet Union possessed some twenty-five hundred strategic delivery vehicles, many with multiple warheads capable of high accuracy. An all-out attack on the United States was technically feasible and strategically not inconceivable (though never very likely). The Chinese strategic force of some thirty liquid-fueled missiles with single warheads, requiring hours to launch, is not an instrument for offensive operations. And when, over the next decades, the Chinese acquire multiple warheads for a larger number of solid-fuel missiles, an American missile defense will serve to maintain the equilibrium.

As for Chinese ground forces, they are capable of defending the home country through a strategy of attrition but not suitable for sustained offensive operations against a major opponent. And around its periphery, China is obliged to cope with a strategic situation far more difficult than the Soviet Union experienced in Europe. The Soviet Union threatened weak neighbors unable to resist Soviet ground forces, either alone or in combination. China faces militarily significant neighbors, including India, Vietnam, Japan, Russia, and the two Koreas, each of which would be difficult to overcome individually and even more so in combination. At a minimum, this imposes on China a diplomacy that does not threaten all its neighbors simultaneously.

To be sure, as China develops what it calls its "comprehensive national strength," its military power will become a more significant challenge. But for the foreseeable decades, the United States possesses diplomatic, economic, and military advantages allowing it to shape the future without resorting to preemptive confrontation with China.

The issue is not whether to oppose Chinese attempts to dominate Asia. If they occur, they must be resisted. But at a moment when the capacity for it does not exist, what is the purpose of a confrontational strategy conducted for its own sake? What is to be the strategic goal? In what way does America gain by conducting relations with China by analogy to the Cold War unless Beijing gives the United States no other choice? To what extent is America alone in a position to impede China's growth in the face of the near-certainty that such a policy would find no significant international support? A prudent American leadership should balance the risk of stoking Chinese nationalism against the gains from short-term pressures. Even on the assumption that a new Cold War is inevitable—an assumption I do not share—a wise American policy would seek to shift the onus for conflict to Beijing to prevent America's isolation.

If China remains domestically cohesive, it is destined to become a major power and, as such, will have an enhanced capacity to challenge the United States. But it will not be the only one: India,

Brazil, and Russia have options similar to China's and, in some respects, face less daunting obstacles. Is the United States to define its security in terms of preventing the emergence of any possible major power? This would make it the policeman of the world and eventually turn most of the other nations against it. It would exhaust America's resources and psychological equilibrium if permanent interventions and crusades became the defining characteristics of American foreign policy—a subject I shall discuss in the concluding chapter.

China policy should be liberated from slogans. The issue is not how to label the relationship but what content it can be given. Cooperative relations are not a favor either country bestows on the other. They are in the common interest of both. There are enough issues to test the seriousness of both sides. A permanent dialogue on such issues as the future of Korea and proliferation of nuclear weapons and missile technology could test the prospects of a stable relationship. Then there is the entire range of New Age issues: environment, cultural and scholarly exchange, among many others. A permanent dialogue is needed as the best means to create a more stable world or, at a minimum, to demonstrate to the American people and America's allies why it is not possible.

TAIWAN AND CHINA

Normally many of these issues confounding Sino-American relations would be clarified by the passage of time. The ultimate intentions of China would become evident, and a consistent American policy would develop with experience and patience. But there is lurking on the scene a wild card that could force the hand of either Beijing or Washington: the future of Taiwan. It is the subject of domestic pressure on the mainland as well as in the United States, and it is governed above all by a process with its own imperatives.

A part of China since the seventeenth century, Taiwan was annexed by Japan in 1895 in what proved to be the first step toward the eventual attempt to conquer the mainland. It was returned to

China by the victorious World War II allies in 1945 after President
Franklin Roosevelt had declared it to be part of China in 1943. In
1949, after the Communist victory on the mainland, Chiang Kai-
shek withdrew to Taiwan and made it the seat of his Nationalist
government, which claimed to represent all of China and which,
until diplomatic relations with the mainland were restored in 1979,
was recognized by the United States as the government of all of
China. On the outbreak of the Korean War in 1950, President Truman interposed the Seventh Fleet in the Taiwan Strait, thereby preventing a Communist conquest of the island and indirectly making
the United States a party in the Chinese civil war.

By that time, Taiwan had become a deeply symbolic issue for
many Americans. It was the inheritor of the legacy of goodwill acquired by the Nationalists for their staunch resistance to Japanese
imperialism in the Second World War. And it became a symbol for
the so-called China lobby, which was outraged by the Communist
victory in the Chinese civil war and was determined to prevent its
culmination in the takeover of Taiwan. Many—including those of
us who engineered the opening to China—had great sympathy for
the effort of the Chinese on Taiwan to create a meaningful and
democratic basis for an autonomous existence. A wide consensus
has always existed in the United States opposed to the forcible return of Taiwan to China.

But the issue is also profoundly symbolic for Beijing. Taiwan was
where the dismemberment of China started—the first province to
be annexed by colonialists. Its unification with the mainland is considered even by Chinese who do not share the views of the governing party as a "sacred national obligation" which can be deferred for
practical or tactical reasons but never abandoned.

For the first few years after diplomatic contact with Beijing was
reestablished, this issue did not present itself. The question of
which government the United States "really" recognized—Beijing
or Taipei—was shelved in the Shanghai Communiqué of 1972. The
United States "acknowledged" that Chinese living on both sides of
the Taiwan Strait affirmed there was only one China and that it did
not challenge that proposition. Since 1972, every American presi-

dent has confirmed America's commitment to a "one-China" policy and the rejection of a "two-China" or a "one-China, one-Taiwan" policy. The most explicit affirmation of that policy was a joint communiqué with Beijing in 1982 during the Reagan administration, which was repeated by President Clinton when he visited China in late June 1998. Since 1972, every American president has also affirmed his abiding concern for a peaceful resolution of the issue—a euphemism for opposition to the use of force—as did the Taiwan Relations Act of 1979, which enshrined the principle in American law.

Within this framework, Taiwan has prospered, become democratic, and participated in international forums that did not require formal state-to-state relations. At the same time, the United States proceeded in 1979 to recognize Beijing as the legitimate government of China, as did the vast majority of the world's governments—most of them before the United States had. But, unlike other nations, the United States was also supplying the bulk of defense equipment enabling Taiwan to remain free of the political control of what was at the same time recognized as the legitimate government of all of China, including Taiwan.

While insisting on ultimate unification as a sacred principle, China nevertheless expressed on several occasions its willingness to defer a final resolution in the interest of its relationship with other countries, especially the United States, provided Taiwan did not stake a formal claim to sovereignty. (In November 1973, Mao told me that China could wait one hundred years.)[4] For its part, the United States, while reaffirming its opposition to the use of force in every administration of both parties since 1971, did so invariably within the framework of a "one-China" policy.

This tacit bargain began to unravel in 1995 when a visa was granted to President Lee Teng-hui of Taiwan for a visit to Cornell University. This came after Secretary of State Warren Christopher had assured the Chinese foreign minister that the existing policy of nonrecognition of Taiwan as a sovereign state would remain in force and that the ban on visits by Taiwan's top leaders would not change. The Chinese reacted by initiating military exercises and missile launches in the Taiwan Strait—carrying, however, no warheads. The United States responded by sending a two-aircraft-carrier task force by way of warning. The crisis subsided, but Sino-American relations have never fully recovered. Since then, Taiwan has elected a new president whose party platform used to advocate independence, and China has backed off a bit, hinting that it would use force only if Taiwan formally declared itself independent.

The sensitive issue of Taiwan falls into the category of problems—like the future of Palestine—that permit no definitive solution at this point. The debacle of the Camp David Middle East summit of 2000 that ended in a military confrontation demonstrates that even the best-intentioned efforts to produce a final outcome for which the parties are not ready may—indeed, almost must—lead to a blowup.

The challenge is how to live with a problem that should be alleviated but does not yet permit a final agreement. The nature of the issues is clear, and the self-restraint this imposes on all sides has become increasingly obvious. If the United States chips away at the "one-China" principle, first affirmed by Roosevelt in 1943 and reiterated by all six American presidents since Nixon, a military confrontation is probable. If China seeks to bring matters to a head militarily, American resistance is certain. If Taiwan abandons restraint and upsets the tacit bargain that has preserved peace in the Taiwan Strait for decades, either locally or by skillful lobbying in Washington, it will unleash a conflict whose consequences cannot be foreseen but are unlikely to redound to Taiwan's long-term benefit.

All the parties involved have an interest in not driving matters to the point of combustion. The United States must resist the domestic pressures to abandon the "one-China" principle. The groups pressing for this change of policy by a series of seemingly marginal modifications need to understand that an explosion can occur because any one step in a sequence that was barely tolerated could well turn out to be a step too far. A serious effort is needed to find a way to ease the confrontational atmosphere. Indications of restraint and flexibility on Beijing's part should be credited as constructive—such as statements by Deputy Prime Minister Qian Qichen that Taiwan would no longer be viewed as a renegade province of the People's Republic of China but as one of two separate (and presumably equal) components of a single China. This idea, coupled with China's previously mentioned hint that it would not use force to bring about unification short of a formal declaration of independence by Taiwan, deserves careful exploration.

At the same time, even as China rejects the proposition that the United States has a right to intervene in the future of Taiwan, it should take account of the seriousness with which successive presidents have affirmed America's concern for a peaceful resolution of the issue. In this they express not only a personal preference but the overwhelming view of American public opinion. Whatever the legal status of these declarations in Chinese eyes, Beijing must take care to not slip into a confrontation with the United States, with all its attendant consequences, through a miscalculation.

A significant measure of responsibility to exercise restraint falls on Taiwan's leaders as well. Some of their supporters act as if it is in Taiwan's interest to exacerbate tensions between Washington and Beijing and to press for congressional and administration measures implying a de facto "two-China" policy. They are skillful in devising measures which seem marginal to Americans but are certain to inflame Beijing. Such a strategy is shortsighted because the existing framework is very much in Taiwan's interest. For a key constraint on China's Taiwan policy has been China's stake in its relationship with the United States. Were Taiwan to achieve formal American recognition of a separate status, as some of its spokesmen and supporters now seem to seek, this would risk a military confrontation and guarantee a political crisis that would divide Asia and turn Taiwan's role in the resulting tensions into a global issue. Taiwan would be less, not more, secure in such an environment.

INDIA

For most of the Cold War, India was a bystander in American policies concerning Asia, a reality symbolized by the fact that the

State Department administered it within its Near East, and not its East Asia, bureau. Indeed, India faces in three directions at once, looking toward the north where it encounters China and Russia, the west where it adjoins the passions and rivalries of the Middle East, and the east where it borders the teeming populations and vast economic resources of Southeast Asia.

Throughout this period, America's relations with India suffered from the same cultural gap noted in some of its relations with the other Asian countries. In the case of India, this seems at first sight inexplicable because, on the surface, there appears to be every reason for the two countries to understand each other very well. India is a democracy, by far the best functioning and genuine free system of any of the nations achieving independence following the Second World War. Its ruling group speaks excellent English. The Indian civil service, though extremely bureaucratic and influenced by socialist theories imbibed at the London School of Economics, is one of the most effective in the developing world. Almost all of its leaders have studied in Western universities. Yet Americans have, in the past, had great difficulty in coming to grips with the way Indian leaders approach foreign policy.

Bordered on the south by the Indian Ocean, on the north by the towering Himalayas, on the west by the nearly as formidable mountains of the Hindu Kush, and in the east by the marshes and rivers of Bengal, India has existed for millennia as a world apart. Its polyglot peoples attest to the waves of conquerors who have descended on it through the mountain passes, from the adjoining deserts, and occasionally from across the sea. Huns, Mongols, Greeks, Persians, Afghans, Portuguese, and, at the end, Britons established empires and then vanished, leaving behind multitudes clinging to their own ways of life.

Unlike the societies of Northeast Asia with long histories of national existence, India came about in its present extent only with the end of British rule in 1947. For centuries, it achieved the astonishing feat of maintaining its identity without the benefit of a specifically Indian state. While China has had its own political institutions which gradually imposed Chinese culture on conquerors until they became nearly indistinguishable from the Chinese people, India preserved its special character not by coopting foreigners but by segregating them. Indian society might bend to force, but it has prevailed by being all but impermeable to alien cultures.

Like the Middle East, India is the home of great religions. Yet unlike Islam or Christianity, the Hindu religion is one of endurance, not of personal salvation. Instead it offers the solace of inevitable destiny. It accepts no converts; one is either born into it or is forever denied its comforts. The assured position it confers via the caste system is so pervasive that the lower castes chose to remain in that status in the Hindu religion rather than escape it by conversion to one of the available egalitarian religions, such as Islam or Christianity. Foreigners could achieve no status in Hindu society, producing an essential imperviousness to foreign rule.

India became unified in its present dimensions because Britain gave the subcontinent, which had been hitherto a religious, cultural, and geographic expression, a homogeneous structure of government, administration, and law. It brought about an Indian state organized on the basis of Western liberal principles of democracy and nationhood. It saddled India as well with the issue of its Muslim population, about one hundred million of them that have remained in India after Pakistan was created during the partition. For India, the birth of Pakistan has been a challenge not only because it alienated territory Indian leaders consider part of their patrimony but also because the proposition that Muslims cannot live comfortably in India is perceived as a time bomb threatening permanent civil strife. For this reason, the United States military alliance with Pakistan during the 1950s and 1960s, though aimed at the Soviet Union and China, blighted American-Indian relations during the Cold War.

But the basic cause for India's aloofness throughout the Cold War ran deeper. India survived through the centuries by combining cultural imperviousness with extraordinary psychological skill in dealing with foreigners. Mohandas Gandhi's passive resistance to British rule reflected the Mahatma's extraordinary moral qualities; it was also the most effective method to fight the imperial power by turning the values of British society in the twentieth century against it. During the Cold War, India proclaimed itself the neutral moral arbiter of world affairs, and many American intellectuals accepted that it was pursuing a higher moral standard than the superpowers. But the ultimate rationale for India's rejection of what it described as the power politics of the Cold War was that it had no national interest in the disputes at issue. For the sake of the freedom of, say, Berlin, India would not risk the hostility of the Soviet Union only a few hundred miles away and to which it wished to give no incentive to join up with Pakistan. Nor would it risk Muslim hostility on behalf of democratic Israel; indeed, during Gamal Abdel Nasser's most radical anti-Western phase, Jawaharlal Nehru was a staunch friend of Egypt. During the Vietnam War, India found the totalitarian nature of the Hanoi regime no obstacle to giving it vocal political support. India's leaders were determined not to isolate themselves from the radical trends in the developing world. And they calculated correctly that, based on its democratic institutions and elevated rhetoric, it had enough friends in liberal and intellectual circles within the United States to keep American irritation within tolerable bounds.

In fact, India's conduct during the Cold War was not so different from that of the United States in its formative decades. Like the Founding Fathers, India's leaders of the Nehru dynasty believed they would protect their young country best by staying aloof from quarrels not affecting its vital interests. And, again like the United States, India did not apply its rejection of power to the region affecting its immediate security interests. Whatever the United States in the nineteenth century proclaimed about European power politics, it did not shrink from using force against Mexico or in the Caribbean. Nor did India hesitate to insist on its power in Sikkim, Goa, Sri Lanka, Bangladesh, and Nepal. And India has for at least twenty-five years worked on a nuclear weapons program culminating in weapons tests in 1998.

When President Clinton visited India in 1999, he spoke with some eloquence on the bonds of common democratic conditions even while lecturing his hosts on the futility of their nuclear weapons program. Neither proposition is likely to form the basis of a new relationship. India is neither about to conduct a Wilsonian policy nor will it abandon its nuclear weapons program.

Indian foreign policy can best be understood by analogy to the one that had been conducted when Britain governed the country. And that policy was, in fact, formulated in Calcutta (the first seat of government) and then, after 1934, from New Delhi. It based Indian security on naval supremacy in the Indian Ocean, on friendly, or at least nonthreatening, regimes in the area from Singapore to Aden, and a nonhostile regime at the Khyber Pass and the Himalayas. In the north, Britain had insisted on the McMahon Line some distance beyond the historic boundaries between China and the Indian subcontinent. Imperial China never accepted this demarcation but was too weak to contest it. Communist China has reclaimed the traditional border and fought to achieve it in 1962. The issue is at present unresolved.

In the arc from Singapore to Aden, American and Indian interests run quite parallel. Neither country wishes to see a fundamentalist Islam dominate the region even as motives for this attitude differ. In terms of its domestic politics, India is more concerned about Afghan fundamentalism than about Iran's, and far more about Saudi financial support for Muslim fundamentalists than about Saddam's intransigence. At least for tactical reasons, India presents itself as a potential mediator between the United States and the Gulf radicals. This could have its benefits as long as there is clear understanding of the extent of the tolerable.

The same is true in the region between India and Singapore. There, as China grows in strength and Japan in assertiveness, a three-cornered rivalry is likely to develop (or, as Indonesia consolidates, a four-sided one). The dominant American interest is to prevent hegemony by any of the participants; it is a classic balance-of-power problem. Thus, the conditions for close cooperation exist—provided India does not get carried away by its growing military strength and the United States is capable of formulating a policy of equilibrium for the region.

In the north, in the Himalayas, the United States has no national interest to let itself be drawn into border disputes between China and India as long as neither side seeks to achieve its objective by force. This is an issue for which America should not risk its relations with either country. It is a classic case of the need to understand the limits of American interests.

The relationship between China and India affects the United States only if either of these states were to seek to dominate the other. America should avoid presenting its objections to the Indian nuclear program in joint forums with China—as occurred during the Clinton administration—because it must not imply a kind of nuclear tutelage over the Indian subcontinent. But neither is it in America's interest to go along with India's justification that its nuclear program is needed to contain China.

The Indian nuclear weapons program, in fact, became the principal point of contention between India and the United States in the last two years of the Clinton administration. The initial American reaction to Indian nuclear testing was highly emotional. President Clinton said:

> To think that you have to manifest your greatness by behavior that recalls the very worst events of the 20th century on the edge of the 21st century, when everybody else is trying to leave the nuclear age behind, is just wrong. And they clearly don't need it to maintain their security.[5]

Any analysis must begin with the realization that nuclear competition on the subcontinent has a long history. India set off its first nuclear explosion in 1974. China tested its first nuclear weapon in 1964. In 1976, as Secretary of State, I failed to dissuade Pakistan from its incipient nuclear program. The nuclear testing thus serves to remind us that, despite the mantra of globalization, there are geopolitical realities that overwhelm fashionable reveries about universality.

India and Pakistan are testing nuclear weapons because, living as they do in a tough neighborhood, they will not risk their survival on exhortations coming from countries basing their own security on nuclear weapons. While the United States has every reason to pursue nonproliferation objectives, the prime ministers of India and Pakistan are equally rational in pursuing their own nuclear objectives. American policy should therefore move from trying to pressure India and Pakistan to abandon their nuclear weapons programs to making them partners in a regime of nuclear restraint and in easing political tension in South Asia.

Nations have at least three motives for building nuclear weapons programs:

- The desire to be a world power based on the belief that a nation unable to defend itself against the full range of possible dangers cannot be a world power. Such a nation will both acquire nuclear weapons and strive for the capability to reach any potential adversary. Anxious to preserve their special status, these states are least likely to engage in proliferation except, as in Russia, due to a collapse of discipline. They are also least vulnerable to sanctions because the other world powers value their cooperation on other subjects. India is in this category.

- States that feel threatened by neighbors with larger populations or greater resources may see in nuclear weapons a means to pose unacceptable risks or to create a deterrent against threats to their survival. This is especially the case if the powerful neighbor has nuclear weapons. Such states could be kept from developing nuclear weapons only by a credible guarantee from existing nuclear powers, which is unlikely to be extended and even less likely to be believed. Israel and Pakistan are in this category.

- Nations determined to wreck the balance of power in their regions and that see in nuclear weapons a means with which to intimidate their neighbors and discourage outside intervention. Iraq, North Korea, and other so-called rogue states are in this category.

Thus there is far from general consensus "to leave the nuclear age behind." The countries which have renounced nuclear weapons are mostly in Latin America and Africa or in the Southern Pacific, out of reach of the major nuclear powers and having no significant conflict with them or with each other. But in the explosive regions of South and Northeast Asia, the Middle East, and the Persian Gulf, the opposite trend prevails.

The United States must do its utmost to prevent the spread of nuclear weapons technology. But once proliferation has taken place, it should not tilt against windmills. America should relate nonproliferation to other objectives and distinguish between countries whose activities represent no threat to American interests or the peace of the world and those which enter the nuclear weapons program in order to disturb the equilibrium; and between nations that will be prepared to join a nonproliferation regime and those that are either indifferent to or supportive of proliferation. India and Pakistan should undertake not to spread either nuclear or missile technology. They should also demonstrate that a plausible effort is being made to ease tensions between themselves. A second objective should be vigorous diplomacy on both political and arms control issues affecting the subcontinent, including protecting a second-strike capability and the prevention of accidents. But the United States also has other common interests with India that must not be jeopardized by overemphasizing the nuclear issue.

The challenge is not to reargue the debates of decades but to give impetus to the basis of a new Indian-American relationship. For under the conditions of the post–Cold War world, a close cooperative relationship between the two countries is in their mutual and basic interests.

WHERE DO WE GO FROM HERE?

America's Asian policy should liberate itself from facile slogans and begin to act on the basis of some of the following operating principles:

First, America's national interest in Asia is to prevent domination of the continent by any single power, especially an adversarial one; to enlist the contribution of Asian nations to overall global prosperity; and to mitigate intra-Asian conflicts. All of these interests are best served by keeping open the option of constructive relationships with all these countries without declaring any one of them to be an inherent opponent, unless its actions give us no other choice.

Second, the best way for the United States to defend Asia against *any* hegemonic threat is by maintaining a superior military establishment and conducting a foreign policy compatible with the national objectives of those major Asian nations whose goals are compatible with its own. A military defense of the Asian balance of power presupposes that the Asian nations maintain a balance to be defended, and ensuring that will require a much more complex political effort than was the case in Europe.

Third, the alliance with Japan remains the bedrock of America's Asian policy. Special care must be taken to ensure that Japan's leaders understand that the United States has no more important relationship in Asia and that Japan has a major voice in the design of American policy. Access to energy is bound to become a principal concern and perhaps an element of competition. These issues must be on the agenda of any dialogue.

Fourth, a similar intensive dialogue is needed with India, especially for the region from Singapore to Aden. America's interest is primarily geopolitical; India is as much concerned about the impact of Islamic developments on its own population. The United States is mostly concerned about Iran and Iraq; India is more focused on Afghanistan and the subventions the Taliban receives from Saudi Arabia, with which America is allied. Nevertheless, the conditions for a constructive strategic dialogue exist.

Fifth, insofar as Sino-American relations can be shaped by American policy, they should be based on the recognition that China, by virtue of its population, history, culture, and geographic position, is an indispensable component of a constructive Asian policy, and this requires a settled policy, not a slogan. Confrontation should be a last resort, not a preferred option. A constructive relationship between the United States and China is not a favor either country does for the other, and it will withstand the stress of time only if it is based on some conception of a common interest. A sustained geopolitical dialogue between China and the United States is therefore imperative—to create a safer international order should it succeed, to prove to the American public and America's allies that Washington has gone the extra mile should it fail. The challenge is not to invent words to describe the dialogue but to give it a content relevant to the future. The United States and China, the most technologically advanced nation and the country with the largest population, have a special obligation to adjust their differences and to identify parallel interests. Though neither side has much experience in long-term dealings with great powers of equivalent stature and on the basis of equality, they have no better option. For as China develops and extends the range of its international concerns, the two countries will be obliged to interact with each other in such regions as Central Asia, the Middle East—especially Iran—and Korea. Confrontation will create a situation in which both sides lose. America has nothing to gain by engaging in it preemptively because it holds strong cards in any foreseeable situation.

Sixth, the visit of South Korean President Kim Dae Jung to Pyongyang and Washington's flirtation with the North Korean capital have opened a new phase on the Korean peninsula. They would hardly have been possible without China's acquiescence, if not encouragement, and they also require Japan's understanding and support. Now that the process is under way, it will evolve in as yet unpredictable directions which will require the greatest degree of policy coordination among Washington, Beijing, Moscow, and, above all, Seoul, as described in earlier pages.

Seventh, the United States has a national interest to prevent or at least to limit the further spread of nuclear weapons and to enlist the nations of Asia in that effort. China has already joined a number of international agreements designed to inhibit the spread of nuclear and missile technology. It has agreed to stop nuclear and missile cooperation with Iran. Further steps are necessary, particularly bilateral arrangements with India and Pakistan for more stringent controls over the export of nuclear, chemical, and biological materials.

Eighth, world order—or Asian order—cannot emerge from a strategy of equilibrium alone. But neither can it be achieved without it. And maintaining the balance of power in Asia requires a coherent view of the future of the region. The United States must maneuver among the various political constellations emerging in Asia with subtlety, persistence, and a firm long-range perspective. It must be present without appearing to dominate. And it should have a major role in dealing with the dangers without turning itself into the focal point of every controversy.

Any serious dialogue with Asian nations cannot fail to include the subject of human rights. Even the most "realistic" American administration must pursue such goals not as instruments of harassment but as reflecting America's deepest values and necessities. No administration which fails to take account of this reality can maintain public support. The American president speaks for all Americans when, with due regard to the national pride of other societies, he affirms these concerns. No Asian nation which understands its interests should make light of them.

FIVE ◇ ◇ ◇ ◇ ◇ ◇ ◇ ◇ ◇ ◇ ◇ ◇ ◇

The Middle East and Africa: Worlds in Transition

IN the conflicts of the Middle East, the emotional impetus derives from forces comparable to those of Europe during the seventeenth century. Schisms defined either by religion or by ideology tear the region apart. The most prominent is the Arab-Israeli conflict, but the rifts within the Islamic world are not much less intense if less obvious. The United States has devoted much of its diplomatic effort in the region to resolving Arab-Israeli tensions. Yet the challenges in the Gulf and the emergence of a fundamentalist Iran, to cite just two examples, pose as great a direct threat to American security and prosperity and, in the long run, perhaps greater ones.

The irony of the American role in the Arab-Israeli conflict is that the attempt in the last year of the Clinton administration to resolve it once and for all may well have taken it from the difficult to the intractable. Israel seeks recognition for a homeland based on a Biblical claim and a symbolic end of the persecutions that have haunted the Jewish people for two millennia, capped by the Holocaust. To Arabs—and especially Palestinians—Israel's objectives appear as a demand for acquiescence in the amputation of their cultural, religious, and territorial patrimony.

A conflict defined in this manner is rarely subject to compromise—at least not within the short time limits of an American electoral year; in fact, it is generally concluded by exhaustion, either physical or psychological. It is unlikely to be settled definitively by an agreement (even if there should be one). The most realistic proposal is for a definition of coexistence. To seek to go further is to tempt violence, as was experienced after the July 2000 Camp David summit composed of President Clinton, Israeli Prime Minister Ehud Barak, and Chairman Yasser Arafat of the Palestine Liberation Organization (PLO). The challenge now is whether coexistence will be brought about by negotiation or whether it will emerge in further tests of strength of a kind that, in a comparable period in Europe, produced the Thirty Years' War.

Meanwhile, the Muslim world is rent by schisms of its own. Some represent a continuation of the historic conflict between the civilizations of the Nile and those of Mesopotamia; between radical secular regimes, such as Iraq's, and moderate secular regimes, such as Egypt's; between fundamentalists, of which Iran's government is the most important, and secular regimes, such as Syria's; between semifeudal governments, such as those of Saudi Arabia or the Gulf states, and covetous, more modern neighbors; between Arabs and Persians; and between the Sunni and Shiite sects of Islam.

In the last three decades, more wars, and far bloodier ones, have taken place among Muslim countries than between Israel and the Muslim world. Each of these intra-Islamic conflicts has had its own internal gradations and tensions. On occasion, fundamentalist Iran has been the scourge of the Gulf states and Saudi Arabia (even when the Gulf states' fear is so great as to inhibit its being avowed). On the other end, Iran feels threatened by secular Iraq and by the fundamentalism of the Taliban in Afghanistan—more intense than even its own—which encroaches on Iranian security both from the north and, increasingly, from the east via Pakistan. For the West, the pivotal country is Turkey, the strongest military power in the region, allied to the West, friendly to Israel, and, because of the indispensability of its geography, important to all the contending forces.

On this ocean of passion, the United States is striving for a compass course. Few of its traditional navigational aids are of much use. The conflicts in the region are not about democracy because, except for Israel, none of the contestants is a democracy, obliging America to cooperate with a number of states on the basis of common security concerns. The fact is that, quite simply, the industrial democracies cannot permit access to Gulf oil to be denied to them or acquiesce in the Gulf's being dominated by a country or group of countries hostile to their well-being.

Indeed, the concept of "hostility" is itself in as much flux as is the region itself. Until the late 1970s, Iran was the linchpin of American security policy in the Gulf; a domestic revolution, which the United States was unable either to prevent or to master, transformed the country into a major threat to the security of the area. The task of protecting Western interests in the Gulf has been complicated further because Iraq, the second-largest country in the region, also turned again into an adversary after the end of its war with Iran in 1988. Thus the security of the Gulf must be wrested from an environment in which the two strongest countries confront the weakest and most precariously placed—not an enviable assignment.

THE ARAB-ISRAELI CONFLICT

By 2000 the world had become so accustomed to the so-called Middle East peace process that it had nearly lost sight of how torturous and bitter had been the history from which it all emerged. In circumstances where the aspirations of a people reclaiming an ancient homeland clash with the resentments of those who have lived there in the interim, a common basis for dialogue is hard to find and becomes only more elusive as the attempt is made to adjust ancestral beliefs.

Arab-Israeli negotiations are obliged to meld territorial and strategic issues—that is, the stuff of diplomacy—with the mandates of ideology, religion, and legitimacy—the stuff of theology. Israel is being asked by the Arab states to cede conquered territory, which is tangible, in return for recognition of its very right to exist by the

Arab states, which is a revocable act. The starting point of most negotiations—accepting the legitimate existence of the parties—amounts to the uncertain *outcome* of Arab-Israeli peace diplomacy.

The prime obstacle to a culmination of the peace diplomacy is the differing conceptions of it held by the parties. Israeli and American leaders define peace as a normality that ends claims and determines a permanent legal status—in other words, they apply the concepts of twentieth-century liberal democracy. But the Arabs and especially the Palestinians consider the very existence of Israel an intrusion into "holy" Arab territory. They may accept territorial compromises for want of a better alternative, but they will treat it in the same way that France acquiesced in Germany's annexation of Alsace-Lorraine in 1870—as a necessity leavened by the determination to wait for the opportunity to regain what has been lost. (To be fair, sacred rhetoric has been part of the Israeli discourse as well—for example, regarding the indivisibility of Jerusalem.)

This difference of perspective has overshadowed and blighted Arab-Israeli negotiations since the founding of the Jewish state. When Israel was established in 1948 on the basis of a United Nations plan of the previous year partitioning the British mandate of Palestine, its Arab neighbors responded by invading the tiny infant state. Israel won that war and, in the process, managed nearly to double its territory by seizing the essentially uninhabited Negev desert. The fighting was ended by a cease-fire, not a peace agreement. But all the Arab states refused to recognize Israel and set out to throttle it with economic boycotts and sporadic guerrilla actions.

Seven years elapsed before there was any attempt at negotiation. Peace feelers under British aegis took place with Egyptian President Gamal Abdel Nasser in 1954–1955. He demanded Israeli withdrawal to the 1948 borders and the return of all Palestinian refugees to their homes. Egypt's quid pro quo (though Nasser was vague about it) was to be recognition of the Jewish state. Israel was being asked to give up half of its territory and risk being overwhelmed by returning refugees in return for recognition of its existence—the point at which, for every other nation, diplomacy begins rather than ends.

A similar pattern continued for two decades thereafter. In 1967, Nasser triggered a war by blockading the Israeli port of Elat—Israel's only outlet to the Red Sea—and coercing the withdrawal of the U.N. force that, after the Suez crisis of 1956, had been interposed between Israel and Egypt on the Egyptian side of the international border. After victory, Israel once again doubled its territory, occupying the Sinai, the West Bank of the Jordan River, and the Golan Heights. In the wake of that debacle, the Arab states gradually began to edge toward negotiations on the basis of the 1967 frontiers, which they had refused to accept before the lost war. But, unprepared to recognize Israel, they rejected direct negotiations though there were some fitful contacts via intermediaries, principally the United States.

In 1973, the so-called Yom Kippur War broke out when Egypt and Syria attacked Israel on the Jewish religion's most solemn holiday. Israel won the war but less decisively than before and at heavier cost. The United States used the dominance it had established during the war to broker three agreements among the combatants—two between Israel and Egypt, the third between Israel and Syria—establishing dividing lines between the military forces of both sides and limitations of the forward deployments to reduce the danger of surprise attack. The second Sinai agreement also contained political elements regarding the content of peace. But the commitment to nonrecognition between the parties was still so great that the negotiations had to be conducted entirely through an American mediator. The two sides never met except at the military level at the very end of the negotiations to sign the requisite documents; only the second Sinai agreement has signatures from political leaders, and these were affixed to the document separately in each country.

Egyptian President Anwar Sadat made the decisive breakthrough in the peace diplomacy with a dramatic visit to Jerusalem in 1977. He was the only Arab leader at the time to understand that, for the Israelis, the challenge of peace was largely psychological. Having lived unrecognized by their neighbors in a quasi-ghetto existence for their entire history, they were prepared to pay quite a high price for the intangibles of recognition and diplomatic normalization.

The Israeli-Egyptian peace treaty mediated by President Jimmy Carter at the first Camp David summit of 1978 between Sadat and Israeli Prime Minister Menachem Begin provided for an Israeli withdrawal from the Sinai, normalization of relations between Israel and Egypt, and the demilitarization of the Sinai, bringing about a two-hundred-mile-wide buffer zone between the Egyptian and Israeli armed forces. The normalization provisions have not amounted to much; in the intervening decades, Egypt's ambassador to Israel has not been given much to do. Trade has been negligible. But the military provisions of the agreement have greatly enhanced Israel's security in return for the withdrawal.

The only Israeli agreement with an Arab state that actually brought about an increase of normal contacts was with the Hashemite kingdom of Jordan. This was because both parties had a common interest in preventing the Palestinian entity emerging after the 1993 Oslo agreement from threatening the existence of Jordan.

Once Arab-Israeli negotiations turned to the subject of Palestine, however, the different perceptions of peace emerged as a nearly insuperable obstacle. On the West Bank, Arabs and Israelis are condemned to coexistence in a fifty-mile-wide strip of territory between the Jordan River and the sea. Not only is there no physical space for a military buffer zone, there has thus far been discovered no psychological space for a genuine accommodation. The dream of the Israeli doves has been that they might live with their Arab neighbors as, say, Belgium and Holland do with each other. But the majority of Arab doves—Palestinian especially—think of peace not as fulfillment but as acquiescence in facts they are powerless to change. Thus, in negotiations with the Palestinians, the Israeli perception of peace became like a mirage that evaporates the more one appears to approach it—indeed, the more desperately it is being approached. After Ehud Barak had made concessions inconceivable by any previous Israeli prime minister—and I have known all of them since David Ben-Gurion—Arafat found it impossible to accept the Israeli quid pro quo without inflaming his own constituencies. Another obstacle was the Israeli insistence that, after regaining the offered territory, the Palestinians would make no further de-

mands. However reasonable that might sound to Americans and Israelis, Arafat shrank from its finality. He might have been willing to
defer some demands for quite some time, but he could not bring
himself to abandon them altogether and forever.

The peace between Israel and Egypt resulted from Sadat's realization that he could secure Egypt's internationally established
frontiers by meeting Israel's psychological need for recognition.
The diplomacy with Syria has not been consummated, even after
Syria was given to understand that Israel was, in effect, willing to
offer it the same deal as Egypt—that is, to return all of the Golan
Heights. It failed partly because the late Syrian President Hafez
Asad wanted first to regulate his succession and partly because Syria
has continued to consider itself the spokesman for Arab, hence
Palestinian, nationalism. And, since Asad's death, his son Bashar,
who succeeded him, has considered domestic consolidation a
higher priority than negotiating with Israel.

An Israeli-Palestinian negotiation faces unique obstacles. Israel's
1967 borders with Egypt, Syria, and Jordan reflected in essence the
internationally recognized borders of the British mandate of Palestine. But the dividing line on the West Bank is based on a military
cease-fire and, after an agreement, the two peoples must continue
to live together on a daily basis in a very limited space. With its
Arab neighbors, Israel dealt with sovereign states whose territorial
claims were not bound up with the destruction of the Jewish state.
But its negotiations with the PLO involved a partner whose charter
had, until 1998, mandated the destruction of the Jewish state and
whose propaganda to its own people since then has not ceased to affirm this objective.

Despite these obstacles, Israel and the PLO came together at
Oslo in 1993 in an interim agreement that was intended to lay the
foundation for an eventual, all-embracing final agreement. Both Israeli Prime Minister Yitzhak Rabin and Arafat would have preferred victory. They settled for the Oslo agreement because each
came to recognize that he had no alternative. Israel was too strong
to be defeated militarily, and the PLO had too many international
supporters to be defeated politically. No major foreign country was

in a position to furnish arms for an Arab attack on Israel or to support a policy of confrontation diplomatically. No Arab country was sufficiently strong to start a war with Israel and maintain itself long enough to trigger outside intervention. On the other hand, Israel was too dependent on American aid to sustain the moral and political isolation of initiating a showdown.

Israel's inability to crush the 1987–1988 *Intifada* in the West Bank and Gaza left it with four options: ethnic cleansing; annexing the West Bank and creating an apartheid state; annexing the Arab population into the Jewish state; or some form of agreed separation of the two communities—that is, acquiescing in the creation of a Palestinian entity certain to evolve into a state.

Ethnic cleansing and apartheid were incompatible with Israel's moral convictions and political necessities. Nor was Israel prepared to incorporate all the Arabs of the West Bank into Israel, as that would destroy the Jewish character of the state. A negotiated coexistence between the Israeli and Arab populations of Palestine emerged as the only viable option. Shortly before his assassination, Rabin expressed this to Australian Foreign Minister Gareth Evans, who had congratulated him for having converted to the peace process: "Not converted," Rabin replied, "committed."

Similarly, Arafat came to the negotiating table only after it became clear that he had no conventional military option left. The disintegration of the Soviet Union had cut off his principal military supply line; after the Gulf War, Saudi Arabia had ended its financial support, and Kuwait had expelled all Palestinians, terminating the flow of remittances. When I met Arafat in Paris in July 1994 on the occasion of his receiving the Félix Houphouët-Boigny Peace Prize jointly with Rabin and Shimon Peres, I asked him why the Israelis should trust him. "Because the Saudis have cut us off," he replied. "The Jordanians are trying to weaken us, and the Syrians are seeking to dominate us."

This confluence of incongruent motives led to the Oslo agreement, which combined a major breakthrough with an orgy of ambiguity. For the first time, Israel accepted the PLO as a negotiating partner (though not as a state), while the PLO accepted Israel's existence de facto without removing from its charter the requirement of its destruction. The portion of the West Bank occupied in 1967 by Israel was divided into three zones: Zone A, comprising some 45 percent of the West Bank, which contained most of the Palestinian population, and Gaza were placed under complete Palestinian control immediately and would have a Palestinian police force of up to thirty thousand; Zone B denoted Palestinian civil authority but Israeli security control; Zone C, which included Jewish settlements, remained under Israeli authority. Well over 90 percent of the population was assigned to Palestinian-controlled areas, and, as a result of follow-on agreements, now some 95 percent has been. Negotiations for a final settlement were to start in two years and be completed in five (by May 1998). During that process, Israel was obliged to incrementally transfer additional territory from Zone B to Zone A. In return, the Palestinian authorities were supposed to improve progressively the atmosphere for coexistence by arresting known leaders of terrorist groups and ending anti-Israeli propaganda.

The signing of the Oslo agreement on the White House lawn in September 1993 was one of those occasions in which hope suspends all doubt. No one present will ever forget the anguished reluctance with which Rabin shook hands with Arafat or the hope expressed in the nearly Biblical remarks of the usually so taciturn Israeli Prime Minister. Nor could one fail to be affected by the culmination of Arafat's long and tortuous journey from terrorist to acceptance as national leader on a level with the other protagonists. President Clinton's dignified chairmanship of the ceremony and the Russian foreign minister's minimal role also testified to the unchallenged global leadership that, for the moment, had clearly fallen to America.

Only the most churlish could refuse to share in the leap of faith that occasion had represented—even when sober thought should have revealed that the Oslo agreement avoided nearly all the key issues: final borders; the future of Jerusalem; the fate of Palestinian refugees; sovereignty, water rights, and the military status of the Palestinian territories. All these controversies were left to the final status negotiation slated for two years hence. At the time, I wrote an article posing these questions: What exactly was being recognized by each party? With what conviction would the Palestinian police force pursue terrorists? When might that police force become the problem rather than the solution? Was the euphoria inspired by the White House lawn ceremony a spur to the diplomacy ahead? Or would it prove to be an obstacle if it generated disillusionment when the inevitable deadlocks developed?[1]

Conventional wisdom held that a process of reciprocal moves before the final negotiations would build confidence between the parties. In fact, the opposite happened. The Palestinian police force became almost twice as large as permitted by the Oslo agreement and increasingly acquired the characteristics of an army. Nor did it significantly assist the fight against terrorism. And the Palestinian propaganda against Israel did not ease.

The fact was that, with the passage of time after the White House ceremony, the internal politics of both sides grew to be at odds with the so-called final status objectives of the diplomacy. Israel entered the negotiations with the PLO deeply divided between two camps. The Israeli doves treated the talks as a kind of eschatological catharsis that would reconcile the parties, obliterate their mutual suspicions, and, in a genuine atmosphere of cooperation, render the exact location of the border unimportant. The Israeli hawks rejected this as a fantasy. They argued that stonewalling would enable Israel to impose security in the form of an "autonomy" that might make occupation more bearable without ever granting statehood to the PLO.

The Palestinians have been divided in much the same way: into a small counterpart to the Israeli doves holding similar objectives—continually cited by Western and Israeli intellectuals as the genuine expression of the Palestinian soul despite the dearth of evidence to that effect; "moderates," who view the negotiating process as a stage in a continuing struggle to wear Israel down; and, finally, the hawks, who oppose any interruption of the struggle and who surely outnumber the doves.

At the same time, the Oslo process failed in large part because, while it did not settle any of the fundamental issues, it did create enough of a sense of security that both sides came to believe they might be able to procrastinate and let time solve the overriding problem: that their domestic constituencies wanted peace without being prepared to face its consequences. The Palestinians came to rely on a combination of American, European, and Arab pressures to oblige Israel to fulfill, step by step, the PLO program. Israel, divided between doves identifying peace with psychological fulfillment and hawks seeing in the peace process a test of endurance, worked itself into a domestic stalemate, torn between hopes of a blissful peace and paralyzing fears of a national catastrophe. The provision of the Oslo agreement for partial Israeli withdrawals before the final status talks became increasingly controversial. Since defining a Palestinian political quid pro quo proved elusive, the partial withdrawals came to appear to many Israelis as the unilateral admission price to final status talks at which Israel would then be asked to cede even more territory.

In the United States, a Clinton administration desperate to bring the parties together, began to treat Middle East tensions as a misunderstanding to be overcome by a process of splitting the differences between the parties not dissimilar to the legislative process of the United States. In Israel, the hawkish Benjamin Netanyahu, prime minister between 1996 and 1999, attacked the Oslo process for its piecemeal nature. Washington treated his declared preference for a comprehensive negotiation as so much stonewalling and used its "influence" (a diplomatic word for pressure) to persuade Israel to make the called-for partial territorial concessions.

A protracted dispute developed over whether the Israeli down payment for a final status negotiation should be a further 10 percent of the disputed territory (Netanyahu's proposal) or 13 percent (Washington's compromise after Arafat asked for a partial withdrawal of 30 percent). Washington's insistence, abandoning an earlier assurance to Israel that it would not put forward a proposal of its own, obscured the key question of where the negotiation was ultimately heading. The absence of an agreed destination fed the illusion in both camps that, in the end, the United States could deliver a settlement, obviating the need for either side to face the reality that a final peace might require sacrifices neither was prepared to make.

The Wye agreement of October 1998, in which Netanyahu yielded to the American demand regarding the slice of West Bank territory to be given up essentially unilaterally, led to the fracturing of Netanyahu's coalition and new elections, out of which Ehud Barak emerged as the victor with not a little assistance from Washington.

It turned out to be a fateful transition. For Barak was a new kind of Israeli prime minister. All of his predecessors had acted only with the approval of their cabinets, which imposed a certain, usually excessive, caution on them. They had also always taken the position that the United States, crucial as its support was for Israel's survival and international position, should not be allowed to prescribe the terms of Israel's negotiations. When America made recommendations that differed from the preferences of the Israeli cabinet, the prime minister would engage in a protracted rearguard action to reduce, at a minimum, American incentives to take over the entire negotiation. This was even true of Rabin despite the mythical quality he has assumed since his assassination.

From the point of view of the management of negotiations, Barak proved to be the most daring and by far the most conciliatory Israeli prime minister in history. A former commando and chief of staff of the Israeli armed forces, he was willing to take initiatives supported by neither his cabinet nor his parliament. Above all, he brought about a fundamental change in relations with the United States. He drew the conclusion from Netanyahu's clash with the Clinton administration that Israel must avoid at almost any cost a rift with the one ally on whose support Israel depended. Barak was determined to prevent an outcome in which Israel would be blamed for any failure of negotiations. And he was in a hurry to conclude an agreement before his domestic support disintegrated totally.

The result was a rather strange relationship between the Israeli Prime Minister and the American President that can best be described as symbiotic psychological analysis. It is not that Clinton pressed concessions on a reluctant Barak. It is that Clinton invariably conveyed to all the interlocutors that negotiating flexibility was the key to American goodwill, thereby adding—perhaps unintentionally—a kind of undifferentiated American pressure to the demands of the other side.

Barak, seeking to anticipate (and he sometimes overanticipated) Clinton, responded with a subtle and more complex analysis of his own. According to this analysis, Israel had become a high-tech, middle-class society whose morale could not withstand indefinitely the harassment and uncertainty of living in a perpetual state of siege, especially in isolation. Modifications regarding heretofore sacred security principles were, in his view, possible because, with the Soviet Union's collapse, no Arab state or combination of states would, for the foreseeable future, be armed sufficiently to launch a traditional conventional war. The long-range danger to Israel, in this view, would come from guerrilla war and weapons of mass destruction. To resist both, Israel required American political support, guaranteed access to American intelligence, and advanced military technology. This, in Barak's view, was achievable only so long as Israel was perceived as a reliable partner of America's quest for peace in the region.

In this manner, American and Israeli strategy began to intertwine at the precise moment when the Middle East peace diplomacy reached its climactic phase. The step-by-step approach that had served it so well in its early stages had run its course. As Barak (and Netanyahu before him) had urged—and as I had advocated in several op-ed pieces—the negotiation now concentrated on all the issues of a so-called final status together: final borders, Palestinian sovereignty, the military status of a Palestinian state, Jerusalem, refugees, and access to water.[2]

What had not been expected by the advocates of the comprehensive approach was the enormous sense of urgency with which Barak and Clinton pushed the process. In September 1999, at a summit in Sharm el-Sheikh, they committed themselves to a one-year deadline for a final peace treaty, and, in July 2000, they scheduled a period of just one week in which to complete the negotiations at Camp David—despite the fact that there had been very little detailed exploration beforehand and despite Arafat's repeated warnings that he was not ready.

These deadlines were completely unrealistic, even delusional. In the weeks before Camp David, Israeli and American spokesmen were at one in conveying the impression that, on the territorial issue, Arafat would accept eagerly the unprecedented concessions Barak later formally proposed (cession of about 95 percent of the disputed territory), and that, on Jerusalem, he would settle for establishing the Palestinian capital in one of the suburbs of Jerusalem that had been incorporated by Israel in Greater Jerusalem. This explains why Barak and Clinton believed that a breakthrough was achievable in the eight days set aside for Camp David II, despite the experience of Carter's summit with Sadat and Begin on the much less complex problem of the Sinai, which required two weeks. It proved to be an extraordinary miscalculation.

The tight deadlines and, paradoxically, the scope of Israeli proposals made the incompatibility of the two sides' definitions of the concept of peace evident and unbridgeable. The growing number of Israelis embracing the peace process viewed the Oslo agreement as nothing less than a Palestinian conversion to the Western liberal notion of peace. This was one motive behind the extraordinary and unprecedented flood of concessions with which Barak opened the Camp David negotiations even before Arafat had shown his hand. They were designed to break down the psychological block that, in the view of the Israeli doves, was the principal impediment to peace.

It transpired, however, that most Palestinians had not so much a mental block as a rather precise idea of what they were after. Continuing to cling to the perception of Israel as an intrusion on "holy" Arab territory, they treated genuine acceptance of Israel's existence as a concession which could not be sold to their own populations. This attitude was brought home to me on the occasion of the heady day of the White House lawn ceremony in 1993 celebrating the Oslo agreement. At a lunch for the two delegations hosted by Secretary of State Warren Christopher, a member of Arafat's delegation told me that he was looking forward to returning to Palestine for the first time in decades. When I asked him how he would feel if he saw the light of Israeli towns from West Bank territory, he replied: "Though I have not been in Palestine for forty years, I consider my home to be in Jaffa [a suburb of Tel Aviv]. And if you ask my children where their home is, they will also tell you that it is in Jaffa." In other words, the towns along the dividing line were not the principal issue but those on the coast—that is to say, the very existence of Israel—or, at the very least, the return of all Palestinian refugees to Israeli territory.

This is what produced the dialogue of the deaf at Camp David II. What Barak and Clinton rightly considered major concessions of Israel's established positions appeared to Arafat at best as a minimum offering he would not be able to present to his constituency as a significant achievement—especially since the territorial offer was coupled with maintaining most of Israel's settlements on the West Bank. If he risked accepting it at all, Arafat was bound to treat it not as the final ending to the conflict but as a stage in a process toward the ultimate fulfillment of Palestinian demands which he is careful not to make explicit to Western audiences. And he has stayed in power by understanding his constituencies. In addressing them, Arafat never strays far from the vocabulary of *jihad*, the holy war, to extirpate Israel.

This is why Israel's proposed quid pro quo of a formal renunciation by the PLO of all future claims and of the return of refugees proved unacceptable to Arafat. Barak is far too intelligent not to have known that these provisions were quite unenforceable, but he needed them to appease his people's psychology. And Arafat was bound to reject them for the same reason. With three million Palestinians in refugee camps, he could give no such assurance without losing the support of a significant segment of his constituency. In the real world, Arafat might postpone his ultimate demands, perhaps indefinitely, but he was in no position to undertake a formal commitment to that effect and maintain the support of his people.

When Israeli territorial concessions were also made conditional on Palestinian "compromises" regarding the holy places, the stalemate headed for a blowup. The linkage of the holy places to the territorial disputes expanded the negotiations from a Palestinian to a pan-Arab, even a pan-Islamic, issue, simultaneously extending Arafat's influence and constricting his flexibility even further. So long as the negotiations concerned territory, moderate Arab leaders could treat it as a Palestinian problem and even urge some compromises. But once the religious issue was on the table, no Arab leader could ignore the looming fundamentalist threat to his own rule. That meant that Clinton's appeals to Egyptian and Saudi leaders to intervene with Arafat were doomed to frustration.

Ironically, Arafat may have been reinforced in his stonewalling by Clinton's eagerness to reach an agreement before he left office. When the mediator is that anxious for success, he becomes a party to the negotiations and loses his impartial status, turning himself into a lawyer brokering formulae and abandoning a strategic perspective. The confluence of these trends must have convinced Arafat that, if he remained adamant, American pressure and Israeli yearning for peace—which he may have interpreted as panic—would produce further concessions.

The collapse of Camp David II was followed by another *Intifada*, raging for months. Despite initially proclaiming that Israel would not negotiate under pressure, Barak encouraged Clinton to restart the negotiations, this time with an American peace plan. It was the first time an American president had put forward a comprehensive scheme of his own. And it imposed on the United States a heavy responsibility, whether it succeeded or failed. If the American effort succeeded, it would oblige America to accept an unprecedented role, both in the negotiations on implementing details (which had to follow what would at best have been a declaration of principles) and later on with respect to guarantees for the outcome. All this would have had to be carried out by a new administration not involved in the underlying strategy, the drafting of the proposal, or the negotiation of it. And if the negotiations deadlocked, as they did, the new administration would be obliged to cope with an even more intense Middle East crisis in a context in which the American capacity to shape events had been discredited by its previous failures.

Radicals throughout the region were bound to think that there would be no penalty for either rejecting American proposals or for resorting to force. Only the naive can believe that, even if an agreement had been reached, it would have ended tensions. The issues of settlements, of the interaction of the two societies, of the holy places, and of refugees would provide manifold pretexts for continuing the conflicts.

WHERE DO WE GO FROM HERE?

The major diplomatic breakthroughs in the Arab-Israeli conflict have grown out of two related circumstances. The first was a dominant role of the United States in shaping the political and strategic environment of the Middle East. The second was more subtle and, on the surface, paradoxical: an Israeli government, stubbornly defending its national interest, that could not be moved by pressures from its neighbors but was prepared to make adjustments in deference to the American ally. When conditions were propitious, the result was a diplomacy in which neither side achieved everything it sought but more than it could have accomplished without the American role.

The first breakthrough occurred in 1973–1974 as the culmination of a Nixon administration strategy over a period of four years of blocking every diplomatic move based on Soviet arms or Soviet pressure.[3] In the end, Sadat decided that Egypt's reliance on the Soviet Union guaranteed endless deadlock and that progress toward peace would be impossible without the good offices of the United States. Despite the American airlift to Israel during the 1973 war, without which Israel's position would have been much more precarious, Sadat relied on American mediation, and even Syrian President Hafez Asad invoked United States mediation to bring about a disengagement agreement on the Golan Heights.

Almost the same situation developed after America's victory in the Gulf War in 1991. The radical forces in the region were either defeated or isolated (including the PLO). Secretary of State James Baker's initiative for a Middle East peace conference in Madrid in

1991 opened a new phase in the peace process, which two years later led to the Oslo agreement. Though technically brokered by Norwegian officials, the agreement was made possible because the PLO had come to realize that it would have no role until it went along with what were, in fact, America's terms: acceptance of Israel as a negotiating partner and of the key United Nations Security Council resolutions defining the premises of the diplomacy. Despite Arafat's support for Saddam Hussein in the Gulf War, the PLO in the end turned to American mediation because no other road was open to it.

The two conditions for a diplomatic breakthrough gradually weakened in the last decade of the 1990s. The decline of American predominance was in inverse proportion to the recovery of Saddam Hussein. The inability to keep Saddam "in his box," which—in Secretary Albright's words—was the declared aim of American policy, was reflected in the loss of American influence both among friendly countries and among adversaries. By the end of the Clinton administration, the United Nations inspection system of Iraq had collapsed with American acquiescence, and Saddam faced no international obstacle to the production of weapons of mass destruction. The sanctions regimen was in tatters. Renewed terrorism, often sponsored from abroad, was a factor few Arab leaders in the region dared to ignore. The willingness, as well as the ability, to stand up for policies advocated by Washington or to urge moderation on Arafat began to erode.

Similarly, Arab leaders came to believe that, while Israel remained a colossus militarily, it was coming apart politically. However well considered the concept of an Israeli retreat from Lebanon in the summer of 2000, the abrupt manner in which it was carried out—abandoning to their fate thousands of Lebanese who had worked with Israel—conveyed panic rather than purposefulness. And this was reinforced by the flood of concessions with which Barak sought to fuel the final status talks. He opened the negotiations at Camp David with concessions never previously considered by any Israeli prime minister and improved his offers, even in the face of rejection and the *Intifada*. The Palestinians may well have concluded that Israel was psychologically on the run and that stonewalling would create a base from which they could achieve the remainder of their demands in a new U.S. administration.

In this setting, the role of the United States progressively weakened. To the extent that Arafat believed that Barak had offered the maximum of which Israel was capable, there was no longer a function for the United States except to facilitate drafting or to back up the irreducible Israeli demands. America had gone from being the Palestinian deus ex machina—with Arafat perhaps believing that Clinton would be able to deliver the maximum Palestinian program without serious negotiations—to a point where the American role had become marginal. This explains why, in the last phase of the negotiations, Israeli and Palestinian diplomats negotiated directly with each other and also the extremely ungenerous comments by the PLO about Clinton's role after he left office.[4]

America's decline from shaping the strategic and political environment to that of a broker in legal compromise formulae achieved the exact opposite of what had been intended. For when the parties perceive that the mediator is defining his role as finding a position halfway between them, they are tempted to put forward their most intransigent position in order to push the middle ground as close as possible to what they really want. Or else they stonewall—essentially the same thing—to induce the mediator to put forward ever more favorable proposals in order to break the deadlock. The worst position for the United States is the one it reached during and in the aftermath of the Camp David process: of seeming more eager for a settlement than the parties themselves. Such a state of affairs exposes it to blackmail by all sides and, in effect, abandons the mediation by making the United States one of the parties.

When the peace diplomacy is resurrected—as it must be because none of the parties has a viable alternative—the American contribution will depend on its ability to insist on a strategic and political concept for the enterprise. Mediating between the positions of the parties without a clear sense of the destination will lead to a repetition of the Camp David setback.

The following principles should guide any new approach:

First, the parties are not ready for a final settlement, especially in the wake of the failure of so many legalistic formulae—at least not on terms both sides can accept. The issues need more time in which to evolve. A rush to finality is likely to lead to another explosion. At this stage, the diplomatic effort should concentrate on a series of interim agreements. Their purpose should be stated not as final peace but as an extended period of coexistence reflecting what is imposed on the parties by reality: that they share the same small territory which both of them consider sacred and that neither is in a position to impose its will on the other by force.

Second, as part of an extended interim agreement, Israel should abandon its opposition to the creation of a Palestinian state except as part of a final status agreement. Instead it should make the establishment of such a state the occasion for working out terms of coexistence between the two societies.

The Israeli ambivalence about a Palestinian state, however understandable, is incompatible with the long-term prospects of any negotiation, whatever the formula on which it is based. Its value as a bargaining chip has evaporated. A Palestinian state was inherent in Prime Minister Menachem Begin's offer of Palestinian autonomy at the first Camp David summit in 1978. It was implicit in the Oslo agreement. Even today, Arafat is treated as a head of state when he travels. Within a measurable time, a Palestinian state will be recognized by most nations, including most European nations, even were the United States to hold back for a while. Israeli ambivalence on this subject gives Arafat a permanent means to exert pressure. Once the state has been established, the challenge will be coexistence with Israel—which, *Intifada* or not, remains the option neither party will be able to avoid indefinitely.

Third, to avoid the insistence on finality and yet provide an extended duration for the interim agreement, the formula of the second Sinai accord of 1975—that the agreement stands until it is superseded by another agreement—could serve the purpose of combining an indefinite duration with the implication that some issues require further negotiation.

Fourth, the negotiation for an interim agreement should focus on territorial issues and defer those relating to the return of refugees, the holy places, and Palestinian renunciation of future claims. The return of refugees is, above all, a question of relative power. So long as Israel is strong enough to prevent a return of refugees, the clause is unnecessary. Were the balance of power to shift to enable the Palestinians to insist on it, no clause would keep them from imposing it.

While the definition of its security is for Israel to decide, American leaders should avoid proposing borders like those of 1967, in which Israel's major cities are connected by a corridor only nine miles wide, leaving Israel's population centers dangerously exposed and within mortar range of adversaries. It is difficult to imagine this as being compatible with Israel's security.

Fifth, in drawing the borders of the interim arrangement, major consideration should be given to the Palestinians' ability to lead a life of dignity within an economically viable entity. Palestinian territory should be made substantially contiguous, and Israeli checkpoints and interference with daily life within that territory should be sharply curtailed. It is also time for Israel to review its settlement policy, especially with respect to those settlements which are most exposed or isolated and thus a constant invitation to new outbursts of violence. They should be consolidated with or without an agreement. As part of the interim agreement, the de facto arrangements for the governance of Jerusalem could be reviewed in an attempt to give the Arab population a greater role without, however, seeking to settle the issue of sovereignty.

Sixth, the United States needs to be clearheaded about the role of other nations in the peace process. Many European leaders volunteer their services, and others, such as Egypt and Saudi Arabia, are being invited by Washington to play a moderating role. The fact is, however, that the European nations are rarely sufficiently even-handed to play a moderating role. Eager to protect their interests in the Arab and Islamic world that go far beyond their relationship with Israel, the European allies generally distance themselves from the United States on Middle East issues and even more from Israel. America has nothing to gain from involving nations which, on principle, are more reluctant to ask sacrifices from the Arab side than they are from the Israeli. The Middle East should always be a subject of intensive consultations between Washington and its European allies. And, if the parties invite European participation, the United States is in no position to object. But, insofar as direct European participation depends on American acquiescence, it should be agreed to only on the basis of a prior understanding, according to which potential participants ask as much from the Arab side as they do from Israel. Otherwise an international conference will turn into a mechanism to isolate the United States or to induce it to impose a solution on Israel.

Seventh, while America's European allies seem to crave public involvement in the peace process, the attitude of friendly Arab states is more ambiguous. The United States has frequently overestimated the role such countries as Egypt and Saudi Arabia are prepared to play publicly. Egypt, having already achieved the restoration of its national territories, generally supports a moderate outcome. But it also has little incentive to run major risks domestically on behalf of negotiating programs which may be castigated by radical Arab countries.

As for the Saudi kingdom, it governs tribes of fundamentalist nomads as well as urban concentrations comparable to Western metropolises. When Iraq occupied Kuwait, it faced an ominous demonstration of covetousness by a powerful neighbor. Traditionally, the Saudis have sought to obscure their vulnerability by opaqueness, by avoiding exposure to risk until all other parties are irrevocably committed. This guarantees that Saudi rulers will behave with extraordinary circumspection. One does Saudi Arabia no favor by propelling it into the daily give-and-take of a contentious negotiation—all the less so as it has participated in no Arab-Israeli war and is certain to facilitate any final result from behind the scenes as it has in times past. Thus the United States should stay in close touch with moderate Arab nations but take care not to expose them to domestic strain.

Eighth, the United States must take account not only of the position of the principal parties but of the security of friendly countries on which the stability of the region depends. A particular case in point is the Hashemite kingdom of Jordan, precariously situated between Israel, Syria, Iraq, and the eventual Palestinian state and thus highly vulnerable to radical pressures from all directions. The kingdom has been a reliable and staunch friend of the United States and genuinely helpful in the Arab-Israeli diplomacy. Its security must not be jeopardized in a rush to conclude the peace process. An agreement on a Palestinian state should therefore include provisions for Jordan's security, and the issue of an Israeli military presence in the uninhabited parts of the Jordan valley should be addressed with this in mind.

Ninth, the key to the prospects for peace is America's relationship with Israel. Israel's survival depends ultimately on the diplomatic cover and at least as much on the military equipment provided by the United States. In that sense, the American position will never be perceived—and cannot be—as completely impartial. There is no alternative source of supply, and curtailing the military relationship would only increase America's difficulties. For an Israel perceived to be weak or even weakening by its neighbors would invite the very conflicts American policy should seek to avoid. It would raise the issue of an American guarantee of Israel's security, which should be considered only as a last resort. For such a guarantee—American or international—would make the United States party to every local clash, a particular challenge with respect to *Intifada*-type warfare. It would lead to insistence on a veto over Israeli responses to terrorism and, in this manner, either involve the United States in endless guerrilla warfare or become a means for permanent coercion of Israel by the guaranteeing power or powers. The same considerations apply even more strongly to the deployment of American or international forces along Israel's border. An Israel no longer able to defend itself will sooner or later be submerged in the tide of its neighbors' hostility.

AMERICA AND THE GULF

No area of the world confronts American precepts with greater complexities than the Gulf. Wilsonian principles cannot guide America's actions in this region. The rationale for preventing its domination by a hostile power is, from the Wilsonian point of view, a choice among evils; there are no democracies to defend. But the United States—and the other industrial democracies—have a compelling national interest in preventing the region from being dominated by countries whose purposes are inimical to ours. The advanced industrial economies depend on supplies of energy from the Gulf, and a radicalization of the area would have consequences extending from North Africa through Central Asia to India.

But this geopolitical imperative has to be implemented against a background in which the two strongest nations in the Gulf, Iran and Iraq, are hostile to the United States and in their conduct toward their neighbors. How does one achieve stability in the Gulf against its two strongest powers simultaneously without permanent bases and supported only by brittle allies?

Traditional diplomacy would counsel improving relations with either Iraq or Iran so that at least one of them can form part of the balance of power in the region. As these lines are being written, neither option appears very promising. So long as Saddam Hussein remains in power in Iraq, a rapprochement with Baghdad will be perceived throughout the region, probably in the rest of the world, and surely by Saddam as a major American defeat and humiliation. And improved relations with Iran, while desirable in principle, face major internal obstacles in Tehran as the ayatollahs work out their domestic deadlocks.

For the time being, no dramatic initiatives are available to reverse this state of affairs. Watchful waiting, not a favorite American pastime, is required. Challenges to the stability of the Gulf must be firmly rebuffed; any encroachment by Iraq on the existing United Nations framework must be resisted in a manner leaving no doubt that the gradualism of the past decade is over and that challenges will be met decisively.

In that period, it is important to strengthen the relationship with allies whose support in possible confrontations would be crucial. Principal among them is Turkey. Adjoining Iraq, Iran, and the tumultuous Caucasus, its cooperation in any crisis becomes indispensable. There has been too much of a tendency in the United States, and even more so in Europe, to take Turkey for granted, to act as if it could be subordinated to domestic politics without cost and as if Turkish national pride or its special circumstances could be ignored. The industrial democracies—especially Europe and the United States—must remember that crucial elements of their basic national security are at stake. Their preferences regarding Turkey's domestic structure must be balanced against these imperatives.

The same sensibilities should govern our attitudes toward Saudi Arabia and the Gulf states. Their comparative weakness in relation to the two regional giants imposes on them a certain caution which creates a gap between what they recommend publicly and what they hope the United States will carry out. The United States must take care not to compound their insecurity by leaving its commitment uncertain or by excessive intrusion into fragile domestic structures.

With the passage of time, India's role in the region will become more important. There is a certain commonality of interests between India and the United States with respect to stability in the Gulf, especially regarding the spread of fundamentalism in the region. But, as has been pointed out in the previous chapter, India is at least as worried about Saudi and Taliban support for its own dissidents as it is about the security balance in the Gulf. And it is occasionally tempted to play the role of mediator between the United States and the Gulf radicals—a role America will find helpful only if it is coordinated with U.S. long-range strategy. Still, as time passes, the Gulf should play a major role in an increasingly intensive strategic dialogue with India.

IRAQ

Iraq became a British mandate after the First World War when the Ottoman Empire in the Middle East was divided up between

France and Britain. Created to serve strategic and economic interests, the new multiethnic state was governed after independence by
a Hashemite dynasty and served as a pillar of British strategy in the
Gulf. In 1958, the dynasty was overthrown in the wake of Britain's
humiliation in the Suez operation of 1956. The radical nationalist
Baath party took over, led by a group of military officers out of
which Saddam Hussein emerged as the dominant figure in the
1970s.

Since then, Iraq has been the scourge of its neighbors. In 1980, it
invaded Iran, plunging itself into a debilitating ten-year war in the
course of which it was gradually thrown on the defensive. The
United States had no interest in the outcome other than to prevent
the domination of the region by one of the combatants. Iran, because of its greater resources, larger population, and radical fundamentalism, was considered the greater threat. The Reagan
administration restored diplomatic and economic relations with
Iraq and encouraged America's European allies to supply military
equipment to Saddam Hussein. After the conclusion of the war
with Iran in 1988, Saddam chose a new target and annexed Kuwait
in 1990, triggering a massive American military deployment to the
Gulf, followed by a victorious military campaign in 1991.

The end of the 1991 Gulf War brought about yet another
demonstration of America's congenital difficulty with translating
military success into political coin. Because the United States has
traditionally viewed force and power as discrete, separate, and successive phases, it has fought its wars either to unconditional surrender, which obviates the need of establishing a relationship between
force and diplomacy, or it has acted as if, after victory, the military
element is no longer relevant and diplomats are obliged to take
over in a kind of strategic vacuum. This is why the United States
stopped military operations in Korea in 1951 as soon as negotiations began and why it halted the bombing in Vietnam in 1968 as an
entrance price to negotiations. In each case, the easing of military
pressures reduced the incentives that had produced the enemy's
willingness to negotiate. Prolonged stalemates and continued casualties were the consequence.

The end game of the Gulf War revealed that the United States had not learned from this history. For it allowed an utterly defeated adversary to escape the full consequences of its debacle. The war aims had been defined too narrowly and too legalistically. The war having started over the Iraqi occupation of Kuwait, American policymakers concluded that, with the liberation of that country, they had achieved both their objective and the limits of the U.N. authorization. They justified this decision by stressing the risk of casualties in going on to Baghdad and the public impact of inflicting casualties after the battle seemed to be won. They remembered the stalemates in Korea and Vietnam but not the causes of them.

The George H. W. Bush administration, as its predecessors had, made a case for its course of action. The highest officials of the U.S. government had testified before Congress and assured the international community that America's sole objective was the liberation of Kuwait. With that objective accomplished or exceeded, domestic or international support for continuing the war was believed to be in danger of eroding.

Fear of the disintegration of Iraq was another justification for ending the war quickly. A Shiite rebellion had broken out in Basra and might have produced an Iran-leaning republic. In the long term, Iran was considered the ultimate danger in the Gulf. Also it was feared that an independent Kurd republic in the north of Iraq might disquiet Turkey and undermine its commitment to support American policy in the Gulf. Finally, it was expected that the impact of defeat and the return home of tens of thousands of Iraqi prisoners of war would lead to the overthrow of Saddam.

These arguments, plausible as they seemed, underestimated Saddam's staying power and its effect on America's position in the Gulf. So long as Saddam remained in office, Iraq could not be part of any effort to achieve an equilibrium in the region. Too weak to balance Iran, too strong for the safety of its Gulf neighbors, too hostile to the United States, Iraq would turn into a permanent wild card. Nor were the military options adequately defined. The choice was not marching on to Baghdad or ending the war; the best course would have been to continue the destruction of the elite Iraqi units—the Republican Guards—which were, and remain, the foundation of Saddam's rule. Had this strategy been followed, it is probable that the Iraqi army would have removed Saddam. While his successor would have been no great advertisement for democracy, the symbolic effect of Saddam's removal would have been considerable, and the victorious allies could have begun restoring Iraq to a regional system.

The argument that continuing the war another week would have outrun public and international support must be weighed against the scale of respect President Bush had garnered with the victory his leadership had made possible. The Arab leaders most immediately affected, especially in Saudi Arabia, subsequently claimed that they would have preferred to go on until Saddam was removed from power.

The attempt to calibrate the extent of Iraq's defeat created a long-term political dilemma. United Nations Security Council Resolution 687 established a cease-fire; its disarmament provisions could be enforced only by intrusive international supervision, while the rapid withdrawal of American forces progressively eliminated the credibility of a threat to reintervene. Saddam seized the opportunity and has since tenaciously restored his position and that of a radical Iraq.

The Clinton administration accelerated this deterioration. When Saddam remained in office after the Gulf War, the United States was left with three policy options: (1) to reconcile with a hopefully chastened Saddam; (2) to keep Saddam "in his box" by obliging him to fulfill the terms of Resolution 687; (3) to make it a national policy to overthrow him.

The Clinton administration pursued all three options simultaneously and achieved none of them. Once Saddam survived the Gulf War, his conduct reinforced the fears of his neighbors. He systematically undermined the provisions of the cease-fire that had ended the Gulf War. In 1996, he overthrew the autonomous institutions established under American aegis for the Kurdish areas. Hundreds were killed, and at least three thousand individuals associated with the United States were exiled. Starting in November 1997, Saddam methodically sabotaged the U.N. inspection system meant to monitor Iraq's programs for building weapons of mass destruction. The Clinton administration repeatedly threatened to use force and recoiled each time, enabling Saddam to dismantle the U.N. inspection system. When the United States finally used force for four nights in December 1998, it was a threadbare camouflage for giving up on inspections altogether.

With the inspection system dismantled, Saddam turned to undermining the economic sanctions set up to reinforce the inspection system that were supposed to remain in place until the certification of the demolition of all weapons of mass destruction and the means to produce them. Three months after Iraq overthrew the cease-fire arrangements in the Kurdish area, the United States, in December 1996, went along with a United Nations–sponsored program which allowed Iraq to sell $2 billion worth of oil annually for the purchase of food and medicines. The rationale was to "isolate" Saddam by separating enforcement of the military provisions from the well-being of the population. The idea that strengthening Saddam's domestic position would ultimately weaken him showed little grasp of Gulf realities. Since then, the so-called oil-for-food program was increased to $6 billion annually and now has no limit. Thus, in the year 2000, Saddam exported $16 billion in crude—roughly the same as Iraq's annual earnings before the Gulf War. Of course, money being fungible, the resources thus freed can be used for the purchase of far more dangerous materials.

The hesitant American response to all these challenges was motivated by two psychological legacies of the Vietnam protest: the enormous reluctance to use power, and the insistence on justifying any threat of force by enlisting the widest multilateral backing. Thus, in response to an alleged Iraqi plot against former President Bush's life on a visit to Kuwait in 1993, Clinton ordered a few cruise missiles fired into a single building that the Pentagon reassuringly announced had been unoccupied. In 1996, when Saddam crushed the American-sponsored Kurdish forces, the Clinton administration responded with cruise missiles against radar stations situated hundreds of miles to the south. And, as noted, a gesture of four

nights of inconsequential bombing signaled American acquiescence in the collapse of the U.N. inspection regime in December
1998. Throughout this period, the Clinton administration also had
a tendency to take at face value statements by Gulf leaders urging
restraint. These were more likely intended to serve as an alibi
which the various rulers—only too well aware of the threat posed
by Saddam—were secretly hoping the United States would ignore.

Saddam's political survival has forced the United States into a policy of "dual containment" against both Iran and Iraq. Saudi Arabia,
Kuwait, and the Gulf states are not strong enough to resist either of
these countries alone, much less the two together. And there seemed
to be ambiguity about America's purpose with respect to Saddam's
longtime role. Thus, President Clinton, after aborting a retaliatory
attack already, in fact, launched, stated in November 1998:

> If we can keep UNSCOM [the U.N. inspection group] in there
> working and one more time give him [Saddam] a chance to be-
> come honorably reconciled by simply observing U.N. resolu-
> tions, we see that results can be obtained.[5]

None of our allies in the Gulf or in the area remotely believed in
the prospect of an "honorable reconciliation" based on observing
U.N. resolutions for a few months. All were convinced that Iraq
would bend every effort to rearm as soon as sanctions were lifted
and that the major powers were already straining to find pretexts
for lifting U.N. sanctions entirely. The countries in the region that
rely on the United States will, in the end, judge America's relevance
to their security by its ability either to depose Saddam or to weaken
him to a point where he can no longer represent a threat—no matter what their public declaration.

With the United States as de facto guarantor of all the frontiers
in one of the most volatile regions of the world, the security of the
Gulf has come to depend on the widespread perception of
America's ability to deal with the consequences of Saddam's continued rule and growing strength. The Gulf states are at once very
conscious of their dependence on America and very nervous about
too visible a collaboration, especially when America vacillates.

Saddam's strategy is geared to three objectives: (1) to focus the world's attention on Iraq's grievances; (2) to force into the open the latent split between the permanent members of the United Nations Security Council regarding Iraqi sanctions; and (3) to shift the focus of the debate from inspection to lifting the sanctions. He is well on the way to achieving each of these objectives. There is no serious effort to restore the U.N. inspection system; most of the international debate concentrates on easing or lifting the sanctions— indeed, several nations, led by Russia, China, and France, are in open noncompliance with them. Notably, Iraq seems to have become a test case for another French effort to define a European identity distinct from and in opposition to the United States.

At the end of a near-decade of shilly-shallying, the United States has maneuvered itself into a position where, in major parts of the world—especially in Europe—America, not Saddam, appears as the obstacle to easing tensions in the Gulf. Iraq's sponsors in the United Nations have a good chance of obtaining the necessary Security Council majority to suspend sanctions altogether. Though the United States would no doubt exercise its veto, such an outcome would advertise America's growing isolation and probably cause other countries to relax their compliance with the sanctions.

America's yielding to the chorus would gain no advantage. The countries undermining sanctions would learn that there is no penalty for flouting U.S. policy backed by U.N. resolutions. The Gulf states would be relieved about the temporary surcease from Iraqi pressures but worried about American steadfastness during the next crisis.

The issue posed by the "smart sanctions" suggested as an alternative is whether they wind up as a method of abdication or a form of pressure that will, in fact, be sustained. If smart sanctions are interpreted as a way of abandoning sanctions altogether, the question is whether, in a retreat amounting to a rout, the United States is better off leading the parade or should let others assume the responsibility. If the smart sanctions are serious, it depends on their nature and America's willingness to insist on their enforcement.

Comparable considerations apply to the often heard proposal

that covert operations backed by the United States can enable it to sidestep the complexities of the sanctions policy. In principle, I favor encouraging internal Iraqi resistance but, having witnessed such covert enterprises from the inside, I would advance three cautionary notes: such covert operations must be run by professionals, not adventurers; they must take into account the interests of neighboring countries, especially Turkey, Saudi Arabia, Iran, and Jordan, to prevent their being drawn into consequences they are unable or unwilling to tolerate and that the United States is not prepared to sustain; and the United States must be prepared to back the resistance movement militarily when it gets into trouble, or else it will repeat the debacle of the Bay of Pigs and of northern Iraq in 1975 and 1996, when most of those it supported were wiped out or exiled.[6] If these conditions cannot be met, the call for massive covert operations turns into a dangerous trap.

Even America's European allies undermining the sanctions regime cannot wish to bring about an Iraqi capacity to turn OPEC into a weapon against the industrial democracies, in the process gradually undermining moderate governments in the region. Only after Saddam is gone—even if by actuarial causes—is a more flexible American policy toward Iraq possible and indicated.

An ominous development in the fall of 2000 occurred with Saddam's increasing effort to manipulate the light oil market by periodically reducing the flow of oil permitted under the sanctions regime. This effort should be treated for what it is: not a problem of supply and demand in the energy market but a national security challenge. A coherent cooperative energy policy on the part of the industrial democracies is essential, but it cannot be equated with kowtowing to Iraq.

It is not too soon to focus on the kind of Iraq to be hoped for after Saddam's removal from office. Iraq should be neither too strong for the balance of power in the region nor too weak to preserve its independence against covetous neighbors, including especially Iran. One of the causes of the Gulf crisis in 1991 was the laxity of the Western nations in the wake of the Iran-Iraq war by ignoring that Iraq might become the next aggressor. It would be ironic if another bout of tunnel vision produced the opposite outcome: an Iraq so weak that its neighbors, especially Iran, rush to refill the vacuum. But a balanced approach to Iraq cannot be achieved with Saddam in office; it is for the future, after he is removed.

To preserve America's assets in the Gulf, determined purposefulness is preferable to the thrashing about characteristic of the 1990s. It is also—paradoxically—important for America's relationship with Iran, the most powerful and largest country in the region. The United States will not be able to moderate fundamentalist Iran if it cannot handle a defeated Iraq, or if Tehran's leaders, looking across their border, see how easy and effective it is to defy the United States. What incentive would the ayatollahs then have for a moderate course?

IRAN

There are few nations in the world with which the United States has less reason to quarrel or more compatible interests than Iran. Though, in the 1970s, the Shah had come to symbolize the friendship between the two countries, those interests did not depend on one personality. They reflected political and strategic realities that continue to this day. The United States has no conceivable interest in dominating Iran as the ayatollahs now governing it insist. During the Cold War, America's interest had been to preserve Iran's independence from the threat of the Soviet Union, the historical source of pressures and invasions of the country. In the nineteenth century, British intervention, motivated by the defense of India and of the sea lanes to it, prevented large parts of Iran from being incorporated into Imperial Russia in much the same way as the neighboring Central Asian states had been conquered by the tsars. In 1946, but for American intervention, Iran's northwestern province of Azerbaijan would have been seized by the Soviet Union as a first step toward dismembering the country. Throughout the Cold War, Iran helped resist Soviet pressure on Afghanistan and penetration of the Middle East.

America's interest in Iran paralleled Iran's own quest for independence. Many American policymakers of that era, myself included, felt deep gratitude for the Shah's support of the United States in various Cold War crises. But our basic motivation was less sentiment than an appreciation of the importance of the sum total of Iran's geography, resources, and the talents of its people.

There is no American geopolitical motivation for hostility between Iran and the United States. Iran, however, continues to provide reasons for America to keep its distance. In several administrations, the United States has made it clear that it is prepared to normalize relations. Iran is destined to play a vital—in some circumstances, decisive—role in the Gulf and in the Islamic world. A prudent American government needs no instruction on the desirability of improving relations with Iran.

The chief obstacle has been the government in Tehran. Since the overthrow of the Shah in 1979, the ayatollah-based regime has engaged in a series of actions in violation of accepted principles of international conduct, many of them aimed explicitly at the United States. From 1979 to 1981, it held fifty American diplomats hostage for fourteen months. Throughout the 1980s, organizations financed and supported from Tehran were responsible for the kidnappings of Americans and other Westerners in Beirut. The Tehran regime provided the main support to groups which killed several hundred American soldiers in Beirut. It is closely linked with and also finances camps in Sudan for the training of terrorists. Evidence exists linking Iran-sponsored groups to the bombing of the American military barracks at Khobar Towers in Saudi Arabia, which killed nineteen Americans in 1996. In France, a senior Iranian living in exile was assassinated by Iranian agents who were then released from prison in exchange for a French hostage being held in Beirut. The Iranian ayatollahs have pronounced a death sentence on the author Salman Rushdie that has not yet been revoked, though the Tehran government has "distanced" itself from it, whatever that means.

Beyond these individual acts, Iran does its utmost to undermine Middle East peace diplomacy. Tehran is the patron of Hezbollah, which continues armed opposition to peace with Israel. Iran provides substantial financial support to Hamas and the Palestine Islamic Jihad, both of which regularly claim responsibility for terrorist attacks on Israeli civilians.

The Iranian regime is now building long-range missiles capable of striking the Middle East and most of Central Europe. It is developing a clandestine nuclear capability assisted by dual technology from the West and with some support from Russia, despite its signing of the Non-Proliferation Treaty (China seems to have ended its previous assistance).

The key question for American policymakers is whether these acts are integral to the nature of the Tehran regime, or whether a relationship based on reciprocal nonhostility is possible. That issue has become part of an agenda of disagreements with America's European allies that is testing the Atlantic relationship.

On one level, the dispute is over whether European companies and American companies domiciled in Europe are subject to the penalties legislated by the United States Congress against violators of sanctions. I have elsewhere in these pages indicated my concern about the extent to which sanctions have been overused. Extraterritorial application, especially against allies, is difficult to justify and requires a new look. The fundamental issue, however, is not the legal basis of American strategy but whether improvement of relations with Iran is helped by unilateral concessions undertaken without any demand for reciprocity. Or is the rush to Tehran an *obstacle* to a rapprochement which is in itself not in dispute? Will continuing unilateral concessions in the face of rigid Iranian policies help or hinder the agreed goal of a better relationship?

At the heart of the disagreement is the insistence of the European allies on what they call a "critical dialogue" with Iran. The allies argue that their dialogue is designed to explore the prospects of moderating Iran's policy and would always include criticism of Iran's human rights violations and other misdeeds; in short, it would by its very existence contribute to easing tensions (not to speak of the signing of lucrative oil and gas deals).

So far there has been little productive dialogue, critical or otherwise, with Europe although the hint of Iranian President Mohammad Khatami suggesting a "dialogue of civilizations" might in time provide an opening wedge. Nor was there any response to the Clinton administration's offer of an official dialogue. It was rebuffed by an Iranian regime that seems incapable of deciding on rapprochement with the United States and was unimpressed by formal and abject apologies for past American conduct.

In essence, the proposition that unilateral gestures will somehow ease Iranian hostility represents the application of "politically correct" psychiatric theory to politics: the perpetrator of a crime is perceived as victim, allegedly deformed by pressures outside his control. But when applied to Iran's transgressions, there is not a shred of evidence to support it. Unilateral concessions of any magnitude are much more likely to reinforce intransigence than to moderate it. After all, why change when the targets of the ideology-based policy are so abjectly eager to accommodate?

While there is little doubt that Khatami is seeking to implement more moderate domestic policies in the face of considerable resistance, there is little evidence so far that this moderation extends to the international scene or that Khatami will be permitted to execute a change of course if he were to atempt it. It is as likely that he will purchase maneuvering room in domestic reconstruction by demonstrations of ideological vigilance on the international scene. In fact, Khatami has publicly identified himself with support for Islamic and Palestinian terrorist groups in Damascus and Beirut.

The debate should move beyond theoretical speculation. If there is to be an improvement of relations with the Iranian Islamic regime, it seems elementary to link it with abandonment of the export of revolution by force and subversion, a curb on terror, and an end to interference in the Middle East peace diplomacy. Simultaneously, progress must be made with respect to Iran's acquisition of missiles and nuclear weapons.

If there were a serious willingness by Iran to move toward an improvement of relations, a series of reciprocal parallel steps could surely be devised to achieve a significant improvement, provided the rulers in Iran are prepared to embrace a normal relationship. The mechanism of such an approach would not be difficult to construct. The new American administration could designate a trusted representative—or an "unofficial" trusted spokesman—to explore, at first secretly, whether it is possible to agree on a series of reciprocal measures leading to a step-by-step improvement of relations. The United States might even agree after the initial dialogue to take a few symbolic steps first, provided they are followed by Iranian moves in a time frame clearly relevant to the initial action.

If America's allies believe that it has not adequately explored the diplomatic options, the United States should be prepared to undertake a serious effort of joint diplomacy. And, at least theoretically, there should be a community of interests. The European nations will be the first victims of the spread of Islamic fundamentalism and of Iranian medium-range missiles. As a nuclear power, Iran will in the long run prove far more threatening to Europe (and Russia) than to the United States. And, if the Gulf blows up, the European nations will be the first to ask for access to American energy supplies to avoid an economic catastrophe.

Foreign policy always comes down to making choices. An effective counterterrorist and counterproliferation policy for the West requires the willingness to accept sacrifices for the sake of a greater long-term goal. There are times when commercial interests must be prepared to give way to broader security interests. American leadership is essential to reach this trade-off with respect to Iran. At the same time, if an alliance turns into a free ride for one side, it will not be sustained by public opinion.

A major effort should be made to achieve a transatlantic consensus that relates diplomacy to reasonable pressures and agreed diplomatic overtures vis-à-vis Iran. Only by a firm, consistent, and conciliatory policy can the day be hastened when Iran will be prepared to take the concrete policy actions which represent the only reliable basis for a long-term cooperative relationship.

WHITHER AFRICA?

Africa tugs at the American conscience. A significant part of the U.S. population originated there. Their ancestors were brought to these shores under circumstances that remain a blot on this country's history and were obliged to live before and after slavery under conditions of which no American can be proud. But the United States only compounds these indignities if African policy is presented primarily as a sop to the past. For the continent's contemporary problems are a challenge to a world that aspires to build a global order.

Poverty is pervasive. Africa has the lowest economic growth rate of any continent and has lagged far behind in modernization. Genocidal civil wars tear apart vast regions. Corruption is rampant. In the resulting chaos, some African countries have become havens for terrorist groups, money laundering, and crime syndicates. Africa's epidemics ravage a greater proportion of the population than anywhere else; 70 percent of the adults and 80 percent of the children suffering from AIDS in the world live in Africa. It is not possible to speak of an interdependent world based on peace and justice while leaving the problems of the African continent unattended.

At the same time, there are few traditional American security interests involved. With the end of the Cold War, no adversarial outside country is in a position to dominate Africa, and no African country has the economic or military capacity to do so. The standard argument of the Cold War—that Africa's resources must not fall into the hands of adversaries—is not applicable to the foreseeable future. Absent a strategic adversary threatening the continent or an unfriendly African nation seeking hegemony, there is no strategic rationale for a new African policy. Moreover, American investment is far smaller than on other continents, and the trade dependence is inconsequential.

At the same time, the absence of traditional geopolitical interests defines an opportunity peculiar to our age. If the term "world community" has any meaning, it must find an expression in Africa. And history does impose an obligation on America to play the major role in organizing and sustaining such a multilateral effort.

The most pressing task must be to ease Africa's suffering and defeat its epidemics. The long-range need is to reduce Africa's political conflicts, help reform its political system, and, on that basis, bring Africa into the globalized world. Such actions require a better understanding of African conditions.

THE AFRICAN ENVIRONMENT

I have found it useful in this volume to sketch the evolution of the various continents by analogy to epochs of European history. No such framework applies to sub-Saharan Africa, however, for the continent is sui generis. Its history is rich, varied, and tragic, but the present states of Africa do not, in fact, go back to these roots. With the possible exception of South Africa, their contemporary borders and national composition share a single origin: the implosion of colonial rule. In no other continent did national borders emerge so directly and intrinsically from the way the imperial powers delineated their spheres of control.

To be sure, the post-colonial countries in Asia also evolved from colonial borders; India was never governed as a single entity in its present extent, and Indonesia's principal unifying historical experience was, for the most part, Dutch colonial rule. But, in Asia, colonialism had a tendency to consolidate: India, Indonesia, and Malaysia are all larger than the principalities that existed before colonialism. By contrast, post-colonial countries in Africa have tended toward fragmentation.

In Africa, borders not only follow the demarcations *between* the spheres of influence of the European powers, as in Asia; they also reflect the administrative subdivisions *within* each colonial area. In East and West Africa, Britain and France governed colonies with long coastlines. Hence it proved efficient to divide these colonies into a multiplicity of administrative units, each with its own outlet to the sea, which later became independent states. On the other hand, in Central Africa, tiny Belgium governed a region nearly as large as the British and French possessions without, however, any significant coastline. Possessing only a very short outlet to the sea at the mouth of the Congo River, this vast territory was ruled by Belgium as a single unit, which later emerged as a single state with an explosive ethnic mixture.

Most importantly, the administrative borders in each colony were drawn without regard to ethnic or tribal identities; indeed, the colonial powers often found it useful to divide up ethnic or tribal groups in order to complicate the emergence of a unified opposition to imperial rule.

With the exception of South Africa, the sub-Saharan African states face internal challenges that, in their totality, have no equivalent anywhere else. In most countries of the world, a society or nation preceded the state; in most African countries, the state precedes the nation and must wrest a national consciousness from a plethora of tribes, ethnic groups, and, in many cases, different religions.

Inevitably, Western democratic principles of political organization have taken hold in Africa only in the most tenuous way. Western democracy is based on versions of majority rule. But this presupposes that the majority can fluctuate and that the minority of the moment has a prospect of becoming a majority in due course. When the divisions are along tribal, ethnic, or religious lines, however, this equation does not hold. A group consigned to permanent minority status will not consider the political arrangement just. And this is even more true when a minority governs the majority, as has been the case in Rwanda and several other African states.

Neither the parliamentary system of Europe nor the federal system of the United States can function effectively in these circumstances. For if an African federal system were based on ethnic, tribal, or religious identity, it would raise a perpetual danger of secession; and if the federal unit mimics the ethnic, tribal, or religious composition of the country, it would simply repeat in every region the conflicts of the entire country. In these circumstances, the political process boils down to a quest for domination, not alternation, in office, which takes place—if at all—by coups and ethnic conflicts rather than by constitutional processes.

Nor does parliamentary government overcome the problem. The concept of loyal opposition—the essence of modern parliamentary democracy—is difficult to apply when opposition is considered a threat to national cohesion and tends to be equated with treason.

For these reasons, African countries have a high propensity for civil war. And if tribal or ethnic loyalties extend across national frontiers, as they do in an extraordinarily large number of cases, civil wars turn into international wars. In this manner, what started as a civil war in Zaire—abetted by the Western powers in the name of democracy—has led to the disintegration of much of the central authority. Now renamed Congo, the country has become an arena for the competition of other African states—Angola, Zimbabwe, Rwanda, and Uganda. Zimbabwe fights for spoils but, for Angola, Rwanda, and—to some extent—Uganda, this is a struggle for their own domestic stability because the ethnic groups involved overlap national borders.

Ethnic wars are fought everywhere in the world with extraordinary savagery; in Africa, they have verged on the genocidal, as in Rwanda, Sierra Leone, and Sudan. The civil war in Angola has lasted for thirty-eight years, the one in Sudan nearly as long. For the parties involved, the issue is not disagreements over governmental programs but ethnic, tribal, and religious survival or, at a minimum, avoidance of a status of permanent discrimination or institutional persecution.

Constitutions, which, by definition, affirm the prevalence of law over governmental fiat, have little meaning where the notion of an independent judiciary is not only nonexistent but inconceivable. Where there is no institutional concept of legitimacy, raw assertions of personal power become themselves a form of legitimacy. This is why a number of African states once lauded for their progressive institutions—Kenya, for example—have regressed to a brutal form of arbitrary personal rule.

The country that is a substantial exception is South Africa despite the fact that its history is more tragic than that of most others and perhaps because of it. When Dutch settlers arrived on the southern tip of Africa in the seventeenth century, they brought with them a stern fundamentalist Calvinism that turned its back on all the subsequent intellectual trends in Europe. The Boers, or Afrikaners as they came to call themselves, developed a distinct identity unique in the history of European colonialism. They remained unaffected by the rationalism of the Enlightenment and the democratic dispensation of the French Revolution.

So deep was their sense of being distinct that, when Britain annexed the Cape province during the Napoleonic wars, the Afrikaners packed up and moved nearly one thousand miles to the north, not as individual settlers but as a whole people with governmental institutions, churches, and schools. In this new home, the Afrikaners first encountered large black populations which they treated with a condescending sense of religious and racial superiority.

The Afrikaners' isolation did not last long. The discovery of gold lured the English to the new states, leading to the Boer War, in which the tiny Boer republics fought the British Empire at the height of its power nearly to a standstill. The Boer War ended the Afrikaners' separateness; it could not overcome their spiritual distinctness.

By 1948, demographics within the white population, which alone had the vote, favored the Afrikaners. While segregation in the American sense existed at all times, the now dominant Boers set about separating the races with a vengeance. Strict laws were passed prohibiting intermarriage and regulating the living areas, working rights, and movement of the nonwhite population. Enacting the system of apartheid was a singular act of political folly and immorality because it obliged the white population to hold down a growing majority of other races by a brute force as incompatible with common decency as it was with the processes of industrialization and modernization.

Almost miraculously, as the century ended, these obstacles were overcome by two extraordinary leaders, Nelson Mandela and F. W. de Klerk. Nelson Mandela's career is the embodiment of courage fortified by spiritual profundity. As early as the 1964 speech in which he defended himself against the charge of treason, Mandela affirmed his devotion to a multiracial society:

It is not true that the enfranchisement of all will result in racial domination. Political division based on color is entirely artificial and when it disappears, so will the domination of one color group by another. The ANC [African National Congress] has spent half a century fighting against racialism; when it triumphs, it will not change that policy.[7]

Mandela kept his word. Three decades of incarceration left no visible residue of bitterness in him—certainly much less than among some of his colleagues who spent the same interval in exile.

Like the demise of Soviet Communism, the end of apartheid occurred with a speed unimaginable even a decade earlier and with a relative minimum of violence. Philosophical idealism and practical insight forged a partnership between the imprisoned revolutionary and his jailer. By 1990, F. W. de Klerk, who had started his career as an advocate of apartheid, could pronounce as an Afrikaner goal what had only yesterday been illegal:

> [our] aim is a totally new and just constitutional dispensation in which every inhabitant will enjoy equal rights, treatment and opportunity in every sphere of endeavour—constitutional, social and economic.[8]

In overcoming its problems, South Africa had unique advantages. The legitimacy of the state was well established, apartheid notwithstanding; the various ethnic groups had considerable experience in dealing with one another. South Africa possessed vast resources, a solid infrastructure, a significant manufacturing base, and a higher level of education than any of its neighbors—a level, moreover, which the present government has pledged to improve rapidly. And the very multiplicity of its ethnic groupings provided a certain insurance against civil conflict. For once that Pandora's box is opened, the consequences are ultimately unpredictable—as is demonstrated in too many of South Africa's neighboring countries.

Withal South Africa continues to face major problems. Law and order are inadequate to attract a steady flow of foreign investment; the relationship between the government and the Zulu minority is fragile and volatile—though it has improved as of this writing. The white minority feels inadequately protected against acts of lawlessness. AIDS is rampant. The World Health Organization has estimated that, by 2010, the epidemic will reduce the country's GDP to a level 17 percent lower than it would be without AIDS.

Toward an African Policy

The paradox of Africa is that the challenge is vast while the concepts on which any policy for overcoming it can be based are elusive. The policies drawn from the traditional policy arsenal of the Cold War lost their relevance with the collapse of the Soviet Union. There is no overriding threat from the outside. Because of the expanse of sub-Saharan Africa, none of its states is in a position to threaten all the others. No state except Nigeria or South Africa is in a position to play a major role outside its immediate region.

Nor does the spread of democracy, while important, provide a unifying principle. There are no well-established democracies in the American sense in Africa—with the exception of South Africa and possibly Nigeria—around which a democratic African consensus could be built.

On his two trips to the continent, President Clinton told his hosts repeatedly that the United States, due to its preoccupation with the Cold War, was responsible for one-party governments in many parts of Africa. But it is difficult to think of any African country, other than possibly Congo, in which the United States played a dominant role in establishing the post-colonial government. In nearly all the cases, those who headed the anti-colonial movements emerged as leaders of the countries after independence. Almost invariably, they established one-party governments or variations thereof—South Africa again excepted.

To be sure, there are significant differences among the various regimes. And the United States should do what it can to encourage a democratic evolution. It can—and should—ostracize governments that are in flagrant violation of human rights. But beyond this, America's influence on the domestic political evolution is limited.

This is why applying the principles of the humanitarian military intervention followed in the Balkans, as some urge, will be even more dangerous in Africa—apart from the questions that these principles raised even in the Balkans, as I shall discuss in Chapter 7. If the United States were to seek to quell the internal crises from Sudan to Congo by the policies used in the Balkans, a long period of outside supervision would follow a bloody conflict. It would be only a matter of time before a new charge of colonialism would be raised. The American debacle in Somalia in 1993 is illustrative. The intervention there began as a humanitarian effort to distribute food but quickly turned into an exercise in "institution-building" that impelled the United States to take sides in the civil war—a task it was unwilling to sustain.

In the end, civil wars are about who dominates. As political legitimacy erodes, a vacuum develops which must be filled by some new authority. As the United States engages in a humanitarian military intervention, media and other observers descend on the scene, certain to find conditions deeply offensive to Western sensibility. They will urge a whole variety of initiatives, from ending corruption to the administration of justice, that make eminent sense in the Western context. None, however, can be accomplished without greater intervention, drawing the United States ever deeper into the political process. And, sooner or later, no matter how well intentioned, such conduct will begin to grate on African sentiments, and that, in turn, will tend to undermine domestic American and indigenous African support for the operation. Nothing is more likely to end a permanent American contribution to Africa than a military role in its civil wars.

There may be cases of genocide where inaction will clash with America's historic perception of itself that its moral and humane concerns are of universal applicability—especially if the violations occur within nations where they can be quickly brought under control. In these instances, limited military intervention may be a duty. The slaughter in Rwanda and in Sierra Leone belongs in this category. In each case, a relatively small deployment of force could have brought an end to the genocide. International action with some American participation—particularly in logistics—would have been appropriate, provided there was a prior agreement that African forces would replace the international force as soon as order was restored.

The absence of overriding security interests defines the outlines of a new approach to Africa. It is the one continent in which a genuinely global political, economic, and social program merges practical and moral considerations. It should be turned into a test of the ability of the United Nations, nongovernmental organizations, other international institutions, and the private sector to cooperate in pursuit of universal goals. A joint program organized by the United States and other industrial democracies should be urgently put forward by the United States, embodying a more creative approach to development assistance and technical training.

An African development program under United Nations or World Bank aegis must take account of the fact that public development funds will be severely limited. Such a program could help overcome the legacy of too many African governments that are either corrupt or base their economies on outdated socialist models of the 1970s. At the same time, those few countries that have shown a willingness to transcend the lessons taught at the London School of Economics—such as Mozambique, Ghana, and Senegal—and are mobilizing domestic capital or seeking to attract foreign investment are making good progress. An African development program should provide incentives for other countries to adopt sensible fiscal policies and establish commercial codes of law and an independent judiciary.

For countries meeting development criteria, incentives should include lowered trade barriers to African agricultural products and forgiveness of past debts. As the program gathers momentum, a free trade status for African countries adopting market principles should be explored. Some of these measures will be painful for the sponsoring countries; it is at the same time a test of their seriousness of purpose.

African security issues—largely civil wars and ethnic conflicts—should be left largely to African nations, with South Africa and Nigeria playing the principal roles. The industrial nations could assist by supporting the creation of an intervention force drawn from African nations. A center for training in African peacekeeping missions could be created where American and European advisors could assist the projected African force.

Finally, an international effort for the control of epidemics is overdue. The global program for dealing with AIDS should be vastly increased. This would involve the creation of clinics in strategic locations in each participating country, which should serve as centers for AIDS education and for the distribution of medicines. The drug companies should join these efforts and supply the necessary drugs at close to cost—provided they can be assured of patent protection and receive guarantees against transshipment. The international volunteer corps of doctors, nurses, and other specialized personnel should be expanded. If undertaken on a sufficient scale—as it should be—such an Africa-wide effort would necessitate the creation of appropriate infrastructures and thus serve not only humanitarian and social ends but also economic ones.

The continent is a tragedy; it is also a challenge. Africa's variety inhibits concerted action; the scope of its crises nevertheless demands a significant response. The idealism of the American people—its Wilsonian commitment and its basic decency—is being tested here, as well as its practical creativity. Realism should illuminate America's understanding of the underlying problems. But without the moral commitment of the American people and of the international community, Africa's tragedy will turn into the festering disaster of our age.

The Politics
of Globalization

FOR the first time in history, a single worldwide economic system has come into being. Markets in every continent interact continuously. Communications enable capital to respond instantaneously to new opportunities or to lowered expectations. Sophisticated credit instruments provide unprecedented liquidity. Globalization has encouraged an explosion of wealth and a rate of technological advance no previous epoch could even imagine. And by basing growth on interdependence, globalization has served to undermine the role of the nation-state as the sole determinant of a society's well-being—though this is far less true in the United States than in many other regions.

The United States has been the driving force behind the dynamics of globalization; it has also been the prime beneficiary of the forces it has unleashed. During the last decade of the twentieth century, American productivity became the engine of global economic growth; American capital underwrote a staggering array of new technologies and promoted their broad distribution around the world; American enterprise nurtured vast markets and stimulated a level of personal consumption that, in previous centuries, was accessible only to the wealthiest. The last decade of the twentieth century may one day be remembered as the "good old days;" the American economy performed so well that it was hard to imagine it could get any better. Yet, according to Federal Reserve Chairman Alan Greenspan, the United States may still be just at the threshold of the technological and economic revolution.[1]

Success of this magnitude inevitably inspires imitation, and the American model of economic management has become the standard in most parts of the world. It would be satisfying to believe that the spread of deregulation, privatization, and removal of trade barriers resulted from the eloquence of American economists or from the preachings of the U.S. Treasury and International Monetary Fund (IMF). What in fact has persuaded most of the world has been the indispensability of American capital markets and the seemingly limitless growth of the United States economy.

The free market has become dominant nearly everywhere, and the Internet promises to link the various components of the global economy to one another in real time. Foreign investment is generally being encouraged. In most regions—and in all the prospering ones—governments are limiting themselves to facilitating the operation of the market, not to regulating it. Economic growth and job creation are being left in an unprecedented degree to free enterprise and to free trade.

The absence of any realistic alternatives reinforces the trend toward the American model. Because of public disillusionment with corruption and bureaucracy, the availability of public funds for development aid has been sharply reduced. Since growth in developing countries depends so importantly on the availability of private capital, and since private capital insists on a predictable legal system and a satisfactory rate of return at reasonable risk, any country striving to become competitive is obliged to join the process of globalization, both politically and economically.

To be sure, even in the United States, globalization has left individuals and groups behind. Jobs are lost in some sectors even as they multiply in others. Yet the protectionist argument that globalization inherently produces unemployment is, at least in the United States, belied by full employment coupled with rising wages. The world's bewilderment about growing protectionist pressures in advanced industrial countries has been well expressed by Joseph Stiglitz, former chief economist of the World Bank: "What are developing countries to make of the rhetoric in favor of capital liberalization when rich countries—with full employment and strong safety nets—argue that they need to impose protective measures to help those of their own citizens adversely affected by globalization?"[2]

In these circumstances, it would be an irony if the new millennium's most distinctive achievement were to turn into a vulnerability, all the more difficult to deal with because there is no precedent for either its nature or its solution. The very process that has produced greater wealth in more parts of the world than ever before may also provide the mechanism for spreading an economic and social crisis around the world. Just as the American economy has been the world's engine of growth, a major setback for the American economy would have grave consequences transcending the economic realm. Depending on its magnitude, it could threaten political stability in many countries and undermine America's international standing.

Almost all experts agree that the market system runs in cycles and that, sooner or later, a downturn is probable. The seemingly endless U.S. economic expansion is bound to turn into a recession sooner or later; the only issues are its timing and its depth. At this writing (the spring of 2001), there is a widespread conviction that the United States is overdue for a recession, and uncertainty attaches primarily to whether there will be a so-called soft landing. Whenever a recession happens—especially a prolonged one—globalization is likely to spread its consequences quickly around the world. The scenario has often been described: a stock market declining for an extended period will reduce the consumption of Americans, many of whom have a substantial percentage of their savings invested in stocks. This will reduce exports from other industrialized countries, triggering downturns in those countries. Capital—especially speculative capital—will flow out of affected countries. Banks will retrench their lending. Facing an uncertain future, consumers all over the world will increase their savings and, by reducing their spending, accelerate the negative trends. Some of the tendencies that brought Asian and Latin American financial markets to the point of crisis in the 1990s could reemerge in different forms but having the same underlying elements.

But there are significant psychological obstacles in preparing for such a crisis. Those responsible for the economy—the U.S. Treasury, the big investors, bankers, and boards of large multinational corporations—do not doubt the likelihood of a setback. But they are reluctant to act on this assumption lest they actually trigger what they are seeking to postpone into a distant future—hopefully one in which they are no longer in office. On the whole, they find it psychologically easier to manage the consequences of a recession than to take controversial measures to avert it, the necessity of which they cannot demonstrate in advance. Or, they leave it to the chairman of the Federal Reserve System to man the barricades. Moreover, the policymakers, governmental as well as those in the private sector, are traveling on uncharted seas. Very few of them foresaw the scale and duration of the boom; even fewer predicted the financial crises in Latin America, Asia, and Russia that punctuated the economic expansion of the 1980s and 1990s—nor, for that matter, the relative speed with which these crises were overcome.

I have nothing to contribute to the debate about the economic measures needed to avert or to mitigate a recession. I will therefore devote this chapter to the issues a farsighted statesmanship must address to prevent the political world from destroying the economic achievements of globalization.

ECONOMICS AND POLITICS

The global system rewards and penalizes its participants by economic criteria. But, for the public, these criteria are far too esoteric to evoke loyalties and commitments. In a crisis, the population will turn to its political leaders to ease the impact of the economic penalties. This is all the more true because even periods of expansion take their toll on parts of the population, so that there exists in most countries—and especially in the developing world—a near permanent minority ever waiting in the wings to act out the validity of its resentments.

To achieve global competitiveness, political leaders in developing countries are obliged to use up political capital by restructuring their economies, eliminating waste and reducing overhead. This frequently implies massive dislocations and (hopefully temporary) unemployment for the sake of long-range benefits not demonstrable at the moment sacrifices are being demanded. Such an equation is often anathema to political or economic leaders if the promised benefits will arrive only long after they have themselves left the scene.

The massive changes in the structures and procedures of most of the societies participating in globalization are strongly encouraged—and frequently insisted upon as a condition of assistance—by the United States government as well as by leading international financial and economic institutions. Yet the advocates of the new gospel often seem oblivious to the historical record, which shows that the practices of reform took many decades to evolve in their own countries. Adopting the American model is not primarily a technical challenge; for most developing countries, it implies nothing less than a revolutionary upheaval in familiar patterns. Only a very few nations have ever managed to combine conservative fiscal and monetary policy, government intervention through regulation rather than ownership or control, deregulation of financial institutions, encouragement of flexible labor markets, and a widely accepted and transparent legal framework. The American model presupposes that capital is relatively cheap and labor is relatively expensive, so that competitive success in the end depends on improvements in productivity sustained by constant technological progress. Comparative advantage is achieved by reducing the labor content of most productive processes to the greatest extent possible.

The American experience demonstrates that, when all these factors combine and however difficult the initial stages, early dislocations will be justified by dramatic improvements in the standard of living. But the experience of most other countries has also shown that it is not easy to make the American model work rapidly. Continental Europe is still struggling with major domestic obstacles to the necessary structural reforms (especially in the labor market and agriculture)—though it now seems well launched on the process of adjustment. Ten years after the defeat of Communism, Russia, despite all Western exhortations and many billions of dollars in aid, is no closer to a normally functioning market economy than it is to democratic institutions. China's rate of growth is extraordinary, but it has been achieved at the price of giving governmental stability priority over democratic reform. Even in countries with a less inhibiting past—in Southeast Asia and Latin America, for example—globalization has proceeded in fits and starts. During the 1990s, the United States, almost alone in the world, solved the problem of how to create jobs while revolutionizing its industrial technology.

All developing countries have faced the challenge that industrialization, by drawing people from the countryside to the cities, brings with it the weakening of traditional political and social support systems. The urban working and lower middle class becomes a fertile recruiting ground for radical politics or religious fundamentalism. This phenomenon was familiar even before globalization; it contributed to the emergence of Marxism in the nineteenth century and to the Iranian revolution in the twentieth. Even when material conditions of the poor and lower middle classes improve in absolute terms, the migrants become increasingly conscious of the gap between rich and poor, which the early stages of modernization magnify and which television and other media bring graphically into the homes and consciousness of nearly everyone. Political and economic indices therefore frequently slip out of phase with one another. Even when the aggregate economic data indicate growth, benefits may not reach the urban population sufficiently rapidly, or on a large enough scale, to remove the sense of rootlessness and dependence at the core of contemporary unease.

Of course, these phenomena are not entirely novel. Displacement by technology has probably occurred since the invention of the shovel. And migrations have taken place in every economic revolution. What is unique in our age is the scale of the global impact and the rate of technological change. The challenge of humanizing the process is, therefore, unprecedented.

Free market capitalism remains the most effective and, thus far, the only demonstrated instrument for sustained economic growth and for raising the standard of living. But just as the unrestrained laissez-faire capitalism of the nineteenth century spawned Marxism, so too literal a version of globalization of the twenty-first century could generate a worldwide assault on the very concept of free markets. Globalization views the world as one market in which the most efficient and competitive will prosper. It accepts—and even welcomes—the fact that the free market will relentlessly sift the efficient from the inefficient, even at the cost of economic and social dislocation.

But the extreme versions of globalism tend to neglect the mismatch between the world's political and economic systems. Unlike economics, politics divides the world into national units. And while political leaders may accept a certain degree of suffering for the sake of growth in their economies, they cannot survive as advocates of near permanent austerity, especially if their policies can be presented as imposed from abroad. The temptation to reverse—or at least to buffer—austerity by political means can become overwhelming. Protectionism may prove ineffective or even backfire in the long term, but political leaders frequently respond to the short-term pressures of what they view as their political necessities.

Even well-established free market democracies do not accept limitless suffering in the name of the market and have taken measures to provide a social safety net and curb market excesses by regulation. The international financial system does not as yet have comparable firebreaks.

The demonstrations against globalization at meetings of the International Monetary Fund and the World Bank in 2000 and at the Seattle meeting of the World Trade Organization in 1999 were early warning signs of the potential political weight of those who believe themselves at the mercy of forces they feel powerless to influence. To be sure, many of these demonstrations follow an all too familiar leftist, anti-American, and anti-capitalist script from the 1960s and early 1970s, even down to some of the personalities involved. The exaltation of violence and self-indulgence of some of the demonstrators reflects ideological disdain for existing political and economic institutions that is, to a considerable extent, independent of specific grievances.

Nevertheless, the leaders of the industrialized world must not ignore the emotional vacuum which the protests reflect, at least in part, lest globalization, the most effective engine of growth the world has ever seen, becomes submerged in the political assault polarizing especially the developing societies most in need of its benefits. And if there is a serious recession in the industrialized world, it may spread even there.

CRISIS MANAGEMENT AND THE INTERNATIONAL MONETARY FUND

Crises seem as endemic to the modern global economic system as its extraordinary growth. Since 1980, they have recurred with increasing frequency—in Latin America in the 1980s, in Mexico in 1994, in Southeast Asia in 1997, in Russia in 1998, in Brazil in 1999. Each was more severe than its predecessor and each involved a higher risk of spreading elsewhere; each has, so far, been mastered more rapidly than seemed possible at the height of the crisis, if a little bit nearer to the edge of the precipice. Each has demonstrated that the international economic system is perhaps more resilient than it is prescient.

The international financial system often conducts itself like those proverbial generals who learn the lessons of the last war but cannot envision those of the next one. After the 1980s, financial institutions learned to be careful about lending to governments. As a result, the crises of the 1990s concerned excessive lending to the private sector or speculative investments in the stock and bond market. In the first decade of the twenty-first century, the lesson of the hedge funds has been largely learned; investors have grown careful about the simpler forms of speculation. The speculative excesses of the 1990s will not be repeated in the same manner. On the other hand, experience teaches that what will be considered risky speculation a few years from now appears relatively safe today, or it would not be attracting capital. The question then becomes, what hidden areas of volatility exist in the contemporary exposures of the financial system? Is fiber optics the equivalent for the next decade of the high-rise office building of Houston in the 1980s?

The various crises of the 1990s illustrate the international financial system's vulnerability. While each crisis is likely to have a different trigger, each is apt to have the same category of causes: changes in the international environment; the inability of small economies to relate the flow of capital to their own long-term needs; credit policies by lenders that appear profligate in retrospect (but only in retrospect); and policies by the major countries taken with inadequate concern for (or knowledge of) their impact on the economies of developing countries.

Increases in U.S. interest rates helped to precipitate crises in Latin America in 1980 and 1994, while an unexpected rise in the value of the U.S. dollar contributed to the Southeast Asian crisis of 1997. Each crisis was aggravated because of changes in the relative values of the major currencies—the dollar, the Euro (or deutsche mark before the Euro's creation), and the yen. The small economies of emerging countries found it impossible to deal with these fluctuations and had to accept essentially passively their consequences, which they compounded by trying to maintain a fixed rate of exchange.

In the 1990s, two other changes in the international environment altered the situations of countries in Southeast Asia: the first was the emergence of China as a major source of low-cost manufactures; the second was the long-term stagnation of the Japanese economy. The growth of the Chinese economy brought about new and significant competition for the countries of Southeast Asia, while Japanese recession reduced their markets (or at least kept them from growing).

The connecting element in both the Latin American and Asian

crises was the excessive readiness of lenders to incur risk. In the 1970s, it was because they believed that sovereign risk—lending to countries—ran a negligible chance of default. By the 1990s, they had learned this lesson and were confining loans to the private sector, counting on the rate of growth of the borrowing countries and the safety net of the international financial system to hedge the risk. One reason for this profligate lending was the intensity of competition; lenders were concerned lest they fall behind their competitors, and they had the benefit of the experience of previous crises, which had all ended with some kind of bailout.

Then too, by the 1990s, the nature of the lenders had changed, and this made it difficult to learn from experience. In the 1970s, the providers of capital were banks; in the 1980s and 1990s, they were largely corporations or investment funds. The corporations made available direct investment; the funds invested in stocks and bonds.

The international financial system led by the IMF had failed to evolve with the financial markets, and it was put to a severe test in the Asian crisis which started in Thailand in 1997. Thailand had carried out most of the policies recommended by the U.S. Treasury and international financial institutions as a solution for the crises of the 1980s: low inflation, a balanced budget, a high savings rate, and convertibility of its currency. The Thai currency, the baht, was at first pegged by the Thai Central Bank to a basket of hard currencies, then to the U.S. dollar. Thereby protected from devaluation, speculative capital from the outside world—especially from the United States but also from Europe—rushed in. That flow accelerated when local borrowers discovered that windfall profits could be made by borrowing dollars in the United States and converting them into bahts in Thai banks at twice the dollar rate. Large speculative gains increased the value of all assets. All this occurred without any warning from American or international financial institutions which benefited from this profligacy, if they did not actually encourage it and, after the event, too readily placed all the blame on Asian borrowers.

In 1997, the value of the U.S. dollar rose and that of the yen declined—reflecting the performance of the two economies—and the

Chinese currency was devalued to remain competitive in export markets. Thai exports denominated in dollars thereby became more expensive and began to decline, and the Thai current account fell into deficit. Capital flow into Thailand dried up; real estate prices started to weaken, and the value of bank collateral plummeted. Foreign investors and foreign banks withdrew funds while Thai borrowers rushed to exchange bahts for dollars at the guaranteed rate. The Bank of Thailand compounded the problem by huge loans which, converted into dollars, helped push Thailand over the brink. In a matter of weeks, the Thai foreign exchange reserves of $30 billion were all but depleted, and a drastic devaluation of the currency became inevitable. Debts denominated in dollars became unmanageable; what had started as a currency problem turned into a self-reinforcing economic, financial, and, in the end, political crisis.

The crisis in Indonesia, which brought down the Suharto government, started as a speculative reaction to events in Thailand. Less than two months earlier, the World Bank had officially praised Indonesia for its sound economic management. But once the crisis had begun in Thailand, local as well as foreign investors began to question the lessons the Indonesian Central Bank seemed to be drawing from the Thai experience. Refusing to undertake any defense of the Indonesian rupiah, it conserved its reserves, leading to an even more rapid collapse of the Indonesian currency, which fell to about a fifth of its pre-crisis value. Thus, whether the Southeast Asian crisis was dealt with by domestic political decisions as in Thailand or by following the advice of international institutions as in Indonesia, economic chaos followed because the international speculative component was too powerful for the local economies of developing societies. In Indonesia, where the government had been weakened by cronyism and corruption, this combination eventually destroyed the political structure as well.

Equity capital—direct foreign investment in assets—runs the same risks as the host country's internal investors and is subject to substantially the same benefits and risks. The assets cannot be moved and must be made profitable if the investor is to realize any gains. But portfolio capital is geared to rapid speculative returns. The managers of speculative funds seek to hedge by nimbleness in the movement of their funds—in simple terms, by rushing in when they see an opportunity and by heading for the exit at the first sign of trouble. Some adopt a strategy of going short—speculating on a drop in the market by selling stock at the existing price and rebuying it at the eventual price when the market drops—thereby profiting from the very decline in values they accelerate in the process. The trading departments of international banks, institutional investors, and hedge funds try to be in a position to benefit from market swings in either direction, creating a danger that upswings are transformed into bubbles and downward cycles into crises before remedial measures can take effect.

Managers of such investments will argue that they are only exploiting weaknesses in the market, not causing them. In fact, according to their own logic, these institutions and funds are acting rationally, even as they generate a deeper and more intractable crisis. Small and medium-sized countries find themselves defenseless in the face of the operation of the global financial system. On the one hand, the crises described here are the penalties the global market exacts from imprudent borrowing—the market's way of restoring an equilibrium by supply and demand. But it is also true that the IMF-based international financial system penalizes imprudent borrowers far more heavily than it does imprudent lenders.

The measures to contain and resolve crises provided by the international financial system have too frequently aggravated matters. The chosen instrument to prevent meltdown is the International Monetary Fund. Created in 1947 to promote international monetary cooperation, the IMF regularly opens its coffers to member states in times of fiscal crisis—albeit with strings attached. In the globalized world, it has increasingly become the organizer of rescue packages and the lender of last resort. But its remedies have in the past often compounded the problem because they are essentially and abstractly economic, while the deeper the crisis, the more political it becomes. And the IMF is ill equipped to deal with the political consequences of its programs.

The more or less standard IMF program was developed during the Latin American debt crisis of the 1980s, caused by the heavy indebtedness of Latin American governments to financial institutions which had encouraged the borrowing on the theory that a default of sovereign debt was impossible. The lending institutions also had not anticipated—and, in fairness, could not have—that, to fight inflation, the Federal Reserve Bank would sustain high interest rates for long enough to produce a recession in the United States with disastrous consequences in Latin America. When the gamble on sovereign lending threatened to go wrong, the IMF was called in and set about restoring the creditworthiness of the governments in the hope that commercial banks would resume lending when that goal was achieved. It did so by shrinking government services, devaluing the currency, and fostering exports to permit the accumulation of surpluses. What the theory failed to take into account was that the political structure of the debtor country might not be able to sustain the sacrifice during the interval between imminent default and assumed restoration of creditworthiness. The lowering of the standard of living and the rise of unemployment inevitably weakened the domestic standing of the affected governments. The resulting stalemate caused the debt problem to linger for ten years or more until a political solution was negotiated that arranged some de facto relief for hard-pressed governments.

The remedies for Latin America in the 1980s, though drastic and politically insensitive, were at least relevant to crises caused by governmental indebtedness. The same remedies make far less sense in the globalized financial system of the new century, where the typical financial crisis arises in the private, not the governmental, sector, as was the case in the Asian crisis. Like a doctor who specializes in one particular disease and sets about applying its cure to every case before him, the IMF insisted on the Latin American cure regardless of the difference in circumstances between Asia and Latin America. In the process, the IMF sought to solve what it considered the debtor country's economic ills, whether or not they had caused the crisis and without adequate consideration of the political impact of its remedies.

Crony capitalism, corruption, and inadequate supervision of banks occur all too frequently in developing countries. They were surely present in Asia in the 1990s. But they were not the cause of the immediate crisis. Until the very eve of the crisis, Asia was the fastest growing region in the world, its progress sustained by high savings rates, a disciplined work ethic, and responsible fiscal behavior on the part of the governments—though not of the private sector. What triggered the actual crisis were the factors largely out of national or regional control described earlier. When the IMF, backed by the United States, intervened with its standard remedies of massive austerity, a political crisis was inevitable. Thailand's democratic institutions proved resilient enough to weather it, though a 42 percent devaluation of the currency and interest rates as high as 40 percent wiped out much of the middle class. By contrast, in Korea, the U.S. Treasury, recognizing the strategic importance of the country, made available additional assistance, moderating the IMF program to one compatible with political stability. (Fortunately an election brought into the presidency Kim Dae Jung, who had attacked the previous Korean administrations from the left and was thus in a strong position politically to implement austerity.)

However, in Indonesia—the world's most populous Muslim country, with vast resources and a crucial strategic location—the Clinton administration, facing accusations of campaign support from Indonesian companies, chose to take no political risks. The IMF was encouraged to make assistance conditional on the remedying of virtually every ill from which the society suffered, whether relevant to the crisis or not. It demanded the closing of fifteen banks, the ending of monopolies on food and heating oil, and the termination of government subsidies. Each of these measures dealt with a real problem and needed to be solved as part of a long-term program.

Implemented over a period of a few weeks, however, their cumulative impact produced a political debacle. Closing banks in the middle of a crisis made a run on all other banks inevitable. Ending subsidies raised food and fuel prices, causing riots directed at the

Chinese minority that controls much of the economy. As a result, Chinese money fled Indonesia in far greater quantities than the IMF could possibly offset. A currency crisis had been turned into first an economic disaster and then a political vacuum.

Some may argue that the overthrow of the Suharto regime justified the decisions of the IMF (and its sponsors behind the scenes), whatever their motive. But the IMF does not have the political competence to lead political revolutions, nor is this its mission. For the legacy of political upheaval goes far beyond the immediate economic causes of it. In Indonesia, it has left the danger of a breakup of the country, which could cause this vital region to develop characteristics similar to those accompanying the disintegration of Yugoslavia; a religious conflict in the Molucca Islands; and a contest between four or five major political forces inhibiting stable government involving the danger of a rise of fundamentalism. With respect to none of these issues has the outside world mustered either the comprehension or the assistance commensurate with the dislocations its pressures and advice have produced.

One of the key issues in dealing with financial crises is to allocate the burden of overcoming them between the borrowers and the lenders. In the Latin American financial crises of the 1980s, it was possible—though complicated and in the face of strong resistance—to divide the burden of indebtedness between the creditor banks and debtor governments. In the crises of the 1990s, and in most foreseeable crises, the problem is fundamentally different. Local companies and banks attract investments not only from traditional, established financial institutions but, above all, from a wide range of industrial corporations and private investors in the industrial countries. The allocation of pain becomes much more difficult, and the multiplicity of creditors makes it much more likely that future financial crises will spread to hitherto untouched sectors of the economies of advanced industrial countries.

The challenge is to keep crises from developing and instituting an equitable method for sharing the pain of those crises that cannot be prevented. However, IMF programs have been historically biased toward reducing the impact of a crisis on lenders to a much greater extent than on debtors. This is understandable because these institutions will be needed to resume lending if the crisis is to be overcome. Nevertheless, if carried too far, the bias encourages serial recklessness in lending. If there are no penalties for ill-advised loans, the crises are bound to repeat themselves. Then Secretary of the Treasury Robert Rubin stated the issue well in a thoughtful speech in 1998: "It is critically important that we work toward changing the global financial architecture so that creditors and investors bear the consequences of their decision as fully as possible."[3]

But how is an equitable allocation of the burden to be determined? The IMF has been, until very recently, quite simply tone-deaf to the political framework in which it must operate. It either neglects that framework or, in rare cases, is overwhelmed by it. It is not equipped to apply political and social criteria. In Southeast Asia, especially in Indonesia, the IMF worsened the crisis by applying largely technical criteria to a complex social and political challenge; in Russia, under pressure from the U.S. government, the IMF, by abandoning most of its own economic criteria, contributed to the emergence of an oligarchic system lacking any economic foundation. Because of America's all-out backing of President Boris Yeltsin, the IMF extended major loans for which there was no economic justification. (Yeltsin's onetime economic advisor, Anatoly Chubais, later boasted rather ungratefully that Russia had "conned" the IMF into continuing lending.[4])

It may be argued that, despite all its weaknesses, the global system has proved its resilience because Latin America recovered in the 1980s—albeit over a period of a decade—and the Asian countries (with the exception of Indonesia) have returned to growth within less than three years. However, a World Bank report has documented the extraordinary social cost of these crises. According to the report, the poorer segment of the population never regained during the recoveries what it had lost during the cycle of crises. In Korea, real wages declined by 10 percent; in Indonesia, by 42 percent; in Thailand, by 38 percent. In none of these countries have real wages returned to pre-crisis levels; even in Mexico, they are still below the level preceding the 1982 crisis.[5]

The long-term impact of these crises on societies even after they have recovered is shown by the percentage of nonperforming loans after growth has resumed. In September 1999, 45 percent of the total assets of the Thai financial system, 19 percent of Korea's, and 64 percent of Indonesia's represented loans to companies unable to pay the interest and principal. Such a situation jeopardizes the willingness, not to mention the capacity, of lending institutions to make loans to support potentially productive enterprises. Should governments seek to overcome this situation by governmental actions, bailouts would increase the public debt by 16 percent of the gross domestic product in South Korea, by 32 percent in Thailand, and by 58 percent in Indonesia—and this in countries which, at the beginning of the crisis, had a very low level of indebtedness. Thus, even after these crises are seemingly overcome, at least statistically, they show themselves to have been a human disaster, an economic burden, and the seedbed of political crises.[6]

These social upheavals—repeated with comparable consequences in Russia, Brazil, Argentina, Ecuador, and across Africa—occurred at a time of unprecedented growth and wealth creation in the United States and, to a lesser extent, in Europe. After decades of effort to close the gap between emerging and industrialized economies, the financial crises of the 1990s signalled a giant step backward. How many such roller-coaster rides can the international system withstand without political and social debacle? What would happen if a U.S. recession were thrown into the equation? What can be done to forestall these events?

POLITICAL EVOLUTION AND GLOBALIZATION

Many thoughtful observers rely on economic growth and the new information technology to move the world more or less automatically into the new era of global well-being and political stability. But this is an illusion. World order requires consensus, which presupposes that the differences between the advantaged and those disadvantaged who are in a position to undermine stability and progress, be of such a nature that the disadvantaged can still see some prospect of raising themselves by their own effort. In the absence of such a consciousness, turbulence, both within and among societies, will mount.

The world's leaders—especially in the industrialized democracies—cannot ignore the fact that, in many respects, the gap between the beneficiaries of globalization and the rest of the world is growing, again both within and among societies. Globalization has become synonymous with growth; growth requires capital; and capital seeks the highest possible return with the lowest risk, gravitating to where there is the best trade-off between risk and return. In practice, this means that, in one form or another, the United States and the other advanced industrialized countries will absorb an overwhelming percentage of the world's available investment capital. Because the great bull market of the 1990s reflected this reality—indeed was based on it—the gap between industrialized and developing countries has widened even as unprecedented wealth is being created.

Without adequate capital, developing countries cannot grow and create jobs. In the absence of rising employment, politicians will eventually lose their appetite for reforms that are preconditions for the globalization model. Since companies based in emerging markets find it increasingly difficult to achieve access to international capital markets, they must raise capital at home, and they can do so only by paying higher interest rates than are available at financial centers. National companies of developing countries thus become increasingly uncompetitive, particularly in sectors of the economy where the barriers to trade are in the process of being dismantled. Emerging-market companies exposed to international competition face the twin prospects of either failing or joining multinational enterprises. This is precisely the opposite of what advocates of protectionism in industrial countries have been predicting when they warned of the low-wage competition from the developing countries.

Developing countries seeking to join the globalization process have no choice in the long run except to restructure. This effort to become as much like the United States or Europe or Japan as possible is as difficult as it is time-consuming, though it can be accelerated through such institutions as NAFTA, which has proved a great boon to Mexico, or by special trade agreements and by pegging their currency to the dollar—as did Argentina and Ecuador. Some countries are even considering making the dollar their official currency.

Whatever road is chosen, multinational companies based in the United States or Europe emerge increasingly as the engines driving globalization. For them, the rush to size has turned into a goal in itself, almost compulsively pursued, because the ability to drive up the stock prices of their company is becoming the standard by which chief executives are increasingly being judged. As executives turn from being long-range builders into financial operators driven by shareholder value determined in daily stock market quotations, the vulnerability of the entire system grows, its long-term vitality could be weakened and, even more so, its resilience in times of crisis. Alan Greenspan's ruminations about "irrational exuberance" reflect the fear that, when markets become decoupled from the underlying national economies, a day of reckoning looms, however long postponed,[7] and that the exuberance might drive a downward cycle further than the underlying realities suggest.

The globalized world faces two contradictory trends. The globalized market opens prospects of heretofore unimagined wealth. But it also creates new vulnerabilities to political turmoil and the danger of a new gap, not so much between rich and poor as between those in each society that are part of the globalized, Internet world and those who are not. The impact of these new trends on the developing world is profound. In economies driven by a near imperative for the big to acquire the small, companies of developing countries are increasingly being absorbed by American and European multinationals. While this solves the problem of access to capital, it brings about growing vulnerabilities to domestic political tensions, especially in times of crisis. And within the developing countries, it creates political temptations for attacks on the entire system of globalization.

In the process, the typical developing country's economy bifurcates: one set of enterprises is integrated into the global economy, mostly owned by international corporations; the rest, cut off from globalization, employs much of the labor force at the lowest wages and with the bleakest social prospects. The "national" sector is substantially dependent on its ability to manipulate the political process of the developing country. Both kinds of companies pose a political challenge: the multinationals, because they seem to withdraw key decisions affecting the public welfare from domestic political control; the local companies, because they generate political pressures on behalf of protectionism and in opposition to further globalization.

The social world reflects this two-tiered system: globalized elites —often living in fortified suburbs—are linked by shared values and technologies, while the populations at large in the cities are tempted by nationalism, ethnicity, and a variety of movements to free themselves from what they perceive to be the hegemony of globalization, frequently identified with American domination. The global Internet elite is completely at ease with the operation of a technologically based economy, while a majority, especially outside the United States, Western Europe, and Japan, neither shares this experience nor may be prepared to accept its consequences, particularly during periods of economic hardship.

In such an environment, attacks on globalization could evolve into a new ideological radicalism, particularly in countries where the governing elite is small and the gap between rich and poor is vast and growing. A permanent worldwide underclass is in danger of emerging, especially in developing countries, which will make it increasingly difficult to build the political consensus on which domestic stability, international peace, and globalization itself depend.

Overt political challenges to this entire process may not become apparent for some time. But the large industrial countries and their multinationals are now too widely perceived to be the principal beneficiaries of globalization. Were the current period of economic expansion to end and, even more important, were it to reverse, especially in the United States, the tensions between economic realities and what is politically sustainable could shake both the economic and the political systems around the world.

Some of these dangers can be averted by accelerating free trade. But even if multilateral free trade progresses at a fast pace, the leaders of the industrial world must not lose sight of the political challenge. They must keep in mind the many decades it took for the American model to evolve into its present form. What has worked in the United States cannot be exactly replicated, and certainly not any more rapidly, throughout the developing world—in any event, not rapidly enough to forestall a political backlash against globalization.

When vast amounts of capital move around the world in response to individual decisions, periodic crises of disequilibrium will almost inevitably occur. And when global growth depends so much on the performance of the American economy, a downturn of any length could wreak havoc with the international financial and political systems. What then would be the reaction of a generation that has never known economic crisis—much less a political one—and that has failed to prepare for it?

If the other industrialized economies move in tandem with ours rather than balance our fluctuations, pressures for modifying the global economic system are bound to multiply. Democratic publics will turn to their governments for relief to cushion them against excessive suffering or dislocation; they are unlikely to accept prolonged exactions for the sake of an economic theory. It may then be argued that the governments that intervened in the market in the Asian crisis—India, Malaysia, China, and Taiwan—navigated the storm with fewer dislocations than did the disciples of convertibility. The dark cloud that is hanging over globalization is the threat of a global unraveling of the free market system under political pressure, with all its attendant perils to democratic institutions.

Even when there is relatively small danger of such an unraveling, it is important to define its possible character and to delineate the available means to avoid it in addition to the measures to mitigate a crisis, should it occur. Few in the booming 1920s expected the Depression of the 1930s, and no government prepared for it. And, in the end, no democratic public accepted orthodox methods for overcoming the Depression.

No economic system can be sustained without a political base. The challenge for those who believe in globalization is to match economic growth with political imagination, to navigate between those who see the world only in technical economic terms and their critics who yearn to return to some quasi-socialist and discredited model of government control. An international sense of social responsibility must be fostered without strangling a successful economic system in regulations imposed by bureaucrats.

Solutions will not emerge unless the United States helps identify the problems and designs forums to deal with them. The annual meetings of the heads of government of the leading industrial democracies—formerly the G-7, now the G-8, including Russia—were originally conceived a quarter-century ago as a forum for the industrialized democracies to face up to their political as well as economic challenges.[8] Regrettably, the G-8 meeting has degenerated into a cumbersome, almost exclusively public relations exercise. The annual economic summits need to be restored into a forum for deliberate discussion and decision to deal with the long-term challenges of the industrial world.

The historical antitrust policies of the United States have yet to find a global expression. The international financial system needs to reduce its volatility and learn to cushion the impact of crises more effectively. The role of speculative capital remains a challenge. In dealing with economic crises, a better balance needs to be established between the claims of lenders and the social needs of affected societies. The concerns of the United States and other advanced societies to improve conditions of labor and protection of the environment must be addressed while maintaining free trade and without giving developing countries the impression that America's real goal is to throttle their competition.

Leaders driven by short-term electoral pressure are reluctant to take on problems, the existence of which is not yet apparent and the solution of which requires a long-term time frame extending beyond the electoral cycle. They are tempted to go along with the conventional wisdom that treats economic phenomena as autonomous and self-correcting and essentially unrelated to the political process.

Yet the great changes in history, almost without exception, were driven by mankind's need for some kind of political vision and pursuit of a standard of justice. While much of the self-righteousness, nihilism, and violence associated with the demonstrations against globalization that are now spreading around the world is abhorrent, these outbreaks represent a warning that the international economic system may come to face a crisis of legitimacy. The industrial democracies must preserve and extend the extraordinary accomplishments that fostered globalization. But they can do so in the long run only if they endow the economic aspects of globalization with a political construction of comparable sweep and vision.

SEVEN ◇ ◇ ◇ ◇ ◇ ◇ ◇ ◇ ◇ ◇

Peace and Justice

PROBABLY the most dramatic transformation in the nature of contemporary international affairs has been the general acceptance of the proposition that certain universal principles are deemed enforceable, either by the United Nations or, in extreme situations, by a group of states (for example, NATO in Kosovo). Moreover, such international conventions as those condemning genocide, torture, or war crimes, are said to be enforceable by national judges who increasingly claim the right to demand extradition of alleged violators into their own jurisdictions. In addition, an International Criminal Court (ICC) is in the process of being created that, when ratified by sixty nations, will invest a prosecutor with the power to start investigations of alleged violations of international law at the request of any signatory state and, when backed by three of the eighteen judges, to bring indictments against any suspected transgressor anywhere in the world (including against citizens of nations which have refused to accept the ICC's jurisdiction). These innovations reflect the new conventional wisdom, according to which traditional principles of sovereignty and noninterference in the domestic affairs of other countries are the principal obstacles to the universal rule of peace and justice.

These views, treated as commonplace in American and much of contemporary West European public discourse—though far less so in the developing world—amount to a revolution in the way the international system has operated for more than three hundred years. They also represent the widespread acceptance of ideas which, until the last decade of the Cold War, had been held almost uniquely in the United States. And they may usher in a new period of global interventionism with unforeseeable consequences.

The international order that America encountered when it engaged itself in world affairs can be dated fairly precisely: it was created by the Treaty of Westphalia, signed in 1648 to mark the end of the Thirty Years' War. That war had its roots in the Reformation, which split what had heretofore been the universal Catholic Church and challenged the autonomous jurisdiction over its internal administration. Some of the rulers of the various feudal principalities used the opportunity to strengthen their authority by asserting control over the religious allegiance of their subjects and the governance of their churches. The already fragile power of the Holy Roman Emperor, traditionally invested by the Pope, was weakened further. Soon even the princes who had remained Catholic set about restricting the power of the Church to define the reach of political authority.

Whether the various rulers opted for Catholic orthodoxy or Protestant reform, a century of war followed—a mixture of civil war, international conflict, and religious crusade. The Holy Roman Emperor, a Habsburg situated in Vienna, fought to reimpose the Catholic Church throughout Central Europe. The Bourbon rulers of France, though Catholic, allied themselves with the Protestant princes of northern Europe to resist the emergence of a potentially hegemonic Austria. Whatever the motives, the war was conducted in the name of religion, disregarding frontiers. Entire populations were obliged to change their faiths on the basis of whatever army triumphed on the battlefield (with the additional modern *Realpolitik* twist that Catholic France sided with Protestant allies to weaken Austria by reducing the sphere of Catholic rule in Germany). This mix of religion and power politics endowed the conduct of the war with unprecedented ferocity. As noted earlier, by some estimates, nearly 30 percent of the population of Central Europe was killed during the Thirty Years' War.

The Treaty of Westphalia reflected a general determination to put an end to carnage once and for all. Its basic purpose (in modern terms) was to stop the merging of domestic and foreign policy or (in the language of the period) of faith and diplomacy. All signatories confirmed the principle *cujus regio, ejus religio*—whoever rules determines the religion of his subjects. No other country had a right to intervene in this process. Thus was born the concept of noninterference in the domestic affairs of other states, and it was developed for precisely the opposite reason it is being discarded today. It was the human rights slogan of the period; restoring peace and tranquillity was its purpose, not legitimizing domestic oppression. Since the divide between Catholic and Protestant was the most inflammatory issue of the day, the Treaty of Westphalia sought to prevent rulers of one faith from inciting uprisings of their co-religionists ruled by a prince of a different faith. With religion removed as an excuse for domestic subversion, the expectation was that domestic tranquillity would return as well and, with it, more benign government.

On the whole, this expectation was fulfilled in the eighteenth and nineteenth centuries, as the European system evolved into an agglomeration of nation-states. The doctrine of nonintervention in the domestic affairs of other countries became one of the keystones, together with the notions of sovereignty and international law regulating the conduct of states in their relations with each other. This did not prevent wars, but it limited their scope. Indeed, in the twentieth century, one of the democracies' chief criticisms of the totalitarian states—especially of Communism—was that they systematically violated the canons of international order by undermining existing governments through radical movements and parties controlled from abroad—in other words, through a return to the ethos of the religious wars.

The international system based on the Treaty of Westphalia had an answer for the problem of violence between states—that is, recourse to war—but it offered no solution to violence *within* states arising from civil wars, ethnic conflicts, and the entire range of what are today called human rights violations. It dealt with the problem of peace and left justice to the domestic institutions. The contemporary human rights activists are arguing the opposite. In their view, peace flows automatically from justice, and the nation-state, or perhaps any state, cannot be relied on to deliver justice; it must be put under some kind of supranational authority entitled to use force to make its writ run. On the whole, the human rights activists trust jurists more than they do statesmen. The advocates of the Westphalian principles trust statesmen more than jurists.

THE AMERICAN TRADITION

The United States was one of the most vociferous critics of the subversive interventionism of the Soviet Union. Yet it has itself never fully accepted the principle of nonintervention for its own conduct. To be sure, in the early days of the republic, the Founding Fathers showed that they understood and respected the principles of the European equilibrium. Tilting back and forth between Britain and France, generally in opposition to whichever side seemed ascendant but without ever committing fully to either, they practiced the injunction of Alexander Hamilton: "The coolest calculations of interest" required Americans to modulate their support for the European powers while tying themselves to nobody.[1] In a statement that could as easily have originated in the British Cabinet, Thomas Jefferson articulated an American version of the balance-of-power theory: "We especially ought to pray that the powers of Europe may be so poised and counterpoised among themselves that their own security may require the presence of all their forces at home leaving the other parts of the world in undisturbed tranquility."[2]

But even in this Hamiltonian phase when American foreign policy resembled that of the European powers in many respects, the justification for it was quite different: Americans then as now viewed their nation as motivated by principles higher than those of the Old World, which they imagined reflected the basically selfish aspirations of monarchs. By contrast, the American republic was viewed as operating according to the dictates of enlightened rationalism; it was destined to serve as a model for less fortunate peoples obliged to live under less benevolent rule. America's actions could therefore never be purely selfish; by its very nature, America constituted a universal cause. As James Madison put it in 1804: "The United States owe to the world as well as to themselves to let the example of one government at least protest against the corruption which prevails." [3]

This avoided the question of how far that universal cause should be pursued. If America was the hope of the world, did it have an obligation to intervene abroad so that this hope was implemented? And if the answer was in the affirmative, how could the United States pursue its international mission without facing the same practical dilemmas in the application of its power that it condemned in the conduct of the European states?

The quandary acquired some urgency in 1821 when the Greek struggle for independence from Ottoman rule generated a wave of enthusiasm to "do something" to apply America's principles to the cause of liberating the Greek people. Secretary of State John Quincy Adams both framed the dilemma and resolved it in a manner that would become the lodestar of American foreign policy for the next century:

> Wherever the standard of freedom and independence has been or shall be unfurled, there will be America's heart, her benedictions, and her prayers. But she goes not abroad in search of monsters to destroy. She is the well-wisher to the freedom and independence of all. She is the champion and vindicator only of her own. She will recommend the general cause by the countenance of her voice, and by the benignant sympathy of her example. She well knows that by once enlisting under other banners than her own, were they even the banners of foreign independence, she would involve herself beyond the power of extrication, in all the wars of interest and intrigue, of individual avarice, envy and ambition, which assume the colors and usurp the standards of freedom. . . . She might become the dictatress of the world. She would no longer be the ruler of her own spirit. [4]

By insisting that the United States performed its distinctive mission best by steering clear of imposing it by force, Adams scrapped the ideological basis for intervention in the European balance of power. Two years later, President James Monroe removed the practical reasons for a Hamiltonian foreign policy—the fear of European intervention in the Western Hemisphere. In the Monroe Doctrine, he boldly expanded Adams's proposition that the United States refrain from entangling itself in European affairs into a warning to Europe not to entangle itself in American affairs, defined as embracing the entire Western Hemisphere, on pain of having such an intrusion treated "as dangerous to our peace and safety"—in other words, as a *casus belli*.[5]

The Monroe Doctrine removed two European powers—Britain and Spain—from the power calculus of North America. It was based on a tacit understanding with Britain, which had abjured an imperial role in the Americas, while the Spanish empire in Latin America was clearly collapsing. Liberated from the necessity of participating in the European balance of power, the United States could cultivate its self-proclaimed missionary role.

In the isolation America came to enjoy in the nineteenth century, its statesmen elaborated two themes which would have appeared contradictory to any other society: that America's values and institutions were applicable universally but, also, that their spread would be all the more certain if America refined them at home without contaminating them by extensive political interaction with the rest of the world.

An unwavering faith in progress and the conviction that history was, or at least ought to be, a steady march toward greater prosperity, freedom, and justice, of which the American experience was the defining symbol, expressed the optimism of the Enlightenment, untempered by the tragedies and adaptations imposed on European nations by their history and geography. "[America's] ancestors," wrote Alexis de Tocqueville in *Democracy in America*, "give them the love of equality and of freedom; but God Himself gave them the means of remaining equal and free by placing them upon a boundless continent."[6] The writer John Louis O'Sullivan summed up this confidence at about the same time in the phrase "manifest destiny."[7]

By the beginning of the twentieth century, the faith in America's universal mission had evolved into the conviction that the key to international well-being resided in extending to the rest of the world the achievements underlying the American success story. At the turn of the twentieth century, William Jennings Bryan characterized the United States as "a republic gradually but surely becoming the supreme moral factor in the world's progress and the accepted arbiter of the world's disputes."[8]

Harboring these attitudes, the United States disdained the way in which foreign policy was conducted in the rest of the world. The Westphalian state system was castigated and, with it, the acceptance of force as the ultimate sanction. In the period between the Monroe Doctrine and the Spanish-American War, the very notion of foreign policy—its practices and strategies—had little place in American thinking.

ROOSEVELT AND WILSON

The end of the Spanish-American War coincided with the accession of Theodore Roosevelt, the first president since the Founding Fathers to resurrect the Hamiltonian idea of treating the balance of power as the distinctive feature of international relations and to undertake an active American role in shaping it. Unlike his predecessors and most of his successors, Roosevelt did not think of the United States as a messianic cause but as a great power—potentially the greatest. Viewing its mission as that of guardian of the global equilibrium in much the same way Britain was protector of the balance of power in Europe, he was impatient with many of the traditional pieties of American thinking on foreign policy. Roosevelt rejected the supposed efficacy of international law; what nations could not protect with their own strength would not be safeguarded by others. He scorned the concept of disarmament, just emerging on the international agenda: "A milk-and-water righteousness unbacked by force is to the full as wicked as and even more mischievous than force divorced from righteousness."[9]

Conducting a *Realpolitik* of his own, Roosevelt in 1908 acquiesced in the Japanese occupation of Korea on the grounds that Korea was unable to defend itself and no other state, or combination of states, was willing to run the risks of defending Korea:

> Korea is absolutely Japan's. To be sure, by treaty it was solemnly covenanted that Korea should remain independent. But Korea was itself helpless to enforce the treaty, and it was out of the question to suppose that any other nation . . . would attempt to do for the Koreans what they were utterly unable to do for themselves.[10]

In this spirit, Roosevelt developed what came to be known as the "Roosevelt corollary" to the Monroe Doctrine, proclaiming an American right to intervene in the Western Hemisphere—not only to prevent interference from the outside as provided for in the Monroe Doctrine but also, and perhaps above all, to vindicate and protect the national interest of the United States. During Roosevelt's presidency, the United States intervened in Haiti, fostered a revolution in Panama that led to its secession from Colombia and laid the basis for the completion of the Panama Canal, established a financial protectorate over the Dominican Republic, and, in 1906, sent American troops to occupy Cuba.

Convinced that the United States could not confine its international responsibilities to practicing civic virtue, Roosevelt began to involve the country actively in the operation of the global equilibrium. When Japan and Russia went to war in 1904, he did not stigmatize Japan, which contemporary criteria would label as the aggressor, because he feared that a Russian victory might enable it to dominate Asia and thereby threaten the global balance of power. But neither did he transform this geopolitical concern into a moral crusade against Russia. Instead, applying the rules of the balance of power, Roosevelt, though wanting Russia weakened, resisted carrying the defeat of Russia to the point where a Japanese threat would substitute for a Russian one. He therefore invited representatives of the warring parties to his home in Oyster Bay, New York, where he mediated their dispute, ultimately formally resolved by the Treaty of Portsmouth. The settlement was based on the premise of an Asian balance of power in which Japan, backed by Britain, would offset Imperial Russia, with the United States maintaining the ultimate balance between the two sides in Asia, much as Britain protected the equilibrium in Europe.

The same geopolitical approach characterized Roosevelt's attitude toward the First World War. By then out of office, he favored intervention on the side of Britain and France long before the incumbent president, Woodrow Wilson, acknowledged the need to do so. Roosevelt feared that a victorious Germany would begin to meddle in the Western Hemisphere, which, in case of a German victory, would have lost the shield of the British navy. Had Roosevelt been in office, he most probably would have sought a settlement analogous to the Treaty of Portsmouth. He would have tried to reduce the capacity of Germany to dominate Europe while retaining it as a factor in the new balance of power. There would have been no attempt to remove the governments of the enemy nations or to recast political boundaries on the basis of such principles as self-determination.

But Roosevelt was no longer in office; instead, at the helm stood a president of an entirely different cast of mind, whose ideas would shape the conceptual basis of American foreign policy for the rest of the twentieth century. Woodrow Wilson led the United States into war for a set of principles more compatible with the American historical experience than those of the European equilibrium. To participate in a balance-of-power system, a nation must believe that it is facing a genuine threat it is unable to master alone. In 1914, however, the American public could not be persuaded that any conceivable change of the existing European balance could threaten America's security. Though history is likely to view Roosevelt as more prescient about the ultimate challenge to American foreign policy, Wilson's ideas prevailed because, however radical and daring they sounded to foreign ears, they represented a global application of verities burnished during a century of American isolation.

Wilson's initial reaction to the outbreak of World War I had been the traditional isolationist one. On December 8, 1914, he rejected a call by Roosevelt to increase America's armaments because he considered that the European conflagration involved a war "whose causes cannot touch us, whose very existence affords us opportunities for friendship and disinterested service."[11]

Two and a half years later, Wilson decided to take the United States into the war but not as Roosevelt would have done—to preserve and strengthen the European balance of power. Rather, Wilson set out to abolish the balance of power and the Westphalian system altogether. Three months before America entered the war, Wilson, on January 22, 1917, defined the only acceptable outcome as follows:

> The question upon which the whole future peace and policy of the world depends is this: Is the present war a struggle for a just and secure peace, or only for a new balance of power? . . . There must be, not a balance of power, but a community of power; not organized rivalries, but an organized common peace.[12]

America's entry into the war turned into the defining moment for its foreign policy and, because of America's growing role, for the rest of the world as well. After a century of castigating the Westphalian international settlement, the United States saw an opportunity to remake it. Striding onto the international arena, America refused the role of being just another state among many pursuing their national interests. Implicit in Wilson's doctrine was a rejection of the sort of moral equivalence that would place the United States on the same moral ground as other states. The American vocation being on a higher ethical plane, according to Wilson, the only valid purpose for America's entry into the war was to remake the world in its own image. The United States would at long last participate in the great international game but only if it was in a position to rewrite the rules. This is why Wilson defined the purpose of the war in such millennial terms:

> We are glad . . . to fight thus for the ultimate peace of the world. . . . The world must be made safe for democracy. Its

peace must be planted upon the tested foundations of political liberty.[13]

Rejecting the notion of national interest as a "standard of national selfishness," he put forth a new criterion:

> This is an age . . . which demands a new order of things in which the only questions will be: Is it right? Is it just? Is it in the interest of mankind?[14]

Three basic themes of all subsequent American foreign policy were laid down by Wilson. In the first place, harmony is the natural order of international affairs; the matters which have historically disturbed it are neither creditable nor important and should, as George Kennan later explained Wilsonianism, "take second place behind the desirability of an orderly world, untroubled by international violence."[15]

Second, bringing about change by force is inadmissible; all transformation must occur by processes based on law or something akin to law or legal procedure. And because peoples are endowed with a God-given right to determine their own fate, the state should be based on national self-determination and democracy.

Finally, any nation built on such principles would, in Wilson's view, never choose war; states failing to meet these criteria would sooner or later plunge the world into conflict. Hence making the world safe for democracy was a dictate of prudence and not only a requirement of morality. And since democracies in that theory never go to war with each other, they have the luxury of concentrating on the issues that enhance the quality of human life. Democracies, according to the Wilsonian theory, have, in effect, no legitimate interest other than the advancement of universal values.

One of the contemporary ironies is that the current advocacy of these ideas is often interpreted abroad as an expression of America's hegemonic aspirations and of its desire to throw its weight around as a superpower. In fact, the applicability of the American model to the rest of the world has been a basic American theme since the founding of the republic; Wilson's innovation was to translate what had been heretofore conceived as a "shining city on the hill," inspiring others by moral example, into a crusade to spread these values by an active foreign policy. His opponents did not thwart him because they doubted the global relevance of American values. Rather they disagreed on how to apply these values, believing that America's universal mission was best fulfilled by burnishing its domestic institutions, not by dissipating its resources in foreign adventures.

The "isolationists" of the 1920s were, in fact, expressing dominant American policies of nineteenth-century America after the presidency of James Monroe. Professor Walter Russell Mead dubbed them "Jacksonians"—after President Andrew Jackson, the first president to emerge from backwoods America and the creator of the modern Democratic party.[16] The Founding Fathers had come from the ranks of landed gentry and a mercantile class with international interests. For them, the Hamiltonian foreign policy of manipulating the European balance of power to protect the fledgling American state made sense. Andrew Jackson represented an America turning its back on Europe and expanding westward. He reflected the views of the pioneers and, in time, also of the urban middle and working class, especially in small towns.

In the 1920s, Jacksonians at first opposed Wilsonianism, allied with it during the Second World War and the Cold War, and retreated to their earlier principles after the Cold War ended.

Wilsonians wanted to make over the international system by active participation in world affairs; Jacksonians on the whole ignored the maneuvers of European power politics unless these explicitly and directly threatened United States security or values. But once an issue had been so defined, the Jacksonians would turn implacable. In the 1930s, Wilsonians could be rallied by violations of international law or of human rights; the conduct in the 1930s of either Germany or Japan did not greatly rouse the Jacksonians—indeed, Jacksonians on the whole opposed Franklin Roosevelt's drift toward intervention in Europe. But when Pearl Harbor was attacked—and American security was directly challenged—Wilsonians and Jacksonians made common cause. They were unanimous that the destruction of Nazism and the unconditional surrender of Germany and Japan were the only acceptable outcomes. And while Wilson after the First World War had been obliged to take into account the views and interests of his European allies, by the end of the Second World War, the United States had become so dominant that Presidents Franklin Roosevelt and Harry Truman were free to shape the international environment according to quintessetially American principles—collective security, national self-determination, and decolonization—in the process creating the United Nations.

In January 1941, Roosevelt proclaimed as goals of American policy the Four Freedoms—of speech and religion, from want, and from fear—"everywhere in the world." In other words, the United States had donned the mantle John Quincy Adams had warned against—of champion and defender of free peoples everywhere. The very characteristics that had fostered American isolationism in the nineteenth century fueled its messianic globalism in the twentieth.

In 1947, the United States, in the Truman Doctrine, assumed the defense of Greece and Turkey; in 1949, of all of Western Europe; in the succeeding decade, of most of the rest of the world, formally or implicitly. And it justified this role in a uniquely American manner.

In 1953, at the height of the Cold War, Secretary of State John Foster Dulles, at a graduation ceremony of the National War College, expressed America's role in exclusively moral—even spiritual—terms. The United States, he insisted, by its very existence, was a threat to despotism:

> We developed here an area of spiritual, intellectual, and material richness, the like of which the world has never seen. What we did caught the imagination of men everywhere and became known everywhere as "the Great American experiment." Our free society became a menace to every despot because we showed how to meet the hunger of the people for greater opportunity and for greater dignity.[17]

The alliance between Jacksonians and Wilsonians continued all through the Cold War. President John F. Kennedy affirmed

America's goal as "not merely peace for Americans but peace for all men and women—not merely peace in our time but peace in all time."[18] And Lyndon Johnson insisted that, in trying to prevent a Communist takeover of South Vietnam, he was implementing a moral duty, not national interest, because altruism was the underpinning of all of American policy:

> To any in Southeast Asia who ask our help in defending their freedom, we shall give it.
> In that region there is nothing we covet, nothing we seek—no territory, no military position, no political ambition. Our one desire—our one determination—is that the people of Southeast Asia be left in peace to work out their own destinies in their own way.[19]

A combination of missionary zeal and solipsism—the inability even to conceive another way of looking at the world—produced the fateful combination of globalist and missionary impulses that propelled the United States into Vietnam. America attempted at one and the same time to remake a government from the top—easing out the indolent Bao Dai, then replacing his successor, Ngo Dinh Diem, with an American-picked military junta; and to promote American-style democracy and capitalism in a country almost completely lacking a middle class or any experience with self-government. These tasks, monumental in themselves, were pursued in the midst of a brutal guerrilla insurgency and invasion from the North while tolerating sanctuaries and unimpeded supply lines in adjacent countries such as Laos and Cambodia.

The resulting debacle was compounded by America's inability to sort out the various strands of its historic approach to foreign policy: how to reconcile universal principles with the practical necessities of a region which permitted only a piecemeal approach to lofty goals; how, in the crucible of battle, to relate moral maxims, which are absolute, to their implementation by means of power, which depends on circumstances.

One victim of the frustrations was the national consensus based on the coalition between Wilsonians and Jacksonians. When the Wilsonians realized that the goal of promoting freedom, prosperity, and the American institutional pattern was proving chimerical, they abandoned the effort in the middle of a bitter war, choosing not to fight for more limited and perhaps more attainable objectives. The radical wing of the Wilsonians drew the conclusion that American idealism had not so much overreached as that a basic moral flaw had drawn the United States into Indochina. To extirpate that flaw, they undertook an all-out assault on the principles that had guided American postwar policy.

The Jacksonians, on the other hand, would continue to insist on the ultimate validity of their principles. But if the war in Indochina was worth fighting, it had to be won and, if it was not won, it had to be abandoned. The Jacksonians had no category for limited war. Neither the Wilsonians nor the Jacksonians were willing to support a gradual extrication designed to preserve American credibility in the Cold War environment where security still very much depended on America's word.

It fell to Richard Nixon to conduct America's foreign policy amidst this wreckage of the historic consensus. An admirer of Wilson, Nixon had even asked that Wilson's desk be placed in the Oval Office—though, due to a mix-up or perhaps bureaucratic malice, he was given instead the desk of Henry Wilson, Grant's second vice president. (He did manage to get the right Wilson's portrait hung in the Cabinet Room.) But, having studied international politics much of his life, Nixon did not accept the proposition that one formula could explain all history or that every contemporary international problem could be solved by a single strategy. Convinced that an excess of Wilsonianism had mired us in Indochina and aware that the Jacksonians were no longer willing to fight for what remained at stake there, Nixon sought to rally the American people by returning American foreign policy to its Hamiltonian roots, giving first priority to the national interest.

There was nevertheless a strong Wilsonian strain in Nixon's policies with respect to arms control agreements, promoting Jewish emigration from the Soviet Union, and measures such as initiating the peace process in the Middle East and an international convention banning biological warfare. But throughout, Nixon's dominant theme was to relate America's policies to its interests and its interests to its capabilities. "Our objective, in the first instance, is to support our *interests* over the long run with a sound foreign policy," he informed Congress in 1970. "Our interests must shape our commitments, rather than the other way around." [20]

The policy had many remarkable successes—a negotiated extrication from Vietnam, an opening to China, a Berlin agreement, a policy toward the Soviet Union combining containment with negotiations on many subjects, and beginning the Arab-Israeli peace process. But its justification, though classically Hamiltonian, was out of tune with what had been the main theme of American foreign policy for the better part of the century. When Watergate weakened Nixon and the extrication from Vietnam made it seem safe to do so, the established impulse to affirm the global relevance of America's values reasserted itself. Nixon and, to a lesser extent, President Gerald Ford (and I as their Secretary of State) came under increasing attack from the Wilsonians for being too power-oriented (the code word for being too traditionalist and old-world) and from the Jacksonians for being too accommodating (the code word for reluctance to base policy on a series of showdowns). When a wing of the liberals switched sides in the early 1970s and created the neoconservative movement, Wilsonianism reemerged in a more muscular (Reaganite) variant. The contest with the Soviets had a moral as well as a strategic aspect, they reminded us—and compromise was dangerous (and, by definition, so was any negotiation with the Soviet Union).

In 1974, a sea change in the conduct of American foreign policy occurred. Until then, American attempts to affect the domestic policies of other states had been by way of covert operations or quiet diplomacy. Official intervention in the domestic affairs of other countries had not yet become an accepted component of American foreign policy; Westphalian scruples still governed. Thus the Nixon administration had managed to increase Jewish emigration from the Soviet Union—from less than one thousand a year to nearly thirty-five thousand—by appealing to Soviet leaders, using quiet diplomacy because a country's emigration policy was still widely considered a domestic matter. In 1974, Congress for the first time applied legislative sanctions to promote Jewish emigration from the Soviet Union, making it a formal and public part of American foreign policy. That the sanctions were maintained despite the fact that Jewish emigration actually *decreased* by some 70 percent for several years after the sanctions started shows how dominant the commitment to overt pressure on behalf of human rights had become and the degree to which the principles of the Westphalian system regarding nonintervention in the affairs of other states were on the wane.

From then on, intervention in what had been considered domestic policy became increasingly fashionable. The Final Act of the Conference on Security and Cooperation in Europe in August 1975 established the upholding of human rights as an international obligation of the signatories. At the closing session, President Ford challenged the Soviet Union explicitly by stressing in his speech "the deep devotion of the American people and their government to human rights and fundamental freedoms."[21]

President Jimmy Carter affirmed this basic Wilsonianism even more strongly: "We ought to be a beacon for nations who search for peace and who search for freedom, who search for individual liberty, who search for basic human rights."[22] President Ronald Reagan emphasized the same principles in more assertive language still:

America's leadership in the world came to us because of our own strength and because of the values which guide us as a society: free elections, a free press, freedom of religious choice, free trade unions, and above all freedom for the individual and rejection of the arbitrary power of the state. These values are the bedrock of our strength.[23]

The Reagan administration produced a synthesis of all three strands of American thought: the Wilsonian rhetoric of America's exceptionalism; a crusading attack against a hostile ideology ("the Evil Empire") to rally the Jacksonians; and the Hamiltonian tactics of Nixon. Evocations of America's unique moral obligation became fused with a hardheaded assessment of the national interest. As for

Congress, during the 1970s, it increasingly made American foreign aid conditional on acceptable human rights conduct on the part of its recipients. During the 1980s, it began to apply sanctions in an effort to achieve human rights objectives, and scores of nations are now subject to such sanctions. The most successful example—and so far the only unambiguously successful one—was the economic embargo against South Africa passed by Congress in 1986.

THE NEW INTERVENTIONISM

The final transition from John Quincy Adams's proposition that the United States helps to spread democracy abroad best by practicing its virtues at home to turning the promotion of human rights into a principal objective of American foreign policy occurred during the Clinton administration. Bill Clinton was the first president of the post–Cold War period, the first president whose formative political experience had occurred as an activist in the Vietnam protest movement, and he injected its premises into American foreign policy. Distrustful of the role of power, hostile to the very concept of equilibrium (he considered it "Old Think"),[24] Clinton acted as if his predecessors contributed to the Cold War by excessive concern with strategic considerations. As a result, one of the staples of Clinton speeches abroad was an apology for America's alleged moral transgressions by blaming them on American preoccupation with the Cold War.[25]

The Cold War, however, was not invented by the United States; serious men and women of nine administrations of both parties preceding the incumbency of Bill Clinton thought (and had good reason to believe) that they were engaged in a struggle affecting the basic security and values of their country and of free peoples in general. The new dispensation in foreign policy combined a rejection of history with a turning away from traditional notions of security and geopolitics. Explicitly suggesting that America's failings were a contributing cause of the Cold War, implying that most international tensions were social in origin and that diplomacy should therefore concentrate on the so-called soft—that is, nonstrategic—issues, it expressed an unconcealed disdain for much of what had been accomplished in the half-century following the Second World War.

Victory in the Cold War encouraged this self-gratification even in other groups, turning it into a global triumphalism. In that dispensation, the United States having arrived at the optimum political and economic system, the best—indeed, the only viable—option for the rest of the world was to adopt American-style political and economic premises. Absent a Cold War and an alternative power center to the United States, the theory of an "end of history" achieved considerable plausibility. Ideological struggles might well have ended once and for all; the entire world was adopting variations of the American economic and political systems. Competition was meaningful primarily in relation to the rate of achieving this goal.[26] And the Asian financial crisis of 1997 gave an additional impetus to Western triumphalism.

In the process, American foreign policy became increasingly driven by domestic politics. When pressure on foreign countries appears free of risk, there is increasing scope for legislating American domestic preferences as objectives of foreign policy. A revealing example of the new congressional engagement was a comment by Representative Nancy Pelosi of California, a strong supporter of restrictions on Chinese trade. When Clinton, early in his administration, made the granting of Most Favored Nation status to China dependent on Chinese demonstrations of progress on human rights within a year, she said:

Hopefully at the end of this 12 months, if there is freedom of the press in China and the other human rights conditions are met, then we can begin to solve some of the other problems that members of Congress have.[27]

Nothing illustrates better the collapse of the Westphalian notion of noninterference than the proposition that freedom of speech and the press, which has never existed in five millennia of Chinese history, could be brought about through legislation by the American

Congress as the initial twelve-month installment in a continuing series of unilateral American demands.

Congressional expressions of this kind were not an aberration but the voicing of an ever more prevalent theme in American (and, increasingly, West European) public opinion. Strobe Talbott, then Deputy Secretary of State, elaborated on this theme in *Foreign Affairs* in November 1996:

> In an increasingly interdependent world Americans have a grow-
> ing stake in how other countries govern, or misgovern, them-
> selves. The larger and more close-knit the community of nations
> that choose democratic forms of government, the safer and more
> prosperous Americans will be, since democracies are demonstra-
> bly more likely to maintain their international commitments, less
> likely to engage in terrorism or wreak environmental damage,
> and less likely to make war on each other.
>
> That proposition is the essence of the national security ratio-
> nale for vigorously supporting, promoting, and when necessary,
> defending democracy in other countries.[28]

The new doctrine of humanitarian intervention asserts that hu-mane convictions are so integral a part of the American tradition that both treasure and, in the extreme, lives must be risked to vindi-cate them anywhere in the world. No other nation has ever ad-vanced such goals, which risk maneuvering the United States and its allies into the role of world policeman.

Rhetoric affirming a doctrine of permanent intervention was es-pecially explicit in the triumphant aftermath of the NATO opera-tion in Kosovo. British Prime Minister Tony Blair proclaimed the Kosovo mission as a victory for the "progressive" forces in foreign policy, replacing outdated traditional concepts:

> This war . . . was fought for a fundamental principle necessary
> for humanity's progress: that every human being regardless of
> race, religion or birth has an inalienable right to live free from
> persecution.[29]

Chancellor Gerhard Schroeder of Germany made the same point even more strongly: "The Alliance had to demonstrate . . . that the weak have in NATO a strong friend and ally ready and willing to defend their human rights."[30] President Clinton adopted the most sweeping formulation:

> We can then say to the people of the world, whether you live in Africa, or Central Europe, or any other place, if somebody comes after innocent civilians and tries to kill them en masse because of their race, their ethnic background or their religion, and it is within our power to stop it, we will stop it.[31]

That Wilsonianism had triumphed over competing traditions in American foreign policy was dramatically illustrated by events of the six months starting in November 1998. By Jacksonian and Hamiltonian standards, Iraq's threat to dominate the Gulf would be considered a fundamental threat to American national security. In December, Iraq evicted the U.N. inspectors placed there by the United Nations Security Council to prevent the production of weapons of mass destruction as a condition of the cease-fire that ended the Gulf War. This resurrected Iraq's long-term capacity to threaten its neighbors, most of whom are America's allies and all of whom are indispensable suppliers of oil for the industrial democracies. Nevertheless, the American reaction was confined to air attacks for four nights (to limit civilian casualties) and, after that, there was substantial acquiescence in Iraq's flouting of the Security Council resolution. The assumption obviously was that the United States would deal with the long-range consequences when they arose; the risk of Iraqi dominance in the Gulf did not involve moral issues justifying sustained military actions.

By contrast, three months later, NATO, under American prodding, bombed Yugoslavia for seventy-eight days around the clock, in essence to put an end to and to reverse Serbia's human rights violations in Kosovo, even though Kosovo represented no threat to American security in any traditional sense. Wilsonian principles were the dominant driving force of Western foreign policy in the Balkans.

Kosovo was the culmination of a series of interventions conducted in the name of human rights and humane values. The American military was deployed in Somalia, initially to help distribute food, then to bring about civilian government; in Haiti, in order to free the population from a military government having come to power by a coup; in Bosnia, to force an end to a cruel civil war; and, in Kosovo, in effect, to shift authority from Serbia to the majority of the population, which was ethnically Albanian.

All four cases of military intervention—three of which were initiated by the Clinton administration—had certain common features: they reflected no traditional notion of American national interest in the sense that their outcome could in no way affect any historic definition of American security; they were a response to powerful domestic pressures to alleviate undisputed human suffering (Bush had initially intervened in Somalia for the stated purpose of having the American military distribute food to a starving population); the intervention was thought to be free of risk (when significant casualties were incurred in Somalia, the American forces were quickly withdrawn). The interventions occurred without any reference to their historical contexts.

Inevitably, such sweeping Wilsonianism led to the same split with the Jacksonians as had occurred in the 1920s. The Jacksonian wing of the Reagan coalition jumped ship and refused to go along with the quest for the multilateral organization of the world. The Senate refused to ratify the Comprehensive Nuclear Test Ban Treaty; it is reluctant to endorse the International Criminal Court and dubious about a permanent role for United States forces in Kosovo. Ironically, the Wilsonian measures Clinton was best able to carry out were those he could order as commander-in-chief. For the rest, his bipartisan achievements were Hamiltonian in nature, such as the North American Free Trade Agreement or America's membership in the World Trade Organization (WTO).

It is not surprising, therefore, that the little controversy on foreign policy that took place during the 2000 presidential campaign concerned the fault line between Wilsonianism and Jacksonianism. The Clinton administration was charged with going beyond the dictates of the national interest in its various military interventions. But what was actually happening was an attempt by Clinton to redefine the national interest in extreme Wilsonian terms. The defense of human rights and humane values, even by force, was proclaimed as a general principle of the American national interest. Deputy Secretary of State Strobe Talbott, in the *Foreign Affairs* article cited earlier, explained that the support, promotion, and defense of democracy "in other countries" was the quintessence of realism:

> It is the basis for asserting in rebuttal of some self-proclaimed realists' insinuations to the contrary that American values and interests reinforce each other.[32]

HUMANITARIAN INTERVENTION AND THE NATIONAL INTEREST: FOUR PRINCIPLES

To embed humanitarian intervention as a top priority into American foreign policy, four conditions must be met: the principle must be universally applicable; it must lead to actions sustainable by American domestic opinion; it must find resonance in the international community; and it must have some relationship to the historical context. All these conditions are relevant to what is now commonly called an "exit strategy," which determines whether one is fixing a temporary problem or plunging into a permanent bog.

These conditions determine above all whether the United States is simply justifying ad hoc decisions driven by circumstances or laying down a general strategy that can be followed. If the policy is not universally applicable—or at least applicable to the vast majority of foreseeable circumstances—it will appear to the rest of the world as an arbitrary exercise of American dominance and, in time, as an act of selfish hypocrisy. If American opinion does not support the course of action, the failure will undermine America's aspiration to serve as a pillar of world order. If the international community does not go along with American objectives, the United States will be driven either to imposition or abdication. If America's actions do not take account of the historical context, they will sooner or later be defeated by growing local obstacles or require a mobilization of power incompatible with the domestic American consensus.

Clearly, neither alone nor in combination with Europe is the United States in a position to right every wrong, or even every major wrong, in the world by applying military force—as so many NATO leaders asserted in the heady aftermath of Kosovo. Nor did the leaders of the NATO coalition apply in practice their lofty declarations in even remotely so universal a manner. Within months of their proclamation of a new ethical foreign policy, they lapsed into embarrassed silence when Russia launched a crackdown in Chechnya that was, structurally, nearly identical to Serbian actions in Kosovo. In both Kosovo and Chechnya, a ruling country sought to maintain its hold on a province of different ethnic composition and religious persuasion by military pressure against its subjects. Russian actions in Chechnya were, if anything, more sustained and on a much larger scale than those of Serbia in Kosovo and resulted in even greater loss of life.

Confronted by such a challenge, most of those who had proclaimed the Kosovo operation to be a universal precedent fell silent or undertook formalistic measures designed, above all, to calm domestic pressure groups. In abject retreat, they sought solace in changing the label of the victims. Thus the "freedom fighters" of Kosovo became the "rebels" or "militants" of Chechnya—in official documents as well as in the media.

There was a comparable evasion of proclaimed goals of the new foreign policy with respect to Africa. In the face of even more widespread murder and gruesome atrocities in Sierra Leone, the participants in the Kosovo operation announced their refusal to become involved militarily—even though minimal forces (by Kosovo standards) could have rapidly put an end to the slaughter. Nor has intervention been proposed for Sudan or in the Caucasus, where again the scale of casualties cumulatively exceeds those of Kosovo.

On closer examination, it is evident that the general principle of the new ethical foreign policy was not being applied to major countries, to allies of major countries, or to those countries with strong domestic constituencies within the larger democratic states. Thus far it has remained confined to a small, formerly rogue state at the edge of Europe and to an Indonesia in the midst of domestic upheaval and incapable of posing any foreign policy risks.

That there are limits to the applicability of a foreign policy principle does not, of course, invalidate its relevance in particular cases. It does, however, require America to understand the relationship between moral principle and day-to-day foreign policy. Moral principles are universal and timeless. Foreign policy is bounded by circumstance; it is, as Bismarck noted, "the art of the possible," "the science of the relative." When moral principles are applied without regard to historical conditions, the result is usually an increase in suffering rather than its amelioration. And if they are applied in light of domestic or international conditions, the desirable is constrained by the concept of national interest, so often castigated by Wilsonians.

Therefore, the limits of humanitarian (or other) intervention are established by the readiness to pay the necessary price, in casualties or in financial sacrifice. A doctrine of intervention, universal or otherwise, can be sustained only if the public is convinced that the interests at stake justify the cost. That was precisely the missing element in all the examples of universal humanitarian intervention of the 1990s, from Somalia through Kosovo. American forces were withdrawn from Somalia as soon as they incurred casualties. And from the beginning of the Kosovo campaign, NATO's leaders (with Prime Minister Tony Blair as the honorable exception) announced that a ground war was not an option—in other words, that no casualties would be risked—tempting Slobodan Milosevic to test his endurance to sustained bombing. The fear of casualties caused even the bombing campaign to be conducted from altitudes thought to be beyond the range of Serbian antiaircraft batteries—at fifteen thousand feet or above—suggesting that, in Kosovo at least, the Western democracies confined their risk-taking on behalf of morality to specific altitudes.

The third proposition is that, to become an organizing principle of the international order, a concept must find some general acceptance in the international community. This is because, almost by definition, international order implies a wide acceptance. Failing that, a principle could still emerge as the ultimate organizing concept, but it would have to do so by way of imposition. This has happened before: some of the universal religions were spread initially by military conquest and became articles of faith only later. And this has been true as well of political outcomes, including the American Civil War.

The various military humanitarian interventions conducted by the United States in the 1990s found varying degrees of international acceptance. The expedition to Somalia was based on a unanimous United Nations Security Council resolution and launched at the direct request of the U.N. Secretary General. It did not, therefore, raise the question of principle as to whether a military solution might be imposed unilaterally or by a group of nations without international sanction. The consensus evaporated as soon as the mission turned from peacekeeping to peacemaking, from supervising what the parties had accepted to imposing an outcome on one or more parties by force.

The humanitarian intervention in Haiti was undertaken as the expression of a new policy meant to demonstrate America's commitment to multilateralism. Thus the Clinton administration persuaded the United Nations to authorize the use of force in restoring civilian government and, two weeks later, on September 19, 1994, sent American troops as part of a U.N. force composed as well of elements from outside the hemisphere.

This multilateral intervention had the paradoxical effect of reversing—at least juridically—America's historic policy toward the Western Hemisphere. From the time of the proclamation of the Monroe Doctrine to the 1947 Rio Treaty setting up a system of collective security for the Western Hemisphere, and in the decades since, every American administration had insisted that hemispheric problems should be settled by the nations of the Americas and, in the extreme, unilaterally by the United States. With respect to

Haiti, the Clinton administration recoiled from involving the institution specifically designed for that purpose—the Organization of American States—as well as from using force unilaterally because the other nations of this hemisphere would not have approved military intervention, though they were prepared to support diplomatic and economic measures.

Since Somalia lay at the fringe of even the broadest definition of concerns for the vast majority of nations and Haiti was within an envelope of traditional American concerns, neither of these ultimately lent themselves to drawing general conclusions about the applicability of the new principles of humanitarian intervention. The situation was, however, different with respect to both Bosnia and Kosovo. These marked disturbances in Europe; the crises occurred on a continent where memories of the Nazi Holocaust were still vivid, and they grew out of the breakup of a country that, during the Cold War, had been under the tacit protection of NATO. A neuralgic reaction by the nations of the Atlantic Alliance to the brutalities of Balkan warfare was inevitable.

But the two cases also differed in substance. Bosnia concerned a civil war in a country that had been formally recognized by the United Nations in the aftermath of the breakup of Yugoslavia. The conflict produced unspeakable atrocities, the majority committed initially by Serbs but, before the conflict was over, Croats—technically on the side of the NATO and U.N. forces—engaged in massive ethnic cleansing of their own. Nor did the Muslims fail to live up to traditional Balkan standards of brutality. The military phase of the NATO humanitarian intervention in Bosnia, occurring as it did at the request of the recognized Bosnian government and under the aegis of the United Nations, raised no new issues of principle and set no new precedent. And there is a level of violence and atrocities so offensive to the American and democratic conscience as to override considerations of the national interest. The difficulties with respect to Bosnia arose not in regard to the intervention but to the political settlement which followed and which I will discuss below.

Whereas Bosnia, historically a buffer between the Austrian and

Ottoman empires and incorporated into the Austrian Empire only in 1908, had never been legally a part of Serbia, Kosovo was the site of a Serbian national shrine. The struggle for Serb independence started there in a disastrous battle with the Ottoman Empire in 1389. Kosovo was not, in fact, wrested from the Ottoman Empire until 1912, and it became an administrative subdivision of Serbia thereafter. Under Ottoman rule before 1912, a minority of Muslims—mostly Albanian—had dominated the Serb majority in Kosovo. When Serbia took over after the Balkan War of 1912, that relationship was reversed, except for the six years of Nazi occupation when the Muslims used the opportunity to exact revenge.

Over the course of the twentieth century, the ethnic composition of Kosovo kept changing until Albanians constituted some 80 percent of the population. The cycle of mutual hatred never disappeared, though President Tito experimented with granting autonomy to Kosovo in 1974. Slobodan Milosevic put an end to this experiment in 1989, the six hundredth anniversary of the fateful Kosovo battle, announcing that he was doing so in order to stop Albanian mistreatment of the Serb population. Whatever the truth of this charge, the ethnic groups in Bosnia and Kosovo stopped oppressing each other only when peace was imposed by outside forces: the Ottoman Empire, the Austrian Empire, or Tito. Today NATO constitutes that force.

The status of Kosovo was juridically different from that of Bosnia. In Bosnia, the civil war was over the allocation of political power within a state in the process of being created, with the possible alternative of its being broken up into three ethnic units. Kosovo, on the other hand, had been recognized internationally as an integral part of the Yugoslav state, and its status had never been challenged. On the eve of NATO military action, President Clinton, in a speech to the Serbian people, reiterated established U.S. policy: "The NATO allies support Kosovo as part of your country." And he added that "the agreement would guarantee the rights of all people in Kosovo—ethnic Serbs and Albanians alike within Kosovo."[33]

What President Clinton was urging the Serbian government to accept in that speech was an extraordinary proposal being made by the NATO foreign ministers that pushed the principle of humanitarian intervention to unprecedented lengths and defined a mission for NATO never previously contemplated. It was, in effect, an ultimatum demanding a NATO protectorate over Kosovo and free passage of NATO troops through Yugoslav territory. The so-called Rambouillet proposals—named after the castle in France where the talks were held, technically under the chairmanship of the French and British foreign ministers but in fact under the aegis of the U.S. Secretary of State—demanded that Kosovo be made autonomous within Yugoslavia under NATO protection, and that the KLA (Kosovo Liberation Army, the Albanian guerrilla force) turn over its arms to NATO forces. NATO was awarded the ultimate security responsibility, backed up by ten thousand Serbian police and fifteen hundred Serbian frontier guards. At the end of three years, an election would determine the future of Kosovo.

The humanitarian impulses motivating the NATO ultimatum deserve respect. But for anyone familiar with Serbian history, the Rambouillet proposals were certain to lead to war. The country that had fought the Ottoman and Austrian empires, often alone, and had fiercely resisted Hitler and Stalin without the help of allies, would never permit transit of foreign troops or turn a province containing its historic shrines over to NATO. Nor was the KLA an ordinary political movement struggling for autonomy. Beginning as disciples of the Albanian hard-line Stalinist ruler, Enver Hoxha, it was described as late as 1998 by Clinton's Special Representative in the Balkans, Ambassador Robert Gelbard, as "without any question a terrorist group."[34] Its goal was an independent Kosovo and perhaps a Greater Albania, including existing Albania and the Albanian part of Macedonia. A pluralistic, multiethnic democracy including Serbs was not a concept comprehensible in the KLA community.

At the time the Rambouillet ultimatum was issued, a civil war was in train that had already generated some three hundred thousand refugees and approximately two thousand casualties, but ethnic cleansing on a systematic scale had not yet begun. The legions of refugees that filled television screens after the NATO bombing started were to a much greater degree the result of NATO's actions than the precipitating cause of them.

And I believe—though, of course, there is no way to prove it—that the desired outcome of an autonomous Kosovo *within* Yugoslavia—the outcome of the Kosovo military operations—could have been achieved at less cost and in a less convulsive fashion.

To be sure, the NATO allies justified their actions by vague and basically inaccurate historical analogies: that the two world wars had their roots in the Balkans, or that the war was really directed against a single Hitler-like figure, Slobodan Milosevic. But the Second World War did not start in the Balkans, and the First resulted from the way the great powers tied themselves to Balkan factions. And Milosevic was a local Balkan thug, no Hitler, who, in the end, was removed by his own people in a domestic upheaval not unlike those that marked the end of all the other Communist autocrats in Central and Eastern Europe.

Despite many reservations, I supported the Kosovo operation after it began in many television appearances because I felt that failure of such a major NATO enterprise would have been the worst possible outcome. But military success did not alter my unease over NATO's decision to demand the dismemberment of a state with which NATO members were still maintaining full diplomatic relations and with which NATO had concluded an agreement on Bosnia only two years previously. The Rambouillet demands had marked a watershed in the history of the Alliance because they amounted to insistence on war by a group of nations that had always justified their union as purely defensive. This was all the more true because NATO had just repeatedly emphasized its own defensive nature in urging Russia to acquiesce in NATO enlargement.

Whatever one's view of the obsolescence of the doctrine of national sovereignty, the combination of flagrant disregard of it by an alliance of democracies and its truculent diplomacy amounted to a departure from the very international norms on which those democracies had insisted throughout the Cold War. As a consequence, a glaring gap opened up between the claims of the various allied leaders extolling their new ethical foreign policy and the reaction of most of the rest of the world. The developing countries generally interpret the doctrine of humanitarian intervention as a device by which the industrial democracies reassert a neocolonialist hegemony. China rejected it for similar reasons. Russia feared giving NATO a blank check for military intervention in Europe; it had historic ties to Serbia.

Perhaps the most interesting reaction has been that of the European allies who, after the first heady proclamations of the new approach, had second thoughts. Having launched themselves into Kosovo as defenders of universal principles, they soon recoiled before their own audacity. European leaders increasingly speak of never again acting without U.N. approval. And since Russia and China have a veto as two permanent members of the Security Council, the doctrine of humanitarian intervention as elaborated over Kosovo has turned into a paradox—a universal principle in search of a consensus.

In these circumstances, the doctrine of universal interventionism may in time redound against the very concept of humanitarianism. Once the doctrine of universal intervention spreads and competing truths begin to fight each other, we may be entering a world in which, to use G. K. Chesterton's phrase, "virtue runs amok."

Humanitarian Intervention and the Context of History

The success of any foreign policy doctrine depends on its relevance to the historical context in which it must be implemented. Of course, there have been upheavals that swept away the historical context in which they occurred. But those episodes are typically prolonged and very violent. Policy should not become a prisoner of the past, but it must make use of the past to seek the maximum improvement attainable without inviting, in the name of reform, even greater suffering and, ultimately, chaos.

The biggest challenge to the American (and lately also to the West European) approach to humanitarian military intervention is that it is put forward as a universal prescription applicable to all situations, without reference to the historical or cultural context. As a result, the various military interventions of the 1990s described in this chapter have generated a debate about so-called exit strategies—which is another way of defining the limits of the universality of the humanitarian interventions.

The George H. W. Bush administration sent troops to Somalia in December 1992 at the explicit request of the U.N. Secretary General, charged by a unanimous vote of the Security Council with "creating the secure environment which is an inescapable condition for the United Nations to provide humanitarian relief and to promote national reconciliation." The motive was humanitarian and Wilsonian; there was no suggestion of any threat to American security. This was a policy with the single laudable objective of easing human suffering. What that original mission did not consider, however, was how the conditions necessitating the sending of troops could ever permit their departure.

Therefore, after President Clinton came into office, the mission was expanded from peacekeeping to peacemaking based on the enforcement authority under Article VIII of the U.N. Charter. This required disarming the contending factions and bringing about, in the words of the relevant Security Council resolution, "the reestablishment of regional institutions and civil administration in the entire country."[35] For the United States, the objective was described by then U.N. Ambassador Madeleine Albright as follows: "We must stay the course and help lift the country and its people from the category of a failed state into that of an emerging democracy."[36]

Unfortunately, the effort to establish a central authority in Somalia, much less a democracy, came up against the historic reality that Somalia was not a country but a collection of warring tribes, half of which had been governed by Italy before independence, the other half by Britain, so that the new country lacked even a common colonial history. Once nation building was added to the agenda, the political objectives of the Somalia intervention required a major and sustained military effort unachievable without the attendant willingness to incur casualties. Washington's obliviousness to the implications of this "mission creep" was demonstrated when the new Clinton administration reduced the number of American troops from twenty-eight thousand to four thousand. As a result of the new mission, a battle took place costing a score of American lives in October 1993. The remaining American forces were abruptly withdrawn, signifying that, while the United States considered the alleviation of human suffering in Somalia worth a financial and economic sacrifice, it was not prepared to expend American lives—the operational definition of the limits of America's humanitarian interest in Somalia.

In Haiti, a similar outcome was avoided only because the American intervention confined itself to peacekeeping and was not used to help shape the political evolution. As a result, Haiti has remained conspicuously autocratic and corrupt, the chief difference being in the shift of power from a rightist to a leftist authoritarian regime without easing the grinding poverty and abject quality of life of the vast majority of the population.

In the Balkans, the gap between American values and historical context proved impossible to bridge. The United States intervened in Bosnia to end the savagery of warfare among the various ethnic groups. When the military intervention succeeded and the Dayton Accords ending the war were negotiated in 1995, the United States faced a choice between two principles which have shaped its foreign policy at least since Wilson: the principle of the inadmissibility of force in bringing about international change, and the principle of self-determination. Multiethnicity required a unified Bosnia composed of Serbs, Croats, and Muslims. Self-determination implied partitioning Bosnia into three ethnic units. The dilemma arose because Bosnia had been an administrative subdivision of multiethnic Yugoslavia but, unlike other units such as Croatia or Slovenia, it was itself a multiethnic entity composed of Croats, Serbs, and Muslims whose hatred for each other had caused the disintegration of the Yugoslav state in the first place.

That this hatred is of long duration is demonstrated in a speech by Prime Minister Benjamin Disraeli (Lord Beaconsfield) to the House of Lords in 1878:

No language can describe adequately the condition of that portion of the Balkan Peninsula—Serbia, Bosnia, Herzegovina. No words can describe the political intrigue, the constant rivalries, a total absence of all public spirit, a hatred of all races, animosities of rival religions, absence of any controlling power. Nothing short of an army of 50,000 of Europe's best troops would produce anything like order in those parts.[37]

The unwillingness of America's leaders to come to grips with the historic context tied them down in the bottomless pit of Balkan passions. In addressing the people of Bosnia, Clinton compared their plight to America's during the Civil War, out of which America had emerged having "learned that there are great benefits which come from finding common ground."[38] The analogy was totally misleading. The American Civil War was fought to the finish; its outcome was not compromise but unconditional surrender.

Bosnian history simply bears no relationship to America's. Throughout their histories, the Serbs and Croats have considered themselves defenders of their religions—Serbian Orthodox and Roman Catholic—first against a Muslim tide, then against each other. And the Muslims are regarded by the two other religious groups as tools of the hated Turks and therefore—since ethnically they belong to the same people—as turncoats. The deep-seated hatred of each party for both the others has endured because their conflict is more akin to the Thirty Years' War than it is to any contemporary political conflict.

In 1991, the George H. W. Bush administration aborted a plan nearly agreed on by all the Bosnian ethnic groups that would have created a loose confederation amounting to virtual partition. In 1993, the new Clinton administration rejected a similar partition plan devised by former Secretary of State Cyrus Vance and former British Foreign Secretary David Owen. In 1994, the Clinton administration, in order to get around the U.N. arms embargo it did not wish to challenge, encouraged the covert sending of arms from Iran to Bosnia, proving that it considered the principle of multiethnicity in Bosnia more important than the strategic objective of resistance to radical-fundamentalist Iran.

In this manner, the United States, at the Dayton negotiations in 1995, drifted toward insisting on a multiethnic, unified Bosnian state despite the fact that, until it was created in 1992, Bosnia had never been an independent state. For at least five hundred years, Bosnia had been a province at the frontier between the Austrian and Ottoman empires. NATO's 1992 recognition of an independent sovereign state of Bosnia inevitably called into being a civil war, not a country. Given that past, insistence on a multiethnic state at the end of the civil war in effect committed NATO to a permanent occupation role to preserve the peace.

Why should a multiethnic state favored by basically only one of the ethnic groups be imposed by outside military force? What American national interest or larger purpose was served by such a policy?

Humanitarian military intervention in Bosnia expressed the refusal of Western democracies to tolerate genocidal ethnic cleansing near their borders in regions with which they had historic ties. But the political outcome of insisting on a multiethnic state that two of the three nationalities involved openly rejected was not dictated by humanitarian principles. It was a political decision based on giving the principle of nonacquisition of territory by force precedence over the principle of self-determination.

The United States has no national interest for which it must either risk lives or deploy forces to bring about a multiethnic state in Bosnia or permit itself to be tied forever to a political quagmire. The creation of a multiethnic state should be left to the parties— welcomed by the United States if it happens but not pursued at the risk of American lives, through American pressure or American military presence. It is not so much a question of military disengagement by the United States as of a political solution that would permit the major disengagement of *all* outside forces—in the context of an international conference described below. The opportunity for such an approach has become greater since the replacement of Milosevic by a new, democratically elected president of Yugoslavia.

The same ambivalence characterized the humanitarian military intervention in Kosovo. On the one hand, NATO leaders did not want to repeat the vacillations which had caused them to procrastinate about intervening in Bosnia. On the other, their humanitarian concerns related to a province they had always recognized as a part of Yugoslavia. They were, in fact, much clearer on what they were seeking to prevent than on what they were seeking to achieve or how.

American involvement in Kosovo began when, in its last weeks in office in December 1992, the George H. W. Bush administration warned Milosevic that, "in the event of conflict in Kosovo caused by Serbian action, the United States will be prepared to employ military force against Serbians in Kosovo and in Serbia proper."[39] That statement, unaccompanied by any definition of what would be treated as unacceptable behavior or how it would be determined which side had caused the conflict, was to involve the United States in Kosovo without advancing a solution or even an idea for one. For the next five years, the Clinton administration and NATO were "talking loudly but carrying a small stick," in the words of British historian Timothy Garton Ash, perhaps the most consistently astute observer of the Balkan crisis.[40]

The combination of massive threats and equivocal action led to a deadlock. The Serbs misjudged both the threshold for NATO reaction as well as allied determination to see any military response through to a conclusion. On the Albanian side, the heretofore widely accepted leader of the Albanian resistance, Ibrahim Rugova—who had consistently practiced a nonviolent approach—was replaced by the KLA, which was determined to use Western human rights concerns to raise the level of violence to the point that would impel NATO intervention. NATO's policy, in short, gave both sides an incentive to pursue the most intransigent course.

When NATO finally intervened, it did so with the same ambivalence that had characterized its previous conduct. The Rambouillet proposals left no choice except military intervention. At the same time, NATO remained sufficiently committed to Westphalian notions of sovereignty to reiterate that it regarded Kosovo as part of Yugoslavia. And it ended the war by enshrining this precise commitment in the U.N. Security Council resolution which ended the war.

In this manner, the realities of the Balkans have imposed themselves on the moral bravado of a "new" diplomacy. For NATO's role in Bosnia and Kosovo after the end of hostilities is comparable to the previous position of the Austrian and Ottoman empires in the region, which managed to impose an armistice on the contending ethnic factions but could never entirely quell their conflicts with each other. NATO is closer to imposing a traditional protectorate in the areas it governs than to implementing a new morality.

The NATO forces are in Kosovo on the basis of a U.N. mandate which, in effect, runs counter to the aspirations of the local Albanian population. The Albanians did not fight for autonomy but for independence and surely not to remain under Yugoslav suzerainty. And they displayed this attitude when they ethnically cleansed over two hundred thousand Serbs from the territory after the NATO victory. What will happen when the post-Milosevic, democratic Yugoslavia, backed by Russia, appeals to the United Nations to adhere to the Security Council resolution to enable Yugoslavia to exercise its residual rights? What will be the American attitude toward Kosovar demands for independence, which are certain to mount? It would be ironic were the United States, having fought a war on behalf of Kosovar autonomy, *now* to resist (or even fight) attempts to achieve Kosovar independence. But the more NATO turns into an occupation force, the more it will find itself a permanent party in a bitter Balkan struggle over issues that seem arcane to the overwhelming majority of Americans and West Europeans.

On the other hand, independence for Kosovo would have a profound impact on all of its neighbors, especially those with large Albanian populations. At least a third of the population of Macedonia is Albanian, and there are significant Albanian minorities in Montenegro and northern Greece. Independence for Kosovo would almost certainly trigger demands for at least autonomy for these minorities—and probably a guerrilla war—especially in Macedonia. In the process, there could well emerge a drive for a Greater Albania, uniting present-day Albania, Kosovo, and whatever Albanian minorities in other countries are able to achieve autonomy. Fulfillment of all the Albanian aspirations will appear to the nations that struggled for independence in the nineteenth and early twentieth centuries as a film played backward, in which a resurgent Islam is reversing the results of their own independence struggles.

The United States and NATO cannot let matters drift indefinitely. A possible way out would be the convening of an international conference including Russia under the auspices of the OSCE (Organization for Security and Cooperation in Europe) to arrive at a political solution for both Bosnia and Kosovo. It would define steps toward independence for Kosovo and settle the Bosnian issue on the basis of self-determination for each ethnic group. The conference would also agree on guarantees for the resulting arrangements.

The United States has come a long way since John Quincy Adams warned against going abroad in search of monsters to destroy. Today America and NATO have emerged as the chief gendarmes of the Balkans. On one level, the growing concern with human rights is one of the achievements of our age and is certainly a testament to progress toward a more humane international order. But its advocates do their cause no favor by pretending that it can be separated from all traditional notions of foreign policy, and that American self-restraint in the pursuit of its historic values was thoughtless or immoral. There is irony in all this when one recalls that, during the Cold War, the Wilsonians had argued that excessive concern with security was leading to strategic overextension and an illusion of American omnipotence. Yet now, in the post–Cold War era, they are urging a global mission for the United States and on behalf of humanitarian and moral values, which risks an even more sweeping overextension.

This reversal of the fronts of the domestic debates of the Vietnam period is, in fact, a reflection of the same misconception that underlay the original debate. As presidential candidate in 1976,

Jimmy Carter frequently cited Vietnam as an example of what happens to a nation when it abandons its values in favor of power politics. In truth, Vietnam proved the exact opposite. The American foreign policy trauma of the 1960s and 1970s occurred not because the United States was too power-oriented but because its values were being implemented too universally; it was not that America focused too much on its national interests but that it had adopted too undiscriminating an identification of its strategic interests with Wilsonian principles.

The dichotomy between power and morality applies to hardly any period of American history. Moral purpose was a key element of the motivation behind every major American policy and every war in the twentieth century—from the "war to end all wars" in 1917, to resisting totalitarian evil in World War II, to the fight against Communist aggression in Korea and Vietnam, and to resistance to the occupations of Iraq and Kuwait by Saddam Hussein. In each case, American presidents proudly affirmed that the United States was serving universal, not selfish, interests—indeed, that the distinguishing aspect of America's involvement was the absence of any distinctly American national interest. Thus the new approach affirms an extension of the reach of American values, not of the significance attached to them.

To treat strategic interests as if they were somehow of a lower order is to paralyze the United States even in pursuit of objectives considered purely moral. Whenever American lives are at stake, so is a conception of American vital interests; otherwise the sacrifice mocks the anguish of bereaved families. Conversely, to go to war without being prepared to incur casualties implies that the issue is ultimately not vital and that America is willing to go only so far in the defense of its principles, inviting the adversary to seek to outlast it. Every war the United States has fought in the last hundred years has had as at least an unstated premise that to recoil from acting would ultimately lead to far greater American sacrifices. In the new century, comparable judgments will have to be made by American presidents on some as yet unforeseeable issues as well as on others discussed in these pages.

Joseph Nye, Jr., in a thoughtful article in *Foreign Affairs*, has advanced four important principles for humanitarian intervention: having a just cause in the eyes of others; proportionality of means to ends; high probability of success; and, wherever possible, reinforcement of the humanitarian cause by the existence of other strong national interests.[41]

When the issues raised by humanitarian intervention are redefined in this spirit, the rhetorical distinction between humanitarian and national interests begins to erode. The challenge to America's leaders and those of the other democracies is to answer questions such as these: Where and for what humanitarian causes will the United States choose to project its military power? What risks is it prepared to run? What price is it prepared to pay? What measures short of force is it prepared to take? And for what period of time?

The new century demands of the United States a new definition of vital interest, strategic as well as moral. The advocates of humanitarian intervention were not wrong to offer one; the question is whether what they have offered takes account of the range and complexity of America's international challenges.

UNIVERSAL JURISDICTION

In less than a decade, an unprecedented concept has emerged to submit international politics to judicial procedures. It has spread with extraordinary speed and has not been subjected to systematic debate, partly because of the intimidating passion of its advocates. To be sure, violations of human rights, war crimes, genocide, and torture have so disgraced the modern age and in such a variety of places that the effort to interpose legal norms to prevent or punish such outrages does credit to its advocates. The danger is that it is being pushed to extremes which risk substituting the tyranny of judges for that of governments; historically, the dictatorship of the virtuous has often led to inquisitions and even witch hunts.

The doctrine of universal jurisdiction asserts that there are crimes so heinous that their perpetrators should not be able to escape justice by invoking doctrines of sovereignty or the sacrosanct nature of national frontiers. Two specific approaches to achieve this goal have emerged recently. The first seeks to apply the procedures of domestic criminal justice to violations of universal standards—as embodied in a number of U.N. conventions—by authorizing national prosecutors to bring offenders into their jurisdictions through extradition procedures. The second approach is the International Criminal Court (ICC), adopted by a conference in Rome in July 1998 and signed by ninety-five states, including most European countries. It has already been ratified by about a dozen nations and will go into effect when a total of sixty have accepted its provisions. On December 31, 2000, President Clinton signed the ICC treaty with only hours to spare before the cutoff date. But he indicated that he would neither submit it for Senate approval nor recommend that his successor do so while the treaty is in its present form.

The very concept of universal jurisdiction is of recent vintage. The sixth edition of *Black's Law Dictionary*, published in 1990, does not contain even an entry for the term. The closest analogous concept listed is *hostes humani generis* ("enemies of the human race"). To date, it has been applied only to pirates because their operations on the high seas were typically beyond the jurisdictions of any state and therefore not subject to any existing criminal justice system.

In the aftermath of the Holocaust and the many atrocities committed since, major efforts have been made to fill this void, among them the Nuremberg trials of 1945–1946, the Universal Declaration of Human Rights of 1948, the genocide conventions of 1948, and the anti-torture convention of 1988. The Final Act of the Conference on Security and Cooperation in Europe, signed in Helsinki in 1975 by President Ford on behalf of the United States, obliged the thirty-five signatory nations to observe certain stated human rights, subjecting those who violated them to the pressures by which foreign policy commitments are generally sustained.

In the hands of courageous groups in Eastern Europe, the Final Act became one of several weapons by which Communist rule was delegitimized and eventually undermined. In the 1990s, international tribunals to punish crimes committed in Yugoslavia and Rwanda, established ad hoc by the United Nations Security Council, have sought to provide a system of accountability for specific regions ravaged by arbitrary violence.

But none of these steps was conceived at the time as instituting a "universal jurisdiction." It is unlikely that any of the signatories of either the United Nations conventions or the Helsinki Final Act thought it possible that national judges would use them as a basis for extradition requests regarding alleged crimes not committed in their jurisdictions. The drafters almost certainly believed that they were stating general principles, not laws that would be enforced by courts other than those of the countries of the victims or the perpetrators. For example, Eleanor Roosevelt, one of the drafters of the Universal Declaration of Human Rights, referred to it as a "common standard." As one of the negotiators of the Final Act of the Helsinki conference, I can affirm that the administration I represented considered it primarily a diplomatic weapon to use against Soviet pressure on their own and captive peoples, not as a legal weapon against individual leaders before courts of countries not their own. It was never argued until very recently that the various U.N. declarations subjected past and future leaders to the possibility of prosecution by national magistrates of third countries without either due process safeguards or institutional restraints.

Yet this is in essence the precedent that was established when, beginning in October 1998, former Chilean President Augusto Pinochet was detained for sixteen and a half months in Britain as the result of an extradition request of a Spanish judge seeking to try him for crimes committed against Spaniards on Chilean soil. For advocates of universal jurisdiction, that detention is a landmark establishing a just principle. But any universal system should contain procedures not only to punish the wicked but to constrain the righteous. It must not allow legal principles to be used as weapons to settle political scores. Questions such as these must therefore be answered: What legal norms are being applied? What are the rules of evidence? What safeguards exist for the defendant? How will prosecutions affect other fundamental foreign policy objectives and interests?

The world should think carefully about the implications of a procedure by which a single judge anywhere is able, essentially at his personal discretion, to assert jurisdiction over a citizen of another state for alleged crimes committed entirely in that other state and to demand extradition of the accused from a third country without regard to the conciliation procedures that might exist in the country of the accused for dealing with the issue.

It is decidedly unfashionable, to say the least, to express any degree of skepticism about the way the Pinochet case was handled. For almost all the parties of the European left, Augusto Pinochet is the incarnation of a right-wing assault on democracy because he led the coup d'état against an elected leader. At the time, others— including the leaders of Chile's democratic parties—viewed Salvador Allende as a radical Marxist ideologue bent on imposing a Castro-style dictatorship with the aid of Cuban-trained militias and Cuban weapons. This was why the leaders of Chile's democratic parties publicly welcomed—yes, welcomed—Allende's overthrow. (They changed their attitude only after the junta maintained autocratic rule far longer than was warranted by the invocation of an emergency.)[42]

Disapproval of the Allende regime does not exonerate the perpetrators of systematic human rights abuses after it was overthrown. But neither should the applicability of universal jurisdiction as a policy be determined by one's view of the political history of Chile. In the event, the Chilean supreme court has found the appropriate solution by withdrawing Pinochet's senatorial immunity. This has made it possible to deal with the charges against him in the courts of the country most competent to judge its own history and to relate its decisions to the stability and vitality of its democratic institutions.

On November 25, 1998, Britain's House of Lords concluded that "international law has made it plain that certain types of conduct . . . are not acceptable conduct on the part of anyone."[43] But that principle did not necessarily oblige the House of Lords to confer on a Spanish magistrate the right to enforce it in a third country. It could have held that Chile or an international tribunal specifically established for crimes committed in Chile on the model of the courts set up for crimes in Yugoslavia and Rwanda were the appropriate forum. The unprecedented and sweeping interpretation of international law in *Ex parte Pinochet* would arm any magistrate, anywhere in the world, with the unilateral power to invoke a supranational concept of justice; to substitute his own judgment for the reconciliation procedures of even incontestably democratic societies where the alleged violations of human rights occurred; and to subject the accused to the criminal procedures of the magistrate's country, with whose legal system the defendant may be unfamiliar and which forces him to bring evidence and witnesses from long distances. Such a system goes far beyond the explicit and limited mandates established by the United Nations Security Council for the tribunals covering war crimes in Yugoslavia and Rwanda as well as the one being negotiated for Cambodia.

Perhaps the most important issue is the relationship of universal jurisdiction to national reconciliation procedures set up by new democratic governments to deal with their countries' questionable pasts. One would have thought that a Spanish magistrate would have been sensitive to the incongruity of a request by Spain, itself haunted by transgressions during the Spanish Civil War and the Franco period, to try in Spanish courts alleged crimes against humanity committed elsewhere.

The decision of post-Franco Spain to avoid wholesale criminal trials on the human rights violations of the recent past was designed explicitly to foster a process of national reconciliation which undoubtedly contributed much to promote the present vigor of Spanish democracy. Why should Chile's attempt at national reconciliation not have been given the same opportunity? Should any outside group dissatisfied with the reconciliation procedures of, say, South Africa be free to challenge them in their own national courts or those of third countries?

It is an important principle that those who commit war crimes or systematically violate human rights should be held accountable. But the consolidation of law, domestic peace, and representative government in a nation struggling to come to terms with a brutal past has a claim as well. The instinct to punish must be related, as in every constitutional democratic political structure, to a system of checks and balances that includes other elements critical to the survival and expansion of democracy.

Another grave issue is the use of extradition procedures designed for ordinary criminals. If the Pinochet case becomes a precedent, magistrates anywhere will be in a position to put forward an extradition request without warning to the accused and regardless of the policies the accused's country might already have in place for dealing with the charges. The country from which extradition is requested then faces a seemingly technical legal decision which, in fact, amounts to the exercise of political discretion—whether to entertain the claim or not. Once extradition procedures are in train, they develop a momentum of their own. The accused is not allowed to challenge the substantive merit of the case and must confine himself to procedural issues: that there was, say, some technical flaw in the extradition request; that the judicial system of the requesting country is incapable of providing a fair hearing; or that the crime for which the extradition is sought is not treated as a crime in the country from which extradition has been requested—thereby conceding much of the merit of the charge. Meanwhile, while these claims are being considered, the accused remains in some form of detention, possibly for years. Such procedures provide an opportunity for political harassment long before the accused is in a position to present his defense. It would be ironic if a doctrine designed to transcend the political process turns into a means to pursue political enemies rather than universal justice.

The Pinochet precedent, if literally applied, would permit the two sides in the Arab-Israeli conflict, or those in any other passionate international controversy, to project their battles into the various national courts by pursuing adversaries with extradition requests.[44] When discretion on what crimes are subject to universal jurisdiction and whom to prosecute is left to national prosecutors, the scope for arbitrariness is wide indeed. So far universal jurisdiction has involved the prosecution of one fashionably reviled man of the right while scores of East European Communist leaders—not to speak of Caribbean, Middle Eastern, or African leaders who had inflicted their own full measures of torture and suffering—have not been obliged to face similar prosecutions.

It will be argued that a double standard does not excuse violations of international law and that it is better to bring one malefactor to justice than to grant immunity to all. This is not a principle permitted in the domestic jurisdictions of many democracies—in Canada, for example, a charge can be thrown out of court merely by showing that a prosecution has been selective enough to amount to an abuse of process. In any case, a universal standard of justice should not be based on the proposition that a just end justifies unjust means, or that political fashion trumps fair judicial procedures.

The ideological supporters of universal jurisdiction also provide much of the intellectual compass for the emerging International Criminal Court. Their goal is to criminalize certain types of military and political actions and thereby bring about a change to a more humane conduct of international relations. To the extent that the ICC replaces the claim of national judges to universal jurisdiction, it greatly improves the state of international law. And, in time, it may be possible to negotiate modifications of the present statute to make the ICC more compatible with American constitutional practice. But in its present form of assigning the ultimate dilemmas of international politics to unelected jurists—and to an international judiciary at that—it represents such a fundamental change in American constitutional practice that a full national debate and the full participation of Congress are imperative. Such a momentous revolution should not come about by tacit acquiescence in the decision of the House of Lords or by dealing with the ICC issue with a strategy of improving specific clauses rather than as a fundamental issue of principle.

The doctrine of universal jurisdiction is based on the proposition that the individuals or cases subject to it have been clearly identified. In some instances, especially those based on Nuremberg precedents, the definition is self-evident. But many issues are much more vague and depend on an understanding of the historical and political context. It is this fuzziness which risks arbitrariness on the part of prosecutors and judges years after the event and which became apparent with respect to existing tribunals. For example, can any leader of the United States or of other countries be hauled before international tribunals established for other purposes? This is precisely what Amnesty International implies when, in the summer of 1999, it supported a "complaint" by a group of European and Canadian law professors to Louise Arbour, then the prosecutor of the International Criminal Tribunal for the Former Yugoslavia (ICTY), alleging that crimes against humanity had been committed during the NATO air campaign in Kosovo. Arbour ordered an internal staff review, thereby implying that she did have jurisdiction if such violations could, in fact, be demonstrated. Her successor, Carla Del Ponte, in the end declined to indict any NATO official because of a general inability "to pinpoint individual responsibilities"—thereby once again implying that the court had jurisdiction over NATO and American leaders in the Balkans and would have issued an indictment had it been able to identify the particular leaders allegedly involved.[45]

Most Americans would be amazed to learn that the ICTY, created at American behest in 1993 to deal with Balkan war criminals, asserts a right to investigate America's political and military leaders for allegedly criminal conduct—and for the indefinite future, since no statute of limitations applies. Though the ICTY prosecutor chose not to pursue the charge—on the ambiguous ground of an inability to collect evidence—some national prosecutor may wish later to take up the matter as a valid subject for universal jurisdiction.

The pressures to achieve the widest scope for the doctrine of universal jurisdiction were demonstrated as well by a suit before the European Court of Human Rights in June 2000 by families of Argentine sailors who died in the sinking of the Argentine cruiser *General Belgano* during the Falklands war.[46] The concept of universal jurisdiction has moved from judging alleged political crimes against humanity to second-guessing, eighteen years after the event, military operations in which neither civilians nor civilian targets were involved.

Distrusting national governments, many of the advocates of universal jurisdiction seek to place governments under the supervision of magistrates and the judicial system. But the prosecutor's discretion without accountability is precisely one of the flaws of the International Criminal Court. Definitions of the relevant crimes are vague and highly susceptible to politicized application. Defendants will not enjoy due process as understood in the United States. Any signatory state has the right to trigger an investigation. As the experience of the American special prosecutor shows, such a procedure is likely to develop its own momentum without time limits and can turn into an instrument of political warfare. And the extraordinary attempt of the ICC to assert jurisdiction over Americans even in the absence of America's accession to the treaty has already triggered legislation in Congress to resist it.

The independent prosecutor of the ICC has the power to issue indictments, subject only to review by a panel of three judges. According to the Rome statute, the United Nations Security Council has the right to quash any indictment. But since revoking an indictment is subject to the veto of any permanent member, and since the prosecutor is unlikely to issue an indictment without the backing of at least one permanent member of the Security Council, he or she has virtually unlimited discretion in practice. Another provision permits the country whose citizen is accused to take over the investigation and trial. But the ICC retains the ultimate authority on whether that function has been adequately exercised and, if it finds it has not, the ICC can reassert jurisdiction. While these procedures are taking place, which may take years, the accused will be under some restraint and certainly under new public shadow.

The advocates of universal jurisdiction argue that the state is the basic cause of war and cannot be trusted to deliver justice. If law replaced politics, peace and justice would prevail. But even a cursory examination of history shows that there is no evidence to support such a theory. The role of the statesman is to choose the best option when seeking to advance peace and justice, realizing that there is frequently a tension between the two and that any reconciliation is likely to be partial. The choice, however, is not simply between universal and national jurisdictions. The precedents set by international tribunals established to deal with situations where the enormity of the crime is evident and the local judicial system is clearly incapable of administering justice, as in Yugoslavia and Rwanda, have shown that it is possible to punish without removing from the process all political judgment and experience. In time, it may be possible to renegotiate the ICC statute to avoid its shortcomings and dangers. Until then, the United States should go no further toward a more formal system than one containing the following provisions:

• The U.N. Security Council would create a Human Rights Commission or a special subcommittee to report whenever systematic human rights violations seem to warrant judicial action.

• When the government under which the alleged crime occurred is not authentically representative, or where the domestic judicial system is incapable of sitting in judgment on the crime, the Security Council would set up an ad hoc international tribunal on the model of those of Yugoslavia or Rwanda.

• The procedures for these international tribunals as well as the scope of the prosecution should be precisely defined by the Security Council, and the accused should be entitled to the due process safeguards accorded in common law jurisdictions.

In this manner, internationally agreed procedures to deal with war crimes, genocide, or crimes against humanity could become institutionalized. On the other hand, the one-sidedness of the current pursuit of universal jurisdiction would be avoided. For this could threaten the very purpose for which the concept has been developed. In the end, an excessive reliance on universal jurisdiction may undermine the political will to sustain the humane norms of international behavior so necessary to temper the violent times in which we live.

Conclusion

When a society faces challenges as complex as those before the United States, it is often said to be at a "turning point." But it is not only the challenges which are unique; equally unprecedented is the definition of what constitutes a turning point. Historically, the term has been attached to a specific set of options, the choice then determining the direction of future policy.

At the beginning of a new century and of a new millennium, the United States will not discover any panacea. Less in need of a specific policy than of a long-range concept, America is obliged for the first time to devise a global strategy stretching into the indefinite future. Fate has propelled a nation convinced of the universal applicability of a single set of maxims into a world characterized by a multiplicity of historical evolutions requiring selective strategies.

America's success in such a world will be measured by a gradual amelioration of a wide variety of political, economic, strategic, and social problems. The fewest of them are susceptible to final solutions; each resonates to a different, perhaps unique, historical rhythm. The American role will prove central to the resolution of many of these, but the United States will drain its psychological and material resources if it does not learn to distinguish between what it must do, what it would like to do, and what is beyond its capacities. It must forge this balance at a moment when not only the objective circumstances affecting foreign policy are in flux but the very way in which knowledge is acquired and perceptions are being formed is changing as well.

It is commonplace to describe the information age as one of the great intellectual revolutions of history—probably the greatest— and to focus on its social, economic, and political ramifications. How it affects the conduct of international relations is rarely discussed except in terms of the global reach of modern communications—the effect, that is, of sheer numbers and the speed of transmission. But what shapes the conduct of international relations and therefore the course of history is not only the number of people with access to information; it is, even more importantly, how they analyze it. Since the mass of information available tends to exceed the capacity to evaluate it, a gap has opened up between information and knowledge and, even beyond that, between knowledge and wisdom.

No previous generation imagined the range of information available today, much less having immediate access to it in the almost mechanical manner of operating a keyboard. The closest analogy to the impact of the contemporary communications revolution is the invention of printing. Before printing, knowledge depended on memory or on methods of storage so complicated as to preclude widespread availability. Printing vastly expanded the amount of information that could be stored and transmitted. But books are very cumbersome repositories compared to electronic databases, and their content has to be collated through time-consuming indexing devices. Acquisition of knowledge through books, therefore, required concepts whose function it is to relate individual items of information to one another and to group comparable events into categories. Reading also produced an emphasis on style designed to facilitate the task by making it an aesthetic pleasure.

Despite all its limitations—with which, of course, our age is more familiar than were the contemporaries—the invention of printing brought with it a vast revolution in religious, philosophical, and political thought. It made possible the proliferation of knowledge, providing the means by which scientific information became generally available. The monopoly of information enjoyed by the church disintegrated. Printing created the conditions for the breakup of the Universal Church, produced the nation-state, spawned rationalism, and ushered in the age of science and discovery. It also led to two centuries of upheaval as these changes were being absorbed into human consciousness and into political and religious institutions.

Our age is at the beginning of intellectual and political transformations likely to prove more sweeping than those produced by the invention of printing and certain to evolve more rapidly. Meanwhile, the question arises of whether the new ways of processing information may not actually inhibit our capacity to learn in the field of international relations. For while the technological revolution provides extraordinary tools for the ordering of information, the successful conduct of foreign policy demands, above all, the intuitive ability to sense the future and thereby to master it. Leadership is the art of bridging the gap between experience and vision.

This is why most great statesmen were less distinguished by their detailed knowledge (though a certain minimum is indispensable) than by their instinctive grasp of historical currents, by an ability to discern amidst the myriad of impressions that impinge on consciousness those most likely to shape the future. This caused that ultimate "realist" Otto von Bismarck to sum up his vision of statesmanship in a reverential statement:

> The best a statesman can do is to listen to the footsteps of God, get hold of the hem of His cloak, and walk with Him a few steps of the way.[1]

Few modern idealists would speak of their purpose in such unassuming ways, and "realists" would reject the invocation of the divine. Little in the era of instantaneous communications encourages this sort of humility. The study of history and philosophy, the disciplines most relevant to perfecting the art of statesmanship, are neglected everywhere or given such utilitarian interpretations that they can be enlisted in support of whatever passes for conventional wisdom. Leaders rise to eminence by exploiting and manipulating the mood of the moment. They define their aims by consulting focus groups rather than following their own perceptions. They view the future as a projection forward of the familiar.

The computer has solved the problem of storing knowledge and making a vast amount of data available. Simultaneously it exacts the price of shrinking perspective—especially in dealing with foreign policy problems. Policymakers are tempted to wait on events and to be distracted by their echo in the media. Indeed, they have few other criteria by which to judge their performance. In the process, a view of the future is too often submerged in tactics. The problem is not the inadequacy of individual leaders but rather the systemic problem of their cultural preparation. The educational challenge to the United States is how to graduate the computer age from the processing of information to the fostering of a vision of our society's destiny.

The ultimate dilemma of the statesman is to strike a balance between values and interests and, occasionally, between peace and justice. The dichotomy postulated by many between morality and interest, between idealism and realism, is one of the standard clichés of the ongoing debate over international affairs. No such stark choice is, in fact, available. Excessive "realism" produces stagnation; excessive "idealism" leads to crusades and eventual disillusionment.

This is because the pursuit of moral ends in international affairs has a different context from that in domestic politics. Successful foreign policy requires the management of nuances in a continuous process; domestic politics is about marshaling interests and passing laws which are subsequently enforced by an accepted judicial system. In diplomacy, morality expresses itself in the willingness to persevere through a series of steps, each of which is inevitably incomplete in terms of the ultimate goal. Domestic politics measures its achievements in shorter time frames and in more absolute terms.

What it comes down to, in the end, is how the United States perceives itself. Though it rejects imperial pretensions and has no imperial structure, it is, for all its protestations of goodwill, perceived in many parts of the world as peremptory and domineering—imperial, in fact. America's ascendancy is prompting responses ranging from the European Union to the Russo-Chinese "strategic partnership," to Mercosur in Latin America, to the incipient Asian free trade zone, to the drive to build up the authority of the United Nations Security Council—all designed to reclaim greater freedom of action vis-à-vis the United States or, at a minimum, to limit American freedom of action.

To some extent, these reactions are the inevitable result of America's unique position as the sole remaining superpower and would exist no matter how the United States conducts its diplomacy. Dominant power evokes nearly automatically a quest by other societies to achieve a greater voice over their decisions and to reduce the relative position of the strongest. But even if these various groupings are conceived as the inevitable building blocks of an emerging new international order, the future shape of the world depends on whether they find their identity compatible with cooperation with the United States or in reflexive opposition to it.

Some Americans, exulting in their country's power, urge the explicit affirmation of a benevolent American hegemony.[2] But such an aspiration would impose on the United States a burden no society has ever managed successfully for an indefinite period of time. No matter how selfless America perceives its aims, an explicit insistence on predominance would gradually unite the world against the United States and force it into impositions that would eventually leave it isolated and drained.

The road to empire leads to domestic decay because, in time, the claims of omnipotence erode domestic restraints. No empire has avoided the road to Caesarism unless, like the British Empire, it devolved its power before this process could develop. In long-lasting empires, every problem turns into a domestic issue because the outside world no longer provides a counterweight. And as challenges grow more diffuse and increasingly remote from the historic domestic base, internal struggles become ever more bitter and in time violent. A deliberate quest for hegemony is the surest way to destroy the values that made the United States great.

American preeminence is a fact of life for the near- and almost certainly the mid-term future. The way the United States handles it will determine what kind of long-term-future emerges. President George W. Bush is wise in calling for a measure of humility for America. The Australian scholar Coral Bell has brilliantly described America's challenge: to recognize its own preeminence but to conduct its policy as if it were still living in a world of many centers of power.[3] In such a world, the United States will find partners not only for sharing the psychological burdens of leadership but also for shaping an international order consistent with freedom and democracy.

While traditional patterns are in transition and the very basis of experience and knowledge is being revolutionized, America's ultimate challenge is to transform its power into moral consensus, promoting its values not by imposition but by their willing acceptance in a world that, for all its seeming resistance, desperately needs enlightened leadership.

Afterword

The New Challenge of Terrorism

The seminal event since this book was written was the terrorist attack on the United States on September 11, 2001. It was a wrenching human tragedy, but it also marked a turning point, separating surface phenomena from underlying trends, forcing the discarding of the fashionable and self-indulgent and demanding a vision of the future.

For a decade, the democracies had progressively fallen prey to the illusion that threats from abroad had virtually disappeared; that dangers, if any, were primarily psychological or sociological in origin; that, in a sense, history itself as heretofore recorded had been transformed into a subdivision of economics or psychiatry.

Although America had experienced terrorism, it was generally aimed at U.S. installations abroad; the impact was largely symbolic, and stopped well short of threatening lives and civil society within the United States.

Before September 11, America's response had been condemnation, one or two retaliatory raids, and criminal prosecution of such perpetrators as could be found. But the attacks on the World Trade Center and the Pentagon went beyond symbolic pinpricks; they were a fundamental challenge to U.S. civil society and security, and to civil society everywhere. The target was the morale and way of life of the civilian population. That is why President George W. Bush, supported by an overwhelming national consensus, defined the challenge from its very beginning as a war. And in a war, it is not enough to endure—it is essential to prevail.

At the same time, the disaster taught America that some of the comfortable assumptions of the globalized world do not apply to that portion of it which resorts to terrorism. That segment seems motivated by a hatred of Western values so deep that its representatives are prepared to face death and inflict vast suffering on innocents in pursuit of the destruction of our societies, in the name of what is perceived by them as a clash of incompatible values.

As these realities penetrated the consciousness of the democratic world, the terrorists lost an important battle at the very beginning. In America, they faced a united people determined to eradicate the evil of terrorism. Within the Western alliance, they ended—at least for a time—the debate about whether there still existed a common purpose in the post-Cold War world. The Western democracies—at least in their first reaction—became aware that the assault on the United States demonstrated as well the perhaps even greater vulnerabilities of their own societies.

In the "coalition diplomacy" that followed, it became clear that the major countries of Europe preferred direct contact with Washington over a mediating role by the institutions of a unified Europe. If Europe did not want to become marginalized, a return to alliance diplomacy needed to take precedence over the emphasis on Europe's distinctiveness from the United States. On the issue of terrorism, European institutions took second place to the more traditional relationship between the nations of the North Atlantic. In the first reaction to the attack on the United States, Europe's leaders understood that their influence on the new diplomacy and strategy depended far more on cooperation with Washington than on challenging American policies—a task eased by the coalition diplomacy of the Bush administration.

This coalition diplomacy did not imply American hostility to an independent European identity. On the contrary, the new Atlantic diplomacy has created a basis for a more constructive relationship between America and Europe. Recognizing that European institutions are not yet ready to play a global strategic role, Europe's leaders used national policies to stress the underlying unity of purpose and values between Europe and the United States on the issue of terrorism, but, in the process, they created the basis on which the next stage of European integration can take place in a much more constructive atmosphere.

British Prime Minister Tony Blair took the lead in creating the moral and political framework for Atlantic cooperation regarding terrorism. But it is also clear that he had more long-range objectives: to demonstrate to the United States the underlying British perception of Atlantic unity and to use the impact of these policies on Washington to participate in the latest stage of European integration. German Chancellor Gerhard Schröder adopted a parallel policy. In the new atmosphere in which Europe volunteered a military participation, occasionally beyond what the United States might have requested or would immediately use, the trans-Atlantic relationship was given a new and more constructive direction—at least during the first phase of the antiterrorism campaign. This is why the NATO allies immediately applied Article 5 of the NATO treaty calling for collective self-defense—a clause that had never been invoked in the fifty years of NATO's existence.

Our Asian allies, Japan and Korea, being democratic and industrialized, rallied with comparable decisiveness and promptness.

But the coalition extended far beyond the Cold War framework. India, profoundly threatened should Islamic fundamentalism spread to its Muslim population, which makes it the second largest Muslim country in the world, has much to lose by not adopting a common course with the United States. Due to the contiguous Islamic southern regions, Russia perceives a shared interest, as does China with respect to its western regions. China had the added incentive to bring an end to global terrorism well before the 2008

Olympics in Beijing. Paradoxically, terrorism evoked a sense of world community that has eluded advocates for world order when that was based on a mere philosophical concept.

In the Islamic world, attitudes were, of course, more ambiguous. Many secular Islamic nations, though deeply concerned about fundamentalism, were constrained by public opinion from avowing their support of the United States, and a few probably even sympathized with aspects of the terrorist agenda. An understanding American attitude toward traditional friends of the United States and the West, such as Saudi Arabia and Egypt, helped to broaden the coalition in the Arabic world.

In building this coalition, the Bush administration, in the direct aftermath of the attacks on American soil, resisted arguments urging immediate military action against known terrorist centers. Instead, Secretary of State Colin Powell very skillfully brought about a global coalition that legitimized the use of military power against Afghanistan, the most flagrant provider of a safe haven for the most egregious symbol of international terrorism, Osama bin Laden. The objective was defined as the destruction of state-supported terrorism. And for all its novelty, the new warfare permitted a clear definition of the strategic objective.

The terrorists are ruthless but not numerous. They control no territory permanently. If their activities are harassed by the security forces and administrative organs of all their potential victims—if no country will harbor them—they will become outlaws, increasingly obliged to devote their efforts to their own survival. If they attempt to commandeer a part of a country, as happened to some extent in Afghanistan, they can be defeated by military operations. The key to antiterrorism strategy, therefore, is to eliminate safe havens.

These safe havens come about in various ways. In some countries, domestic legislation or constitutional restraints inhibit action unless there are demonstrated criminal acts, or they prevent transmitting what is ostensibly domestic intelligence to other countries—as was the case in Germany and, to some extent, the United States. Remedial measures with respect to these situations were taken in the aftermath of the September 11 attacks.

But the overwhelming majority of safe havens occur where a government closes its eyes because it sympathizes with at least some of the objectives of the terrorists—as in Afghanistan, Yemen, and Somalia, and to some extent Iran and Syria, and, until it changed course, Pakistan, which had originally supported the Taliban. Even ostensibly friendly countries that have been cooperating with the United States on general strategy, such as Saudi Arabia, made a tacit bargain with terrorists, so long as terrorist actions were not directed against the host government.

The antiterrorism coalition brought together by the United States sought to break this connection. Many of the host governments knew more than they were prepared to communicate before September 11. Incentives were created for the sharing of intelligence. Security cooperation was improved, designed to interrupt the flow of funds, harass terrorist communications, and subject the countries that provide safe havens to pressures, including, in the extreme case, military pressure.

Though the elimination of bin Laden and his network and associates as a unified force was a significant achievement, it was only the opening engagement of a continuing worldwide campaign.

THE ATLANTIC ALLIANCE AND IRAQ

When the target of the American effort went beyond the destruction of identified terrorist groups in a particular country to the elimination of the capacity to distribute weapons of mass destruction, the coalition consensus began to weaken and, in some respects, to disintegrate. Within months of near unanimity with respect to the Afghan operation, a presidential call to arms evoked an unprecedented degree of acrimony. Remarkably little of the avalanche of disapproval of President Bush's "axis of evil" comment in his January 29, 2002, State of the Union address, referring to North Korea, Iran, and Iraq, and their possession of weapons of mass destruction, addressed the substance; the focus of criticism was on his motives: the imminent congressional election (this from the British Foreign Secretary); American imperialism (the European Commission foreign policy head); simplistic thinking (the French Foreign Minister); the trend toward American isolationism and hegemonism (leading German newspapers).

Yet President Bush had raised an issue central to international security: the nexus between large, well-organized and deadly terrorist organizations (such as al Qaeda), states that have used and supported terrorism (such as Iran and North Korea), and states that have developed (and, in the case of Iraq, used) weapons of mass destruction. Until September 11, the United States and its allies withheld military action until after terrorist attacks had, in fact, occurred; constraint was sought via the same principle of deterrence that was applied to weapons of mass destruction in the hands of the major powers: the expectation that rational leaders would avoid actions leading to their own destruction. But when such weapons are within reach of leaders not constrained by domestic institutions or public opinion, that have employed them against their neighbors and their own people (as has Iraq), that at times have made systematic assassination part of their policy and where hundreds of thousands have been sacrificed to death by starvation (as in North Korea), or that have backed virulent terrorist groups and hostage-takers (as in Iran), and if attacks are made by suicide bombers, these constraints may not operate any longer. Especially where covert use and linkage to terrorists are always possible, preventive action must be considered.

Obviously the three nations cited by President Bush need to be dealt with by methods appropriate to their special situations. Iraq poses the most urgent challenge; Iran will require the most sophisticated policy; North Korea is comparable to Iraq domestically but, in recent years, has occasionally seemed to grope for a new approach. The scope for diplomacy is smallest with respect to Iraq, greatest, one hopes, with respect to Iran. This is why both the President and Secretary of State Colin Powell indicated there was no intention to deal with Iran and North Korea by military means. But, in the end, the test of any policy will be the degree to which the risk to global security inherent in the possession of weapons of mass destruction by dangerous regimes is brought under control.

The Atlantic Alliance, which has been the keystone of the foreign policy of its members for a generation, cannot avoid this issue any longer. On one level, the controversy reflects fundamental differences in historical experience. America has never—at least since the War of 1812—experienced a direct threat on its soil. European countries—with perhaps the exception of Britain—have been periodically devastated by neighbors for 1,000 years. September 11 was therefore a far greater shock to American public opinion than to European. Americans have traditionally sought to overcome a challenge, once it was recognized, in a conclusive manner; European societies have rarely had the resources to do so and have a predisposition, honed by history, to seek to *manage* problems, rather than to solve them.

Another reason for the acrimony so soon after a seeming restoration of allied unity lies in European domestic politics. President Bush's intellectual convictions were shaped by the conservative side of the American political spectrum, and he was elected by espousing its principles. In foreign policy, this translated into a firm commitment to the nation's security, the nurturing of established links with traditional allies, and an emphasis on the national interest, which has been interpreted by some as a move toward unilateralism.

By contrast, the center-left European governments, having moved toward market-oriented policies in domestic affairs, are under pressure from their left wings to maintain familiar leftist principles, at least in foreign policy. These include opposition to any modification in the established nuclear balance (except to reduce its size), suspicion of American military expenditures and purposes, the erosion of European security budgets, and emphasis on the so-called "soft" issues, such as the environment.

The formative political experience of the European leaders was in the anti-Vietnam protests of the 1970s and the antimissile demonstrations of the 1980s, that of the key members of the American administration in the Reagan-era rejection of those attitudes. Clashing perceptions were therefore inevitable.

Generational change is a contributing factor to the acrimony developing so soon after extraordinary solidarity. The Atlantic Alliance's first generation of European leaders, though they led countries weakened and impoverished by the war, had their formative experience when Europe was the center of world affairs. They understood that their ultimate choice was between the alliance or a kind of neutralism. No such consensus as to the danger exists today. Hence attacks on America as violence-prone, unilateralist, and emotionally unbalanced—the slogans of the opposition during the Cold War—have become the standard fare of intellectuals and the media, feebly resisted, if at all, by governments. The most favorable media comment about the United States tends to urge governments to base their policy on "encouraging" moderate members of the Bush administration presumed to be sympathetic, as if it were a revolutionary government in danger of veering out of control.

This trend has been reinforced because for European governments, the dominant foreign policy concern for more than a decade has been the creation of the European Union—a historic task from which the United States is, by definition, excluded. And for many European leaders, European identity has come to be sought in distinction from and, not infrequently, in opposition to the United States. Europe is concentrating on the legalistic, bureaucratic, and constitutional arrangements involved in integrating more than twenty nations with vastly differing histories, languages, and, occasionally, cultures, while the United States celebrates the exceptional nature of its established institutions and declares them relevant to the rest of the world.

The vast gap in military power between Europe and the United States compounds the difference in their perspectives. There is no precedent for the military dominance that the United States has achieved over the rest of the world. There does not exist now—nor will there for the foreseeable future—any country or group of countries capable of posing a military challenge to the United States. This situation tempts adversaries to challenge the United States on a level beyond the conventional, such as by terrorism. Some friendly nations fear that the United States, being able to impose its preferences, will do so in every situation by the naked exercise of power. And occasional gloating by Americans over their single superpower status and American hegemony reinforces those tendencies.

Differences are inevitable. But they should challenge leaders on both sides of the Atlantic to remember the importance of the continued partnership of all democracies in a world of increasing turmoil. The United States owes its coalition partners some warning of the military options it is considering and of the political outcome it is seeking. Allied leaders, if they want to preserve an essential traditional relationship, need to counter the caricature of America as a trigger-happy, domineering colossus. They know—or should know—that thoughtful American leaders recognize that the forcible imposition of an international order is against the character of a nation in which a dominant historical theme has been anti-imperialism and in which an isolationist streak is ever present. Nor can it be in America's long-term interest to turn every issue into a test of strength, for such a course would create incentives for other countries to unite against America—and history shows that empires usually collapse from within when every issue has become domestic, and psychological and physical exhaustion sets in.

The United States has put forward a definition of the dangers posed by Iraq and similar countries: the possession of weapons of mass destruction by governments that have demonstrated their willingness to use them, have professed hostility toward America or its allies, and are not restrained by domestic institutions. Do our allies reject the American definition of the danger? Or do they accept it but reject the military means for dealing with it? And if the military means are rejected, what is the alternative? If "engagement" is defined in psychological terms—the pacification of the adversary—it becomes a synonym for traditional appeasement. What changes has "engagement" achieved in Iraq? What benefits did the British Foreign Secretary's visit to Tehran bring Britain? And in what way did the obsequious mission to Pyongyang of a delegation from the European Union—a gesture of dissociation from statements by Bush that were considered too insistent in Europe—ameliorate Pyongyang's conduct either toward Seoul or the rest of the world?

America's critics generally advance nation-building as an alternative to America's alleged obsession with military means. Even granting this premise, the most sweeping policy of nation-building and alleviation of poverty would still require a time scale irrelevant to the immediate problem of terrorism and of the present weapons of mass destruction in the possession of potential terrorist states. Indeed, a case can be made for the proposition that nation-building becomes relevant only *after* the change of a terrorist regime, such as with the Taliban and probably Iraq, and is either impossible or counterproductive before then.

The principal concrete alternative put forward to the Bush administration's approach—especially with respect to Iraq—is for an inspection scheme to discover weapons of mass destruction. But no scheme now on the table has even remotely remedied the failure of previous inspection regimes that failed to uncover Iraq's nuclear weapons program before the Gulf war and afterward was unable to find most of Iraq's biological-weapons facilities.

All this has elevated the problem of Iraq to a high priority. The issue is essentially geopolitical. Iraq's policy is implacably hostile to the United States. It possesses growing stockpiles of biological and chemical weapons, which Saddam Hussein has used in the war against Iran and on his own population. It is working to develop a nuclear capability. If these capabilities remain intact, they could in time be used for terrorist acts or to stoke some new regional or international upheaval.

But if the overthrow of Saddam Hussein is to be seriously considered, three prerequisites must be met: (a) development of a military plan that is quick and decisive, (b) some prior agreement on what kind of political structure is to replace Hussein, and (c) the support or acquiescence of the key countries needed for implementation of the military plan.

A military operation against Saddam Hussein cannot be long and drawn out. If it is, the battle may turn into a struggle of the West against Islam. It would also enable Hussein to try to involve Israel by launching attacks on it—perhaps using chemical and biological weapons—in the process sowing confusion within the Muslim world. A long war would also make it more difficult to keep allies and countries such as Russia and China from dissociating formally from what they are unlikely to join but equally unlikely to strenuously oppose.

Before proceeding to a confrontation with Iraq, the Bush administration will therefore wish to examine with great care the military strategy involved. Forces of the magnitude of the Gulf War of a decade ago are unlikely to be needed. At the same time, it would be dangerous to rely on a combination of U.S. airpower and indigenous opposition alone. To be sure, the contemporary precision weaponry was not available in the presently existing quantities during the Gulf War, and the no-fly zones will complicate Iraqi troop movements. They could be strengthened by being turned into no-movement zones, proscribing the movement of particular categories of weapons.

Still, we cannot stake American national security entirely, or even largely, on local opposition forces that do not yet exist and whose combat capabilities are untested. Perhaps Iraqi forces would collapse at the first confrontation, as some argue, but the likelihood of this happening is greatly increased if it is clear American military power is available in overwhelming force.

A second prerequisite for a military campaign against Iraq is to define the political outcome. Local opposition would in all likelihood be sustained by the Kurdish minority in the north and the Shiite minority in the south. But if we are to enlist the Sunni majority, which now dominates Iraq, in the overthrow of Saddam Hussein, we need to make clear that Iraq's disintegration is not the goal of American policy. This is all the more important because a military operation in Iraq would require the support of Turkey and the acquiescence of Saudi Arabia and the Gulf states. None of them is likely to cooperate if they foresee an independent Kurdish state in the north and a Shiite republic in the south as the probable outcome. A Kurdish state would inflame the Kurdish minority in Turkey, and a Shiite state in the south would threaten the Dhahran region in Saudi Arabia and might give Iran a new base to seek to dominate the Gulf region. A federal structure for a unified Iraq would have to be clearly in prospect. In any event, a clear idea of the proposed outcome should exist before military operations are attempted.

Creating an appropriate coalition for such an effort and finding bases for the necessary American deployment will be difficult. The effort is likely to separate those members of the coalition that joined in order to have veto power over American actions from those that are willing to pursue a long-range strategy. Nevertheless, the skillful diplomacy that shaped the first phase of the antiterrorism campaign would have much to build on. Saddam Hussein has no friends in the Gulf region. Britain will not easily abandon its pivotal role, based on its special relationship with the United States, that it has earned for itself in the evolution of the crisis. Nor will Germany move into active opposition to the United States. The same is true of Russia, China, and Japan. A determined American policy thus has more latitude than is generally assumed.

There is a need to prepare the ground diplomatically with great care. The United States cannot make issues affecting its own fundamental national security depend entirely on the consensus of other nations, but neither should it start actions affecting fundamental interests of other societies without a major effort to create understanding, even when consensus is not possible. As the most powerful country in the world, we should not rest our claim to leadership on hegemony, as I have pointed out elsewhere in this book.

In the aftermath of September 11, a global coalition was formed on the premise that members of the global coalition were free to choose the degree of their involvement. A la carte coalition management worked well when membership required little more than affirming opposition to terrorism in principle. Its continued usefulness in the case of Iraq will depend on how coalition obligations are defined. Should the convoy move at the pace of the slowest ship, or should some parts of it be able to sail by themselves? If the former, the coalition effort will gradually be defined by the least-common-denominator compromises that killed the U.N. inspection system in Iraq. Alternatively, the coalition can be conceived as a group united by common objectives but permitting autonomous action by whatever consensus can be created—or, in the extreme case, by the United States alone.

The balance between American leadership and international consensus is shown by the experience of the Gulf War of 1990. That war was triggered by a clear case of aggression that threatened Saudi Arabia, whose security has been deemed crucial by a bipartisan succession of American presidents. The United States decided to undo Saddam's adventure in the few months available before the summer heat made large-scale ground operations impossible. Several hundred thousand American troops were dispatched before any attempt at coalition-building was undertaken. Since the United States would obviously act alone if necessary, participating in the coalition became the most effective means for influencing events.

At issue then is not America's attempt to impose an international order but whether every member of a coalition should have a veto over our fundamental perceptions of security. It must be remembered that one country's perception of unilateralism is another's perception of leadership. A definition of consensus based on unanimity leads to paralysis; a definition of leadership insisting on unilateralism on every issue leads to an imperialism that, in the long run, will exhaust the imperial power. To navigate between these extremes is the challenge for American and allied policy.

With respect to Iran and North Korea, there is more scope for devising a common long-range diplomatic strategy. And it involves a fundamental choice. The debate on dealing with these regimes generally focuses on how to encourage moderate elements within the existing structure, especially those around President Mohammad Khatami in Iran. But a strong case can be made for the proposition that the real struggle is between the increasingly sophisticated public and a repressive regime. Dialogue with the ayatollahs is important, but it must not become a device to strengthen their hold on power. Room must be left for appealing to the democratic aspirations of the general public. As for diplomacy toward the ayatollahs, at some point engagement must lead to reciprocity; it must not become an exercise in psychological self-fulfillment.

However the issue of weapons of mass destruction in the hands of potential terrorist states is resolved, the longer-range goal must be to devise an international system for dealing with new attempts by additional countries to acquire weapons of mass destruction or biological and chemical weapons. The survival of civilized life requires that this problem be dealt with preemptively, and it cannot be done by unilateral American action. Thus the issue of terrorism merges with the challenge of international order.

THE ISRAELI-PALESTINIAN CONFLICT

Side-by-side with the challenge of terrorism—and partially related to it—has been the Arab-Israeli conflict. Convinced that America's intensive diplomatic activity contributed to the deadlock and the outbreak of the *Intifada* in 2000, the Bush administration in its early days took an aloof attitude, insisting that the parties narrow their differences before American mediation would resume. After September 11, the war on terrorism was inevitably given priority. But with violence in the Middle East escalating, the Bush administration in April 2002 reengaged itself in the diplomatic process.

The reappearance of active American diplomacy in the Middle East was greeted with a mixture of hope and trepidation. Hope, because the rage of both parties was giving way to exhaustion. Trepidation, because both sides knew their stated objectives were in essence incompatible. The secret dream of Israelis is legitimization of the status quo. For Palestinians, the goal is the imposition of terms reducing Israel at least to its 1967 borders or perhaps to those of the U.N. resolutions of 1947, which could facilitate the destruction of the Jewish state altogether.

Many who generally criticize America's foreign policy (and count among its sins obliviousness to their advice) are joining the widespread call for Washington to play a dominant role. These pleas have been given fresh impetus by the initiative of Crown Prince Abdullah of Saudi Arabia, which proposed normalization of relations between the Arab world and Israel if Israel returns to the 1967 frontiers. At the same time, the near unanimity in Europe and the Arab world urging American intervention stems from the hope that, in the end, the United States will impose on Israel a settlement essentially identical to the Abdullah plan.

In the past thirty years, American diplomacy has been the catalyst for practically all the progress the peace process has made. But given the explosive politics of the region, it is all too easy to overestimate what is possible. In 2000, the impetuous attempt to settle all issues in one negotiation of limited duration at Camp David contributed to the outbreak of the current warfare, as I have explained in Chapter 5.

In present conditions, a comparison of both sides' positions demonstrates that another attempt at a negotiated solution would probably not fare any better. The only formal plan by an Israeli government was put forward by Prime Minister Ehud Barak at Camp David. This offered over 90 percent of the disputed territories (the formula was complex and somewhat vague on how the 90 percent was to be calculated) but retained about 70 percent of the settlements. In exchange, the Palestinians were asked to renounce any future claims, including the right to return into Israel proper (though they would be free to return to a Palestinian state). Prime Minister Ariel Sharon has disavowed this proposal. Yasir Arafat preferred the *Intifada* to accepting it.

The most forthcoming Arab proposal has come from Crown Prince Abdullah. According to its imprecise outline, Israel would return to the dividing lines of 1967 in exchange for the normalization of relations with the Arab states. Literally, this would imply Israeli abandonment of all settlements and Arab control of the Old City of Jerusalem, including the holy places. The Abdullah plan does not define what is meant by normalization and is silent about such issues as the right of refugees to return (though this would surely be put forward in an actual negotiation).

Welcome as this engagement in the peace process is—the first by an Arab state not having a direct national conflict with Israel—its specific terms represent a restatement of a position that has produced the existing deadlock. The pre-1967 "border" in Palestine—unlike the Egyptian, Syrian, or Jordanian frontiers with Israel—was never an international frontier; it was a cease-fire line established at the end of the 1948 war. It was never recognized by any Arab state for fifty years and has been grudgingly accepted recently by states that do not, however, recognize the legitimacy of the state of Israel. I have never encountered an Israeli Prime Minister or chief of staff who considered the '67 border defensible, and especially if coupled with an abandonment of a security position along the Jordan River. This is because the '67 borders leave a corridor only eight miles wide between Haifa and Tel Aviv and put the border of Palestine at the edge of Israel's only international airport. Moreover, Israel would have to give up settlements containing approximately 200,000 inhabitants (about 4 percent of its Jewish population), including the most ideological part of the population. Many of them would have to be extricated by force to abandon what they consider a biblical territorial claim.

In return, Israel would achieve diplomatic relations with its neighbors. But in almost all other negotiations, mutual recognition of the parties is taken for granted, not treated as a concession. In fact, nonrecognition implies the legal nonexistence of the other state, which, in the context of the Middle East, is tantamount to retaining an option to destroy it. Once granted, recognition can always be withdrawn; breaking diplomatic relations is a recognized diplomatic tool. Nor does formal normalization involve much else: Israel's peace agreement with Egypt of twenty-three years ago has brought little in the way of enhanced economic or cultural relations other than an exchange of ambassadors who are rarely brought into play.

While the terms of the Crown Prince's proposal represent no breakthrough, Saudi engagement could be important if it is used to produce a cease-fire and to start negotiations without preconditions from either side. But if its ultimate purpose is to induce the United States to impose its specific provisions, it would undermine the security of Israel and ultimately the stability of the region.

This is why a negotiation focused on the 1967 frontiers is likely to end in deadlock. For after the experiences of the Oslo agreement and eighteen months of suicide bombings, Israelis know (as should the rest of the world) that the real division among Palestinians is not between those who want peace in the Western sense—as a point after which the world lives free of tensions with a consciousness of reconciliation—a tiny minority among Palestinian leaders, and so-called extremists. On the contrary, the fundamental schism is between those who want to bring about the destruction of Israel by continuing the present struggle and those who believe that an agreement now would be a better strategy to rally forces for the ultimate showdown later on.

Even if those Palestinians and other Arab leaders who sign a "final" agreement have no afterthoughts, no one can guarantee that they will not be replaced by more radical successors. A peace agreement will not quell but may stimulate the intransigence of radical groups or states. If, as is asserted, Arafat cannot be asked to accept a permanent cease-fire as an entrance price into negotiations because his radical opponents would have a veto, why would the same condition not apply after a peace settlement? Thus the differences between a permanent and an interim settlement are more a matter of semantics than substance. The real question is whether it is possible to create a period of coexistence of sufficient duration to permit an approach to the issue of final frontiers free of theoretical assessments and based on the actual experience of Palestinians and Israelis living together.

The precariousness of Israel's position is paradoxical. Israel has never been more powerful and, at the same time, never more vulnerable. Israel is militarily stronger than any conceivable Arab adversary or combination of them; it is clearly able to inflict heavy losses on Palestinian terrorist groups. But it has evolved into a middle-class advanced society, and the strain of guerrilla warfare on such a society is psychologically draining. The *Intifada* has generated an ambivalent rigidity in Israeli society. Prior to the Oslo agreement, the Israeli peace movement viewed reconciliation with the Arab world primarily in terms of psychological reassurance; land would be traded for peace, even though the Arab quid pro quo would be revocable. But since the *Intifada*, the vast majority of Israelis no longer believe in reconciliation—they want victory and the crushing of their Arab adversaries.

At the same time, there is growing despair over the seeming futility of the enterprise. With the ratio of Israeli casualties to the guerrillas' going up, and the fact that Israel's retaliation beyond a certain point will not be tolerated by the United States and the rest of the world, a sense of resignation is spreading. The desire to turn on the tormentors is beginning to be balanced by signs of a hunger for peace at any price.

Israel finds itself facing the classic dynamic of guerrilla warfare as it has played out for two generations now. The guerrillas not only do not recoil from terrorism, but practice an extreme form of it because a violent, emotional, and—to bystanders—excessive retaliation by Israel serves their purpose: to trigger intervention by the international community, especially the United States. In the process, Israeli sanctuaries are established that, to all intents and purposes, hamstring the counterterrorist forces' capacity to get to the root of the guerrilla challenge. That process gradually threatens to erode Israel's margin of survival, even while the world's media and diplomats bewail Israeli excesses. Torn between a recognition of strategic necessities and the pull of emotional imperatives, Israel runs the risk of ultimately descending into paralysis.

NATO, American, or other third-party guarantees are of marginal utility in overcoming this psychological problem. Nobody can seriously believe that the European countries would go to war for Israel, especially against challenges that are likely to be ambiguous. The only possible solution would be an American guarantee against invasion from neighboring states. Aside from raising profound domestic questions in the United States, this would bring with it an American veto of Israeli retaliation against less than all-out attack and, vis-à-vis guerrilla warfare, would add America as a target without significantly improving the capability of Israel's defending forces.

Therefore, the beginning of wisdom is to recognize the impossibility of a final settlement under current conditions. Some crises can only be managed, not solved. The constant invocation of unattainable goals will foster a general climate of irresponsibility. Yet a less ambitious mediation may have some prospects for success, if for no other reason than that the status quo is becoming increasingly intolerable for Palestinians as well. They have fought ferociously on behalf of the classic paradigm of asymmetrical warfare: the guerrilla wins if he does not lose. Still, a point may be approaching where the costs of the war will exhaust, or perhaps even destroy, the civil society the guerrillas are seeking to establish. This is particularly the case after the Israeli incursions into Palestinian territory severely damaged the Palestinian infrastructure. As for the other Arab states, their impotence on the Palestine issue threatens in time to radicalize their domestic politics. They have a stake in a settlement that brings about coexistence, even if they are not able for domestic reasons to modify the historic Arab terms for a comprehensive solution in the initial stages.

If the United States launches itself into a major diplomatic effort, it must be clear about what is at stake. Will the mediation be interpreted in the region as being produced by terrorism or as an attempt to shape an outcome based on familiar American principles? Will the perceived lesson be that September 11 in the end obliged America to adopt positions it had rejected previously? Or will terrorism be viewed as obstructing rather than inspiring a positive American role? If negotiations start, will the military prowess displayed by the Palestinians in the *Intifada* provide an excuse for them to play the constructive role Anwar Sadat did after the initial Arab successes of the 1973 war? Or will the Palestinians view America as being in retreat and Israel on the verge of an abyss, toward which Arafat, with the help of outside mediation, will push it step by step? The answers to these questions will determine the prospects for a peaceful evolution of the region and also, to a large extent, the prospects for America's war against terrorism.

By themselves, the Palestinians will not accept anything less than their maximum demands because they believe they have the momentum of international support behind them; the Israelis will not accept these demands because they fear for their very existence. The United States can bridge this gap only by making clear to both sides that the one feasible goal is a settlement in which each will achieve less than its maximum aim, but more than it can accomplish by the continuation of the conflict. It must urge Israel toward a peace program; it must impress upon its Arab interlocutors the limits of achievable concessions.

In pursuit of this goal, the Bush administration proposed a Middle East peace conference with a wide membership. At long intervals, the caldron of the Middle East generates an opportunity for a possible breakthrough. It usually occurs after an explosion that brings home to the parties their necessities as well as their limits and permits a balancing of concessions with the help of interested bystanders. The Middle East conference called by Secretary of State Colin Powell may relate occasion to opportunity. But for this to happen, it is important to be clear not only about the opportunity, but also about its limits.

A broad-based Middle East conference is not the most appropriate forum for achieving a comprehensive solution, and the United States has generally avoided this venue, for the composition of such conferences tends to isolate America. The vast majority of the potential participants in the proposed conference other than Israel— the European Union, the United Nations, Russia, moderate Arab states—will, in the quest for a comprehensive solution, endorse variations of the Saudi plan. For its part, the United States has supported—albeit halfheartedly—the phraseology of U.N. Security Council resolutions calling for "secure borders," not necessarily those of 1967. The quest for a comprehensive solution thus sets up precisely the United States-and-Israel-vs.-the-world equation, which jihadists seek to promote.

Nor is a general conference the best forum to induce compromise regarding a comprehensive agreement. In the face of broad-based opposition, Israel will dig in reflexively. Under pressure from radical colleagues, the moderate Arab participants will not modify their position. This is why the United States saw to it that previous general conferences were merely token. The Geneva conference of the 1970s met only once, in a plenary session, after which the negotiations for two disengagement agreements and two political agreements, culminating in a peace agreement with Egypt, were conducted in separate forums. And the Madrid conference of 1991 led to the PLO-Israeli agreement negotiated in Oslo under Norwegian aegis, without reference to the original meeting.

While Prince Abdullah deserves credit for stating a willingness to accept Israel under some conditions, the substance of the Saudi plan is inherently one-sided. Israel is asked to cede territory—a tangible and irrevocable act; the Arab states in return offer normalization and recognition, which are psychological and revocable. And the content of normalization has never been defined. Nor are Palestinian leaders in a position to make a general agreement. No Palestinian leader has been willing to renounce the right of return of Palestinians to Israel. This implies an option to overwhelm Israel demographically, or to extinguish it.

A fashionable argument is to invoke the Camp David talks of 2000, during which Israel proposed giving up some 90 percent of the West Bank, and the subsequent Taba talks, which raised that percentage to 96 percent, as proof that the Saudi plan is not so far from reality. But the Taba "agreement" is a strange concoction. It was negotiated in the last weeks of the Clinton presidency and while Israeli Prime Minister Ehud Barak was heading for an overwhelming electoral defeat, and no written record of it seems to exist; no map reflecting what the percentages represent has ever been published. The Israeli proposal—which was a minority position within Israel and was rejected by Arafat—was based on the assumption that major territorial concessions would change the psychological framework and result in genuine coexistence. It cannot be resurrected after months of suicide bombings; it could come about, if ever, only at the end of an extended period of coexistence.

Should the United States or an international consensus pursue a comprehensive agreement nevertheless, if only, as some claim, to save Israel from a strategy that is multiplying its enemies and eroding America's position in Islam? Imposition of the Saudi plan would not reconcile the Arab world. Whether the United States garners credit in the Islamic world for diplomatic initiatives will depend on perceptions of the choices made available. Any imposition viewed as having been extorted by Islamic militancy would encourage *jihad* groups around the world, which would demand the destruction of Israel next. Such a seeming concession would not even help Arab moderate leaders; to the extent that militant Islam gains momentum, the position of moderate Arab leaders is progressively undermined. And it would gravely weaken America's war on terrorism.

Imposition would break Israel's back, psychologically. Israel, under irresistible American pressure, would end the period of the *Intifada* with borders insecure, all settlements abandoned and Jerusalem partitioned, while having no assurance of long-term Arab reciprocity. This would transform Israel into a client state of America, totally dependent on American military support in every crisis by means of a defense agreement (useless against suicide bombers); it would surely lead to an upheaval in Israeli society, wrecking its faith in the future (no matter what polls would show at any moment of despair). This in turn would tempt those in the Arab world who would treat an agreement as an interim stage in the destruction of Israel to magnify their pressure.

America's influence—and that of its European allies as well—is enhanced to the degree that its diplomatic initiatives are perceived as resulting from free choice and not from either terrorism or other pressures, such as oil boycotts. The American strategy should be to help bring about a change in the calculations that have produced the current impasse—not a paper plan reconfiguring conventional wisdom. The United States must urge a strategy reflecting the fundamental reality that progress toward a settlement can come only by stages, and that the quest for a comprehensive peace in the abstract will guarantee another explosion.

At this stage of the Middle East crisis, the fundamental challenge is to establish a framework for coexistence for the two sides. Only then will it be possible to address the long-term issues of peace and final frontiers realistically. America's special position obliges it to act as mediator, but also to define the limits of its mediation. The moderate Arab nations must understand that the United States is not able to obtain their maximum demands for them but will do its utmost to achieve more than they can hope for without American mediation. And Israel must accept that the status quo is not sustainable.

The quest for an overall settlement is equivalent to an extended stalemate, in which a desperate Israel may seek to weaken its neighbors to a point where the terms in dispute become irrelevant and in which Arab terrorists seek to weaken Israeli cohesion. While keeping open an ultimate comprehensive agreement, the only feasible strategy at this point is to strive for peaceful coexistence; comprehensive peace should then be the next stage after a specified interval, during which new conditions have been created for both sides.

In outline, such an interim agreement would bring about a Palestinian state on territories substantially larger than those controlled by the present Palestinian Authority—though short of the 1967 borders—with a unified territory ending the many Israeli checkpoints offensive to Palestinian dignity and self-respect. It would end new Israeli settlement and leave existing settlements the option of being evacuated or living under Palestinian rule. This is the maximum Israel can concede under present conditions and would be a great step forward for the Palestinians. Whether the area between the borders of the Palestinian state and the 1967 borders could be constituted as a buffer zone with a special status deserves exploration.

In return, the Palestinians would need to stop hostile propaganda, abandon terrorist bases, and end terrorist attacks on Israeli territory. To accomplish this, the Palestinian Authority would need to reconstitute itself in a way that generates confidence in its ability to honor its obligations and to establish a functioning state on democratic and representative foundations.

Such an interim agreement is the only conceivable outcome that has any chance of being negotiated relatively rapidly and of lasting for some period. It contains an equilibrium of concessions; it provides a framework within which coexistence can be tested and from which a comprehensive agreement can emerge.

Thus, the proposed conference can play a useful role if it adopts a division of labor:

• The United States would play the principal mediating role in the negotiation of an interim agreement, which would be buttressed by a general statement of objectives for the overall goals, providing a link between an interim and a comprehensive settlement. Our European allies could contribute by suspending the myriad plans by which they seek to improve their position in the Arab world, but which in reality radicalize that world by raising unfulfillable expectations.

• Because the distrust between the parties is so great, Israel will not accept the word of the existing Palestinian Authority. But since it is inappropriate for Israel to designate the leaders with whom it is prepared to negotiate, Arafat should be made the responsibility of the Arab states participating in the conference. They should guarantee the Palestinian Authority's commitments and facilitate the negotiations.

• Europe and the United Nations, backed by the United States, could generate an international commitment to assist in the creation of a viable Palestinian entity, at first under an interim agreement and later on when a permanent settlement is reached. That commitment would imply a level of assistance that could be effective only in the context of a new set of institutions, in the creation of which the conference—or a relevant subgroup—could play a major role. The criteria for attracting international support must include what the Palestinian Authority lacks now: commitment to a legislature responsible for the designation of the executive, an administrative structure beyond corruption, and a system of laws.

In this way, the conference could help bring about a reconstituted Palestinian Authority, more predictable and capable of a genuine cooperative relationship. That outcome could provide an interval which makes it likely that the final step toward an overall agreement will be taken in conditions less shadowed by hatred and bloodshed and by leaders on both sides less encumbered by the battles of the past.

RELATIONS WITH RUSSIA

September 11 accelerated trends that had already begun in the U.S.-Russia relationship before that fateful date. This relationship has the potential of becoming as symbolic of the new era as the opening to China was after 1972. President Vladimir Putin's conduct both before and since the September 11 attacks shows that the first leader of a genuinely post-Communist Russia is adapting Russia's historic policies to the emerging international realities.

Mikhail Gorbachev and Boris Yeltsin had made their careers in the life-and-death struggles that culminated in positions on the Politburo. They were brought up in a world in which the Soviet Union saw itself as a superpower equal in reach—at least in its own perception—to the United States. Instinctively believing that Russia's turmoil was but a brief interruption before resumption of a global mission, they oscillated between posing as the leader of a superpower side-by-side with America and fitful stabs at traditional Soviet policies based on strategic opposition to the United States.

By contrast, Putin's career was made in the bureaucracy of the KGB and later as the deputy mayor of St. Petersburg. The former position placed a premium on analysis of the international situation; the latter brought Putin face to face with the dilemmas of post-Soviet reconstruction. Like his immediate predecessors, he seeks to restore a significant role for Russia, but, unlike them, he understands this is a long-term process requiring a different trajectory from that of Russia's imperialist history.

In terms of Russian history, Putin is best understood as comparable to Prince Alexander Gorchakov, who conducted Russian foreign policy for twenty-five years after the Russian debacle in the Crimean War in 1856. Patient, conciliatory policies and the avoidance of international military crises allowed Gorchakov to restore an isolated and gravely weakened country to a leading international position.

Putin's priorities appear to be the recovery of the Russian economy; the restoration of Russia as a great power, preferably by cooperation with the United States but, if necessary, by building countervailing power centers together with China or Europe; combating Islamic fundamentalism; establishing a new security relationship toward Europe, especially with respect to NATO expansion to the Baltic states; and solving the strategic nuclear issue with the United States.

Because of these priorities, Putin did not push his disagreement on missile defense to the point of confrontation. A clash with the United States would have drained Russian resources and encouraged a return to Cold War patterns. Cooperation would symbolize a new era and perhaps bring some technological progress in shared antimissile technology. And the price would be tolerable: the size of the Russian nuclear and missile arsenal will prevent any missile defense foreseeable for the next quarter-century from threatening Russia's ultimate retaliatory capability. This is why Putin has, above all, striven for and achieved agreed limits on offensive deployments and acquiesced in the United States' abrogation of the ABM treaty.

On the political plane, the challenge of Islamic fundamentalism is probably the dominant Russian concern. Russia's leaders perceived Afghanistan's Taliban and similar movements as threats to the newly independent Uzbekistan, Azerbaijan, Kazakhstan, Tajikistan, and Turkmenistan, formerly Soviet republics and still regions of major relevance to Russia's security. Furthermore, Moscow fears that militant ideologies could stimulate irredentism in Russia's southern Muslim provinces.

These concerns caused Putin to treat the terrorist attacks of September 11 as an opportunity for the kind of cooperation regarding the fundamentalist challenge toward which he was feeling his way in any event. He established a policy of partnership with the United States, which is another way of saying that he was pursuing Russia's objectives by enlisting American power in their support.

President Bush decisively seized this opening, but it is important to keep in mind that the new Russian policy results not from Putin's personal preference for the American President—helpful as their personal relations are—but from a cool assessment of Russia's interest. Putin has left himself other options, with China and with Europe, should his reliance on the United States founder. Accordingly, personal relations between leaders—necessary to create an initial psychological framework—must be translated into agreed, permanent common interests. Otherwise, there is the risk of repeating the experience of previous Western leaders who relied on their ties to Mikhail Gorbachev or Boris Yeltsin (and, before that, to Joseph Stalin and his successors). One does Putin no favor by ascribing his policies to his personality, impressive as it is; it is an argument that domestic opponents may, in time, turn against him.

There is hope for improved American and Atlantic relations with Russia precisely because there is an objective new basis for them. It is not only that the current political structure of Europe obviates the kind of Napoleonic or Hitlerite invasions that magnified Russian security concerns, or that wars between nuclear powers are now perceived as out of the question, inevitably exacting costs out of all proportion to any rational objective.

Above all, it is the political calculus that has changed, especially in regions of historic contention, such as the Middle East. The previous conception of a zero-sum game between two dominant powers is no longer applicable. During the Cold War—and for some period afterward—both Russian and American leaders thought that a political gain for one side was a strategic loss for the other and systematically attempted to reduce each other's influence in the Middle East. Under post–September 11 conditions, such policies would weaken both countries against Islamic fundamentalism and undermine the stability of the region in which they both have a vital interest.

There are, however, clear limits beyond which neither country may be able to go. The United States cannot, in the name of opposition to Islamic fundamentalism, acquiesce in Russia's methods for suppressing the upheavals in Chechnya. Nor can America be indifferent should the fight against Islamic fundamentalism become a pretext to force the newly independent states of Central Asia back under Russian strategic domination. The safety of Israel remains a fundamental American goal. Russia has not in the past displayed a similar concern, though this attitude may be changing on the part of some Russian leaders—especially Putin—who are beginning to view Israel as a strategic counterweight to Islamic fundamentalism. Finally, it is possible that the competition for access to oil and the routes for its delivery will prove a major obstacle to policy coordination. In the end, the possibilities of Russo-American cooperation regarding Islamic fundamentalism depend on the ability to carve out a passage between starry-eyed optimism and a new competition in defined strategic areas.

The challenge is how to create consulting mechanisms capable of dealing jointly with the new common realities without giving

Europe the sense that it is facing a Russo-American condominium. Europe itself attempted to broaden these mechanisms when NATO adopted a scheme to fit Russia into a new relationship with NATO. A new NATO council including Russia is supposed to deal with specifically defined policy areas while the existing NATO council without Russia deals with all other matters. Decisions by the new body would be unanimous, thus giving Russia a veto together with all other members. The topics include nuclear proliferation, terrorism, and refugee displacements—leaving little for traditional NATO except dealing with a receding Russian threat.

These subjects deserve common exploration with Russia. But Russian de facto membership in NATO was not the wisest solution—though it is, at this writing, an accomplished fact. NATO is basically a military alliance, part of whose purpose is the protection of Europe against a reimperializing Russia. Since the end of the Cold War and the advent of the common front against terrorism, this danger has disappeared for the foreseeable future. Nevertheless, the reason why former members of the Warsaw Pact have joined NATO, and others are in the process of seeking to do so, is that Central Europeans consider history more relevant to their security concerns than personalities. NATO does not protect its members against one another. To couple NATO expansion with even partial Russian membership in NATO was, in a sense, merging two contradictory courses of action.

It will be argued that this problem can be avoided by the careful definition of objectives assigned to the new NATO-Russian council. But that would not solve Russia's problem, nor that of NATO. The distinction between the subjects appropriate for each forum will be highly ambiguous. And if it is to be established by the same group of ambassadors who, wearing another hat and having offices in the same building, are practicing cooperation, the members of the council will be in an impossible psychological position. But as Russia becomes a de facto NATO member, NATO ceases to be an alliance, or becomes a vague collective security instrument.

Nor is a permanent assembly of NATO ambassadors the best forum for exploring issues such as terrorism, nuclear proliferation, or other global issues. For NATO is not now the principal forum for such issues. A new pattern of consultation outside the NATO framework is needed.

Now that the decision for Russian quasi-membership in NATO has been taken, the challenge is to work out a relationship that provides a serious forum for consultation with Russia without destroying the security safety net heretofore provided by the Atlantic Alliance.

As I have discussed in Chapter 2 on Europe, the problem is analogous to that posed by the collapse of the Napoleonic empire. The end of Napoleon did not end the fears of a resurgent France. But it was also recognized that permanent peace required the full participation of France in international diplomacy. The solution was the creation of the Quadruple Alliance to guard Europe against a renewal of French expansionism. France was not a member of the security undertaking. But it was invited to join as an equal partner in the so-called Concert of Europe that dealt with political issues affecting the political stability of Europe.

The American-European-Russian relationship must deal with four basic challenges:

• Relationships must be lifted from the psychological to the political level; they cannot be made to depend on the personal relationship of the leaders. Concreteness of objectives and especially programs and understandings is necessary. In the nuclear field, this requires the ability to pursue two courses simultaneously: the agreements of a previous generation based on the assumption of superpower rivalry (and a very limited number of nuclear powers) have lost a great deal of their relevancy, but at the same time the nuclear world cannot be left to an unconstrained multiplication of nuclear weapons and other means of mass destruction. Nonproliferation must become a principal objective of the diplomacy, especially of nuclear powers.

• In the political field, the necessities of the present must not be overwhelmed by hopes for the future. This applies especially to America's NATO relationship, which is its only institutional link to Europe. But it applies as well to America's relations with China, Japan, and Israel. These must not be sacrificed to the tactics of the moment.

• By the same token, Russia will seek to maintain its influence in regions of geopolitical and historical importance to the Russian state and as a hedge should the effort to create a new basis for Russo-American relations flounder—as is seen in its recent friendship treaties with China and North Korea.

• All this imposes a new need for imagination in American and Western foreign policy. With a wise foreign policy, America for the foreseeable future should be in a position to create incentives that cause both Russia and China to stand to gain more from cooperative relations with the United States than from confrontation with it.

The frozen relationships of the Cold War no longer fit a world in which there are no principal adversaries and in which the very distinction between friends and adversaries is in transition in many regions. In such circumstances, the United States needs to design a diplomacy that prevents threats to fundamental American interests and values without designating a specific adversary in advance, and above all by a policy based on the widest possible international consensus on positive goals.

A Final Word

The war on terrorism is not the ultimate test of American foreign policy, which is, above all, to protect the extraordinary opportunity that has come about to recast the international system. The North Atlantic nations, having understood their common dangers, can turn to a new definition of common purposes. Relations with former adversaries can go beyond liquidating the vestiges of the Cold War and find a new role for Russia in its post-imperial phase, and for China as it emerges into great power status. India is emerging as an important global player. The Middle East peace process should be urgently resumed and provides an ultimate challenge. These and other prospects must not be allowed to vanish because those who have the ability to prevail shrink from what their opportunities require.

◇ ◇ ◇ ◇ ◇ ◇ ◇ ◇ ◇ ◇ ◇ # NOTES

One: AMERICA AT THE APEX: EMPIRE OR LEADER?

1. The Chicago Council on Foreign Relations polls purport to show continuing interest in international engagement. But other indices, such as media coverage and congressional interest, suggest otherwise.

2. Tom Brokaw, *The Greatest Generation* (New York: Random House, 1998).

Two: AMERICA AND EUROPE: THE WORLD OF DEMOCRACIES I

1. European Union–Russia Summit press conference, October 30, 2000.

2. Joschka Fischer, address to the German Society for Foreign Affairs, Berlin, June 8, 1998.

3. See, e.g., article by later-to-be President Clinton's Deputy Secretary of State Strobe Talbott, "Rethinking the Red Menace," *Time*, January 1, 1990, p. 69.

4. President Bill Clinton, press conference with Russian President Boris Yeltsin, Helsinki, March 21, 1997.

5. President Bill Clinton, remarks at the United States Military Academy commencement, West Point, New York, May 31, 1997.

6. Protocols to the North Atlantic Treaty of 1949 on the Accession of Poland, Hungary, and the Czech Republic, May 4, 1998, especially Section 3, *Congressional Record* (Senate), pp. S4217–20.

7. For examples of European rhetoric, see Peter W. Rodman, *Drifting Apart? Trends in U.S.-European Relations* (Washington, D.C.: The Nixon Center, June 1999), pp. 11–13, 29–31, 55–57.

8. President John F. Kennedy, address at the Paulskirche, Frankfurt, Germany, June 24, 1963, *Department of State Bulletin*, Vol. XLIX, No. 1256 (July 22, 1963), p. 122.

9. Minister of Foreign Affairs Hubert Védrine, address at the opening of the French Institute of International Relations (IFRI in its French acronym) conference, "Into the 21st [Century]," Paris, November 3, 1999.

10. Joschka Fischer, "From a Union of States to Federation: Thoughts on the Goal of European Integration," address at Humboldt University, Berlin, May 12, 2000.

11. Védrine, *loc. cit.*

12. The idea of overlapping circles of integration—an integrated core group and a wider one involving the core and the remainder arranged in various combinations—has been endorsed by a number of advocates of European integration, among them former French President Valéry Giscard d'Estaing, former German Chancellor Helmut Schmidt, and former head of the European Commission Jacques Delors.

13. Prime Minister Tony Blair, speech to the Polish Stock Exchange, Warsaw, October 6, 2000.

14. *Diário Noticias*, January 8, 2000.

15. Prime Minister Tony Blair, statement following the European Council meeting, Helsinki, December 13, 1999.

16. For an elaboration, see Rodman, *Drifting Apart*, pp. 38–39, 70, 76–77.

17. Report of the Commission to Assess the Ballistic Missile Threat to the United States, Executive Summary (Washington, D.C.: July 15, 1998), p. 5.

18. Ibid., p. 6.

19. President Bill Clinton, "Remembering Yeltsin," *Time*, January 1, 2000.

20. Vladimir Putin, "Russia at the Turn of the Millennium," December 31, 1999.

21. President Vladimir Putin, inaugural speech, Moscow, May 7, 2000.

22. "Russia's National Security Concept," January 10, 2000, in *Arms Control Today*, January/February 2000, p. 18.

Three: THE WESTERN HEMISPHERE:
THE WORLD OF DEMOCRACIES II

1. Interview with Council of the European Union president António Guterres, *Le Monde*, January 1, 2000.

2. Larry Rohter, "South American Trade Bloc Under Siege," *New York Times*, March 24, 2001, p. B2.

3. See Council on Foreign Relations Independent Task Force on Brazil, "A Letter to the President and a Memorandum on U.S. Policy Toward Brazil," February 2001.

Four: ASIA: THE WORLD OF EQUILIBRIUM

1. Winston S. Churchill, *The Gathering Storm* (Cambridge: Riverside Press, 1948), pp. 207–8.

2. *Canadian International Business Strategy, 1996–97: Aerospace and Defence*, p. 5.

3. See Andrew Nathan and Perry Link, eds., *The Tiananmen Papers: The Chinese Leadership's Decision to Use Force Against Their Own People* (New York: Council on Foreign Relations, 2001). This compilation regarding the leadership decisions during the Tiananmen Square revolt provides a fascinating insight. I cannot judge its authenticity; it sounds plausible.

4. Henry Kissinger, *Years of Upheaval* (Boston: Little, Brown, 1982), p. 692.

5. President Bill Clinton, joint press statement with Chancellor Helmut Kohl, Potsdam, Germany, May 13, 1998.

Five: THE MIDDLE EAST AND AFRICA: WORLDS IN TRANSITION

1. Henry A. Kissinger, "Turning a Fairy Tale into Reality," *Newsweek*, September 27, 1993.

2. See, e.g., Henry Kissinger, "The Bottom Line of the Mideast Peace Process," *New York Post*, November 19, 1996; and "The Oslo Piecemeal Process," *Washington Post*, August 24, 1997.

3. See Henry Kissinger, *White House Years* (Boston: Little, Brown, 1979), pp. 559–60, 1276; and Henry Kissinger, *Years of Upheaval* (Boston: Little, Brown, 1982), pp. 201–2.

4. Tracy Wilkinson, "Once Applauded as a Hero, Clinton Bows Out amid Palestinian Catcalls," *Los Angeles Times*, January 19, 2001, p. A-10.

5. President Bill Clinton, statement in the White House briefing room, November 15, 1998.

6. On the abandonment of the Iraqi Kurds in 1975, see Henry Kissinger, *Years of Renewal* (New York: Simon & Schuster, 1999), pp. 576–96.

7. Nelson R. Mandela, statement during the Rivonia trial, April 20, 1964.

8. F. W. deKlerk, speech to the opening of parliament, Cape Town, South Africa, February 2, 1990.

Six: THE POLITICS OF GLOBALIZATION

1. Testimony by Alan Greenspan on the Federal Reserve's semiannual report on the economy and monetary policy before the House Committee on Banking and Financial Services, February 17, 2000.

2. Joseph E. Stiglitz, "Two Principles for the Next Round, or, How to Bring Developing Countries in from the Cold," address at the International Centre for Trade and Sustainable Development, Geneva, September 21, 1999.

3. Robert Rubin, address on the Asian financial situation, Georgetown University, January 21, 1998.

4. Interview with Anatoly Chubais, *Kommersant Daily*, September 8, 1998. See also Stephen Fidler, "Russian Central Bank Lied to the IMF," *Financial Times*, July 30, 1999.

5. *Global Economic Prospects and the Developing Countries 2000* (Washington, D.C.: The World Bank, 1999).

6. See Martin Wolf, "Asia's Future Burning Bright," *Financial Times*, February 23, 2000.

7. Alan Greenspan, Francis Boyer Lecture of the American Enterprise Institute, December 5, 1996.

8. See Kissinger, *Years of Renewal,* Chapter 20.

Seven: PEACE AND JUSTICE

1. Henry Cabot Lodge, ed., *The Works of Alexander Hamilton,* Vol. V (London and New York: G. P. Putnam's Sons, 1885–1886), pp. 369–70.

2. Andrew A. Lipscomb and Albert Ellery Bergh, eds., *The Writings of Thomas Jefferson,* Vol. XV (Washington, DC: The Thomas Jefferson Memorial Association, 1903–1904), pp. 435–36.

3. Gaillard Hunt, ed., *The Writings of James Madison,* Vol. VII (New York: G. P. Putnam's Sons, 1901), p. 183.

4. John Quincy Adams, Address of July 4, 1821, in Walter LaFeber, ed., *John Quincy Adams and American Continental Empire* (Chicago: Times Books, 1965), p. 45.

5. Message of President James Monroe to Congress, December 2, 1823, in Ruhl J. Bartlett, ed., *The Record of American Diplomacy* (New York: Alfred A. Knopf, 1956), p. 182.

6. Alexis de Tocqueville, *Democracy in America,* Book I (New York: Alfred A. Knopf, 1994), pp. 290–291.

7. See David L. Larson, "Objectivity, Propaganda, and the Puritan Ethic," in David L. Larson, ed., *The Puritan Ethic in United States Foreign Policy* (Princeton: Van Nostrand, 1966), p. 15.

8. William Jennings Bryan, "The Paralyzing Influence of Imperialism," Speech to the Democratic National Convention, Kansas City, July 6, 1900.

9. Roosevelt letter to Hugo Munsterberg, October 3, 1914, in Elting E. Morison, ed., *The Letters of Theodore Roosevelt* (Cambridge: Harvard University Press, 1954), Vol. 8, pp. 824–25.

10. In John Morton Blum, *The Republican Roosevelt* (Cambridge: Harvard University Press, 1967), p. 131.

11. Woodrow Wilson, Annual Message to Congress, December 8, 1914, in Arthur S. Link, ed., *The Papers of Woodrow Wilson* (Princeton: Princeton University Press, 1966–94), Vol. 31, p. 423.

12. President Woodrow Wilson, Address to the U.S. Senate, January 12, 1917, in ibid., Vol. 40, pp. 536–37.

13. President Woodrow Wilson, "War Message," April 2, 1917, in ibid., Vol. 41.
14. Woodrow Wilson, remarks at Suresnes Cemetery on Memorial Day, May 30, 1919 in Link, ed., *Papers of Woodrow Wilson*, Vol. 59, pp. 608–9.
15. George Kennan, *American Diplomacy, 1900–1950* (Chicago: University of Chicago Press, 1951), p. 96.
16. Walter Russell Mead, "The Jacksonian Tradition," *The National Interest*, No. 58, Winter 1999/2000.
17. John Foster Dulles, "Morals and Power," in Larson, ed., *The Puritan Ethic in United States Foreign Policy*, p. 143.
18. President John F. Kennedy, remarks at American University, June 10, 1963.
19. President Lyndon B. Johnson, news conference, March 13, 1965.
20. President Richard Nixon, "U.S. Foreign Policy for the 1970s: A New Strategy for Peace," Report to the Congress, February 18, 1970, Introduction.
21. President Gerald R. Ford, address to the Conference on Security and Cooperation in Europe, Helsinki, August 1, 1975.
22. Second Carter-Ford presidential debate, October 6, 1976.
23. Ronald Reagan, State of the Union Address, January 25, 1983.
24. Jim Hoagland, "Russia into the Vacuum," *Washington Post*, November 21, 1997, p. A27.
25. See, e.g., President Clinton's remarks to the Community of Kusowera School, Mukono, Uganda, March 24, 1998 (on Africa), and Secretary of State Madeleine Albright's remarks before the American-Iranian Council, Washington, D.C., March 17, 2000 (on Iran).
26. Francis Fukuyama, *The End of History and the Last Man* (New York: Free Press, 1992).
27. *Los Angeles Times*, May 29, 1993.
28. Strobe Talbott, "Democracy and the National Interest," *Foreign Affairs*, November/December 1996, pp. 48–49.
29. Prime Minister Tony Blair, Statement on the Suspension of NATO Air Strikes Against Yugoslavia, London, June 10, 1999.
30. Chancellor Gerhard Schroeder, Policy Statement to the German Bundestag on the Fiftieth Anniversary of NATO, April 22, 1999.

31. President Bill Clinton, remarks to the Kosovo Force (KFOR) troops, Skopje, Macedonia, June 22, 1999.

32. Talbott, "Democracy and the National Interest," p. 49.

33. President Bill Clinton, videotaped address to the Serbian people, March 25, 1999.

34. U.S. Department of State press briefing on Belgrade, Serbia, and Montenegro, February 23, 1998.

35. U.N. Security Council Resolution 814 of March 26, 1993.

36. Madeleine Albright, remarks to the National War College, National Defense University, Fort Leslie McNair, Washington, D.C., September 23, 1993.

37. Hansard Parliamentary Debates, Fifth Series, Vol. 241, August 1878, Columns 1759–60.

38. President Bill Clinton, taped address to the people of Bosnia, January 12, 1996.

39. Cable from Secretary of State Lawrence Eagleburger to the U.S. Embassy, Belgrade, December 24, 1992, cited in *Washington Post*, April 18, 1999, p. A1.

40. Timothy Garton Ash, "Kosovo: Was It Worth It?," *New York Review of Books*, September 21, 2000.

41. Joseph S. Nye, Jr., "Redefining the National Interest," *Foreign Affairs*, July/August 1999.

42. I was in high office at the time of these events and have described in my memoirs the views and actions of the Nixon and Ford administrations in which I served (see Henry Kissinger, *White House Years* (Boston: Little, Brown, 1979), Chapter 17; *Years of Upheaval* (Boston: Little, Brown, 1982), Chapter 9; *Years of Renewal* (New York: Simon & Schuster, 1999), Chapter 24). Like that of the three administrations that followed us, our aim was to mitigate Pinochet's human rights abuses without reviving the radical and Castroite threat to the political evolution of Chile. And the Reagan administration, in fact, did a great deal to promote a restoration of democracy in Chile.

43. Lord Nicholls of Birkenhead, Appellate Judgment in *Ex parte Pinochet*, British House of Lords, November 25, 1998.

44. The Cairo Arab summit of October 2000 pledged that Arab states "will, under international law, prosecute those responsible for the

savage practices" allegedly committed by Israeli officials and military personnel during the Palestinian uprising of that period.

45. *La República*, June 2, 2000.

46. Robert Shrimsley and Ken Warn, "Britain Faces Legal Action over Sinking of Belgrano," *Financial Times*, June 30, 2000, p. 2; Andy McSmith, "Belgrano Families to Sue Britain," *Daily Telegraph*, June 30, 2000, p. 2. The ECHR rejected the case on July 19, 2000, because it was made outside legal time limits.

CONCLUSION

1. Paul Liman, *Fürst Bismarck nach seiner Entlassung. Neue vermehrte Volksausgabe* (Leipzig: Historisch-politischer Verlag, 1901), p. 3.

2. See, e.g., Robert Kagan, "The Benevolent Empire," *Foreign Policy*, Summer 1998.

3. Coral Bell, "American Ascendancy and the Pretense of Power," *The National Interest*, No. 57, Fall 1999, pp. 55–63.

◇◇◇◇◇◇◇◇◇◇◇ INDEX

Look for these other Henry Kissinger books available in paperback.

Ending the Vietnam War
0-7432-1532-X • $16.00

Years of Renewal
0-684-85572-0 • $24.00

Diplomacy
0-671-51099-1 • $22.00